Religious Radicalism
after the Arab Uprisings

Religious Radicalism after the Arab Uprisings

Editor
Jon B. Alterman

CSIS | CENTER FOR STRATEGIC &
INTERNATIONAL STUDIES

ROWMAN & LITTLEFIELD
Lanham • Boulder • New York • London

Center for Strategic & International Studies
1616 Rhode Island Avenue, NW
Washington, DC 20036
202-887-0200 | www.csis.org

Published by Rowman & Littlefield
A wholly owned subsidiary of The Rowman & Littlefield Publishing Group, Inc.
4501 Forbes Boulevard, Suite 200, Lanham, Maryland 20706
www.rowman.com

Unit A, Whitacre Mews, 26-34 Stannary Street, London SE11 4AB

ISBN 978-1-4422-4067-4 (cloth alk. paper)
ISBN 978-1-4422-4068-1 (paperback)
ISBN 978-1-4422-4069-8 (electronic)

♾™ The paper used in this publication meets the minimum requirements of American
National Standard for Information Sciences—Permanence of Paper for Printed Library
Materials, ANSI/NISO Z39.48-1992.

Printed in the United States of America

Contents

ACKNOWLEDGMENTS

This book would not have been possible without invaluable contributions from a distinguished group of international security practitioners and experts. The project's Senior Advisory Group offered continued guidance and substantive feedback to the research team throughout the project. Members included Arnaud de Borchgrave, director of the CSIS Transnational Threats Project and a senior adviser to the Center; Juan Zarate, senior adviser to the CSIS Transnational Threats Project and CSIS Homeland Security and Counterterrorism Program; Bernard Haykel, professor of Near Eastern Studies and director of the Institute for Transregional Study of the Contemporary Middle East, North Africa and Central Asia at Princeton University; Stephen R. Kappes, partner and chief operating officer at Torch Hill Investment Partners and a former deputy director of the Central Intelligence Agency; John MacGaffin, senior adviser to the CSIS Transnational Threats Project and a former associate deputy director for operations at the Central Intelligence Agency; Ziad Munson, associate professor of sociology at Lehigh University; Richard O'Neill, founder and president of the Highlands Group and a former deputy for strategy and policy at the Office of the Assistant Secretary of Defense at the U.S. Department of Defense; as well as representatives from the Defense Intelligence Agency at the U.S. Department of Defense and the National Security Research Centre at Singapore's National Security Coordination Secretariat. Additional appreciation is extended to both Arnaud de Borchgrave and Juan

Zarate who, in addition to serving on the Senior Advisory Group, also worked closely as project advisers with the authors of the "Key Elements of the Counterterrorism Challenge" chapter in the final stages of its writing.

The study also benefited from interviews with individuals and meetings with representatives from a wide range of organizations in Egypt, Jordan, Kuwait, Lebanon, Saudi Arabia, Singapore, Tunisia, Turkey, the United Arab Emirates, Qatar, and the United States. We would like to thank all those who were kind enough to make time, both formally and informally, to meet with the study team, answer our questions, and challenge our findings and recommendations.

Special acknowledgment is owed to Carolyn Barnett, who coordinated the background research for and critically edited many of the chapters, and to Zack Fellman, for his contributions to the field research used in the "Key Elements of the Counterterrorism Challenge" chapter.

Additionally, the following contributors deserve particular credit and a great deal of thanks for their contributions to this project: Rebecka Shirazi, Waleed Al Bassam, Basil Bastaki, Nicole Beittenmiller, Meaghan DeWaters, Sandra Geahchan, Christopher Looney, Jason Mullins, Dan Paltiel, Breanna Thompson, and David Wiese.

We are also grateful to the government of Singapore and the U.S. Defense Intelligence Agency for their generous support of this study.

While this book benefited greatly from the guidance of numerous people, the content is the sole responsibility of the authors and should not be construed to represent the opinions of anyone associated with the project. Any mistakes contained herein are the sole responsibility of the chapters' authors.

1. INTRODUCTION: THE CHANGING GEOPOLITICAL LANDSCAPE

Jon B. Alterman

The breadth, depth, and persistence of religiously inspired violence in the Arab world have made the region an outlier for many decades. While religious wars and pogroms feature in the history of many countries, the tensions that caused them have attenuated in the modern period. In the Arab world, however, religious and sectarian conflicts seem to have deepened and accelerated, coloring not only how Arabs see their own societies, but also how Arab states interact with non-Arab powers.

Varying explanations have been offered for this phenomenon. One is that the violence is a natural outgrowth of Islam itself. According to this view, Islam is a religion that brooks no compromise and is bent on domination; it has bloody borders because it is a religion of conquest. Further, Islam is coercive and patriarchal by nature, and thus it inspires coercive and patriarchal societies. It is essentially a premodern religion in a modern world, and it carries with it premodern levels of violence and repression.

Another explanation is that the religiously inspired discord in the Arab world is an outgrowth of the region's modern politics. This argument suggests that the colonial and mandate periods, followed by decades of authoritarian rule, have created publics who are estranged from their rulers and who naturally flow to the least regulated space in society—the mosque—to express their discontent. The scant prospects of liberalization or more broadly participatory governance, this argument goes, pushed a hardened minority to support violent and/or revolutionary change. Rigorous repression of dissent hardened the opposition and made it more extreme; the growing extremism of the opposition frightened and alienated much of the general public and, in the eyes of many, justified increasing repression.

Most religions, it seems, have been used to justify most things at some point in history. It is hard to accept the idea that Islam is uniquely receptive to violence given the justifications religion has given for violence throughout the world. And yet, other regions have emerged from colonialism without the high levels of endemic violence of the Arab world. The durability of religiously inspired violence in the Arab world, and the seemingly widespread acceptance of violence against civilians, demands some explanation.

The terrorist attacks of September 2001 brought focus and urgency to the problem. The collective tendency in the West was toward the political explanation of the Arab world's malaise, and the George W. Bush administration made the Middle East's democratization a priority. If governance became more inclusive, the thinking went, it would push politics toward consensus rather than polarization. If political activity held out the prospect of victory, it would undermine the argument that only violent action could bring about change.

The Arab uprisings of 2011—often referred to as the "Arab Spring"—seemed to offer just the opportunity that democratization advocates sought. Suddenly political groups who believed they had no chance of ever sharing power found themselves holding power. At the same time, many who believed that they one day would be able to pass power to their children found themselves thrown from office.

For radical groups using violence, these political changes created a new set of challenges. If the new rulers were not violent, how could the use of violence by the opposition be justified? How could any opposition group long accustomed to saying "no" transition to putting forward a positive agenda? How would opposition groups rising to power decide who is too extreme among them, and how would radical groups decide who is too radical? If groups had long accustomed themselves to being out of power, how could they accommodate themselves to the compromises and inconsistencies that complex modern government requires?

We began the study that follows in mid-2013 in order to explore the effects of the Arab transitions on radicalism in the region. At the time this study began, the trajectory of the Arab uprisings was still deeply uncertain. The Muslim Brotherhood was still in power in Egypt, the avowedly Islamist Ennahda Party led the government in Tunisia, and the Islamic State had neither consolidated its position in the anti-Syrian opposition nor proclaimed the resurrection of the caliphate. It was clear that all three contests for power would profoundly influence the shape of radicalism in the Middle East going forward. We also set out to understand Saudi Arabia's actions in this sphere, and not only because the country uses its custodianship of the holy mosques in Mecca and Medina and its vast oil wealth to have a prominent voice in Muslim matters. Saudi Arabia has also had a long struggle with domestic political Islam, which blended the austere puritanism of Muhammad ibn Abd al-Wahhab with the impulse toward action of Hassan al-Banna, the Muslim Brotherhood's founder. Any change in regional understandings of the connection between religion and politics would resonate deeply in the Kingdom, and Saudi Arabia would certainly seek to influence those understandings using its various tools of influence in the Arab world.

While the broader regional debate was about religion and politics broadly, we were especially interested in the effects of that debate on radicalism. It was clear that governments would have hard choices to make about whether to seek to include or suppress radical groups, and radical groups would have hard choices to make about whether they would seek to partner with governments or continue to struggle against them. It seemed possible that the region was facing a very different future.

The initial trends seemed to indicate at least short-term victories for radical forces. At a basic level, several of the secular governments that had sought to crush radical forces had been crushed themselves. While many of the new Islamist rulers differed with the radical groups on ideology and theology, they were certainly more sympathetic to them than their predecessors. The other advantage radical groups found regarded policing. On a practical level, the Arab uprisings represented the failure of internal security organizations to suppress uprisings in their early phases. For new governments, successful uprisings left internal security forces badly wounded, or worse. Those forces certainly lacked the trust of the new generation of politicians, many of whom they had been oppressing for decades. For existing governments, the threat of a mass uprising shifted the attention of the security services away from small and violent groups, on which they had focused for a decade, and toward the prospect of mass mobilization. While Osama bin Laden's death in May 2011 represented a profound blow to the jihadi movement, the contemporaneous melting away of police and security forces in many countries represented an opportunity for the movement. The endurance of anti-state violence in Syria, Iraq, and Libya gave a further boost to the radical camp, providing a cause for which young men could gather and fight, regardless of their origins around the world.

And yet, as we survey the Arab world in late 2014, radicals have not secured control over any country, although the Islamic State has at least temporarily carved territory out of two states. For all of the openings that the Arab uprisings provided long-time oppositions, it somewhat improbably reinforced most governments' advantages. In part, this is because the bloodiness of long-running conflicts in Syria, Iraq, and Libya, and the further empowerment of radical groups throughout the region, persuaded many formerly disaffected—or even hostile—citizens that they were in fact better off with the governments they had and should not take a chance on a transition. The Bahraini government's ability to reassert control after large-scale protests, and the Egyptian military's ability to reinsert itself at the center of Egyptian political life after a year-long interregnum of Muslim Brotherhood rule, undermined the argument that the status quo could no longer hold. In many cases, governments relied on the old tools at their disposal: the mass media and the religious authorities to rally support, state repression to silence critics, and the promise of reward from state systems to consolidate alliances.

Jihadi groups and hard-line salafi groups sympathetic to them had not worked out the details of how to hold actual power, and they soon became marginalized. They seemed to take the attraction of their movement for granted, expecting that in the absence of repression they could swiftly become mass movements. Groups allied to the Muslim Brotherhood, by contrast, got more traction in the initial months of the uprisings. They had long aspired to political participation, seeing democratization as a vehicle to accumulate power and influence (even if actual control had once seemed a far-off prospect).

In practice, even groups like the Muslim Brotherhood, which had long labored among the public, had problems holding on to power. In places where Islamists won elections, such as Egypt, the new governments never fully established their control over the system. In many cases, elements of the old regime bitterly complained about what they called *"ikhwanat al-dawla,"* or the "Brotherhood-ization" of the state, and they were able to resist it.

In that resistance was one of the most interesting phenomena of the Arab uprisings, and one of the most unexpected: the wide-scale vilification of the Muslim Brotherhood, which had been tolerated in much of the Arab world for decades. Although the Muslim Brotherhood as an organization has many authoritarian characteristics, its decades of effectively and efficiently providing schools, hospitals, and other public services persuaded many that the group's sights were firmly set on politics, not violence. Yet as populations reflected on the poor job performance of Muslim Brotherhood officials once in power, and as governments viewed themselves locked in a battle against the Brotherhood for their survival, the Brotherhood went in the public eye from attractive alternative to failed experiment. Violence crept back, and much of it was ascribed to the Brotherhood. While many populations were merely disappointed that the Brotherhood had not met expectations, resurgent governments saw something more threatening in the organization. The Brotherhood's unabashed search for monopoly power had represented an existential threat to the status quo, and it had to be fought at all costs.

The establishment's conflict with the Muslim Brotherhood highlighted what was really at stake in the Arab uprisings: the exercise of legitimate authority. Governments had become used to not being questioned and to relying on religious authorities to support their claims. The religious community was essentially a conservative community, and it reminded Muslims of numerous teachings that call for loyalty to the ruler. What the establishment found most threatening about many of the opposition movements that flowered after 2011 was the unity of religious and secular forces. Historically, traditional interpretations of Islam led conservative forces to support legitimacy of the state, and horror at the excesses of the radical right led liberal forces to support the legitimacy of the state. The Arab uprisings unified conservative and liberal forces, and combined them with the energy and innovation of young people. This coalition threatened the entire arrangement. Governments tried desperately to tear it apart, and up to now they have been largely successful.

These findings and others are captured in the chapters that follow. Chapter 2 explores competition for authority in the jihadi-salafi sphere, and chapter 3 examines the jihadi context on the ground in Syria and Iraq and in surrounding countries. Chapters 4, 5 and 6 discuss the shifting relationships between oppositions and governments in Tunisia, Egypt and Saudi Arabia respectively, and chapter 7 draws some conclusions from what we have learned.

With the benefit of hindsight, we understand that the changes of 2011 were less fundamental than many had hoped. Jihadi groups have experimented, and governments have experimented. Each has adapted to the other. The threats have not gone away. Perhaps most surprising is continued uncertainty over what lessons one should draw from the events of 2011. Were the uprisings of that year a sign that the status quo could no longer prevail, or did they serve as a wake-up call for governments to attend to the needs of their people? Did the seemingly spontaneous organization of opposition groups inspire young people to take action on their own, or did it demonstrate to young people the futility of political activity? Does the ongoing violence in Libya, Syria, and Iraq serve as a warning to populations not to challenge authoritarian governments for fear of inviting chaos?

On balance, it seems clear that radical groups found opportunity in the Arab uprisings. Taking advantage of the decline of security services as well as governments' failures to address grievances, radical groups remained as a magnet for the region's disaffected young men. Despite early hopes, the Arab uprisings did not provide constructive domestic outlets for the energies and passions of the rising generation. Faced with the choice between mobilizing young people and anesthetizing them, governments have redoubled their pursuit of the latter course.

The whole range of exogenous challenges, possibly including sustained economic dislocation and certainly including more sophisticated and targeted use of social media and networking, will continue to test sitting governments. In addition, the Muslim Brotherhood is down but not out in many places. Many have turned harshly against the Brotherhood, yet it continues to enjoy strong support in numerous areas—far more than most jihadi groups. The Brotherhood will certainly seek opportunities to reintegrate into politics, and members and supporters may use a variety of tactics to make the rulers who pushed them from power fail.

One thing seems clear. The dynamism and innovation that have emerged among radical and opposition groups throughout the Middle East will continue. Governments will need to use many of their existing tools as well as some new ones to face the challenges of this emerging reality. They will need to be not only strong but (as the last four years have demonstrated) also agile. Many may seek to compel, but they will also need to accommodate, and to divide effectively between those who can be reconciled and those who cannot.

2. JIHADI-SALAFI REBELLION AND THE CRISIS OF AUTHORITY

Haim Malka

Jihadi-salafists are in open rebellion. The sheer audacity of the September 11, 2001 attacks, combined with Osama bin Laden's charisma and financial resources, established al Qaeda as the leader of jihad for a decade. Yet, the Arab uprisings of 2011 and the civil war in Syria shifted the ground dramatically. More ambitious jihadi-salafists have challenged al Qaeda's leadership and approach to jihad, creating deep divisions. For the foreseeable future, this crisis will intensify, and al Qaeda and its chief competitor, the Islamic State, will continue to jockey for position.

In late 2010, the self-immolation of a despairing Tunisian street vendor inspired millions of Arabs to rise up against authoritarian governments. In a matter of weeks, seemingly impregnable Arab regimes started to shake, and a single man had sparked what decades of attacks by Islamists, including jihadi-salafi groups, had not: the overthrow of an authoritarian government. In the wake of this change, a new generation of jihadi-salafists saw unprecedented opportunities to promote their own methods, priorities, and strategy of jihad.

Jihadi-salafists had very little to do with the Arab uprisings themselves, though they quickly realized the importance of capitalizing on new regional dynamics. The fall of authoritarian rulers in Tunisia, Libya, and Egypt created contested political and security environments. New governments released thousands of jailed jihadi-salafi leaders and activists. This move not only bolstered the ranks of jihadi-salafi groups, but also provided unprecedented space for them to operate locally with minimal constraints. Meanwhile, the war against the Bashar al-Assad regime in Syria and the ensuing security vacuum in its territory created a new focal point for jihad, attracting thousands of fighters from across the region and beyond. Like others in the region, jihadi-salafists were inspired by a new activist spirit and a growing sense of empowerment. In short, the jihadi-salafists were handed a brand new set of opportunities that could have allowed them to rally together in a stronger-than-ever united front. Instead they began to challenge al Qaeda's central authority and the consensus it had overseen.

New militant groups proliferated across the Middle East and North Africa. In the Sinai Peninsula and Yemen, militants expanded their operations against government targets. In Tunisia, jihadi-salafists promoted da'wa, or proselytization and spiritual outreach, to build new constituencies and contest political space. A variety of groups with diverse goals emerged in Libya. Al Qaeda largely approved of these different approaches because they fell within the broad strategy the organization had pursued for over a decade, and al Qaeda's leaders urged jihadists to take advantage of the opportunities before them.

A mutiny was already brewing when events in Syria and Iraq in 2013 and 2014 exposed deep fissures over leadership, strategy, and what had been largely theoretical debates on Islamic governance. Al Qaeda had worked hard to maintain a consensus for years. After 2011, jihadi-salafists not only rebelled against al Qaeda's authority, they questioned al Qaeda's ultimate goal and how it wages jihad. In June 2014, jihadi-salafists in Iraq declared the caliphate, an unprecedented step in modern times, which shattered the principle of consultation, or *shura*, which many jihadi-salafists respected. More importantly, this rebellion sought to supplant al Qaeda's leadership by forcing jihadists to declare allegiance to and obey a caliph. These jihadi rebels want to set a new course, even if it means creating *fitna* (strife) or dividing the movement.[1] And they are grabbing power from an aging and seemingly out of touch al Qaeda leadership. This new division is reshaping the jihadi-salafi landscape, and it has widespread implications for future jihadi-salafi tactics, strategy, and priorities.

ROOTS OF JIHADI-SALAFISM

Jihadi-salafists are part of the broader salafi movement.[2] According to Bernard Haykel, salafists are religious and social reformers who seek a return to the authentic beliefs and practices of the first three generations of Muslims; they adhere to a particular understanding of *tawhid*, or the unity of God, oppose *shirk* (polytheism), view the Qur'an and Sunna (the canonized practices of Mohammad) as the only valid sources of law and authority,[3] and are hostile to innovation, or *bid'a*, often associated with non-Islamic cultural practices that Muslims have come to adopt.[4] Most salafists argue for obedience to Muslim rulers, including authoritarian ones, and have traditionally opposed jihad against Arab governments because they believe that rebellion is harmful to the umma, or Muslim community.

However, a strain of salafism has emerged over time that embraces violence and articulates this violence as a manifestation of jihad. Diverse groups across the Middle East and North Africa and beyond adhere to this strain; they share a broad goal of waging violent jihad to establish a new Islamic political struc-

---

1. *Fitna* can refer specifically to discord or strife within the Muslim community. It is an important concept to jihadi-salafists who, for example, accuse rival groups of disrupting the unity of the Muslim umma. *Shura*, or consultation, is an important aspect of decisionmaking in groups like al Qaeda: *fitna* is the opposite of *shura*.

2. For a detailed description and definition of salafism, see Bernard Haykel, "On the Nature of Salafi Thought and Action," in *Global Salafism: Islam's New Religious Movement*, ed. Roel Meijer (London: Hurst, 2009): 33–57.

3. Salafists are also referred to as Ahl al Hadith (people of the Hadith or Sunna) for their legal focus on the Qur'an and Sunna rather than the four schools of jurisprudence (Hanbali, Shafi'i, Maliki, and Hanafi). See Roel Meijer, "Introduction," *Global Salafism: Islam's New Religious Movement*, ed. Roel Meijer (London: Hurst, 2009), 4.

4. Haykel, "On the Nature of Salafi Thought," 38–39.

ture and society, although they remain deeply divided over the methodology and strategy, or *manhaj*, that would achieve that goal.

What constitutes jihad has varied over time and place. The first two Muslim dynasties, the Umayyads and Abbasids, used jihad as a tool to consolidate control over territory.[5] Jihad in classical texts distinguishes two forms: offensive jihad, which is the duty of the Muslim community on a collective level (*fard kifaya*), and defensive jihad to repel invaders, which is an individual duty (*fard 'ayn*).[6] The idea of defensive jihad crystallized during the Crusades and throughout the Mongol invasion, when Muslim lands were under attack. Ibn Taymiyya, a fourteenth-century scholar widely quoted by jihadi-salafists, shifted ideas about jihad from a political-territorial action to an action intended to purify Muslim identity and practice.[7] Ibn Taymiyya justified violent jihad against the Mongol rulers, arguing that they were not true Muslims because they maintained their own non-Islamic cultural practices and laws.

Modern jihadi-salafists argue that the Muslim world has been under constant attack since the outset of European colonialism in the nineteenth century and demise of the Ottoman caliphate in the early twentieth century. Thus they justify their violent actions as a defensive jihad to protect Muslims against invaders, whether they are British, American, or Western-supported Arab regimes. This understanding of jihad as a defensive duty is significant because it empowers individuals rather than a head of state or Muslim ruler to declare jihad.

5. Paul L. Heck, "Jihad Revisited," *Journal of Religious Ethics* 32, no. 1 (March 2004): 106.

6. Classical jurists divided jihad into two modalities. Offensive jihad is initiated by a Muslim ruler (the caliph) and is considered by most to be a *fard kifaya*, a collective duty, requiring only a sufficient number of Muslims to participate as needed to ensure its success. The second modality is defensive jihad, which is waged whenever Muslim lands or people are directly attacked. The defensive modality does not require a Muslim ruler to initiate the fight, nor does it have the same limitations on participants. Since it is a *fard 'ayn*, an individual duty, all must participate. The repeated trio of 'things to defend' seen throughout jihadi texts includes land/home, family, and money. See Sherman Jackson, "Jihad and the Modern World," *Journal of Islamic Law and Culture* 7, no. 1 (Spring/Summer 2002): 1–26.

7. Heck, "Jihad Revisited," 115.

Jihadi-salafism also owes much to two more recent thinkers and ideologues: Muhammad ibn Abd al-Wahhab in the eighteenth-century Arabian Peninsula, and Sayyid Qutb in twentieth-century Egypt. The former was a religious reformer who argued for a fundamentalist interpretation of the Qur'an and Sunna as the source for Islamic belief and practice.[8] The latter was a twentieth-century member of the Muslim Brotherhood who was tried and executed for plotting violence against the regime of Gamal Abdel Nasser. Both were outraged by what they perceived as the decay of Islamic society, and both sought—in different ways—to revive the authentic Islam practiced by the first generations of Muslims.[9]

Under the influence of two South Asian revivalist scholars, Abu-l-A'la Mawdudi and Abu-l-Hasan al-Nadwi, Qutb refined two interrelated concepts crucial to jihadi-salafism's justification for violence against Muslim rulers. The first was the notion of *takfir,* or declaring a Muslim an infidel for un-Islamic behavior or thought.[10] The second was a contrast between the existing, corrupt political order in both the Muslim world and the West and an idealized political system based on Islamic law derived from the Qur'an and Sunna which embodied God's sovereignty

---

8. Muhammad ibn Abd al-Wahhab sought to eradicate all vestiges of *bid'a* (unlawful innovations) in the Arabian Peninsula, such as marking the Prophet's birthday, praying at tombs, and use of musical ceremonies in Sufi rituals, which he decried as *shirk,* or idolatry. He argued for a fundamentalist interpretation of Islamic theology, based on the teachings of Ibn Taymiyya and the Hanbali school of law. An alliance between ibn Abd al-Wahhab and the Al Saud family eventually solidified Wahhabism's religious control and the Al Saud's political dominance in the Arabian Peninsula. Wahhabism, then, is a salafi movement in that it seeks to emulate the *salaf* in its teachings and practice. Though the terms salafi and Wahhabi are often confused or used interchangeably, not all salafis are Wahhabi.

9. These early Muslim generations or *salaf* were those who lived during Muhammad's lifetime and for about two centuries after and observed his practices. See "Companions of the Prophet," *The Oxford Encyclopedia of Islam and Women* (New York, NY: Oxford University Press, 2013).

10. Qutb did not invent the notion of *takfir.* In fact, the practice of *takfir* dates back to some of the earliest days of Islam, when a group later known as the Kharijites ("those who withdrew or broke off") declared the rest of the Muslim community infidels and attacked them. Some in the Muslim world today accuse the Islamic State of representing a new incarnation of the Kharijites.

on earth, or *hakimiyya*.[11] Qutb concluded that any system that does not implement *hakimiyya* should be resisted.[12]

In combination with Gulf-inspired salafism, Qutb's ideas provided the ideological foundation for modern jihadi-salafism. Qutb posthumously inspired a generation of militant Sunni thinkers in Egypt and beyond,[13] and many of those who had studied his thought[14] found their way to Afghanistan in the 1980s—where the jihadi-salafi movement would enter a new phase.[15]

11. This contrast opposes *jahiliyya* to *hakimiyya*. *Jahiliyya* refers to the "age of ignorance" and immorality that characterized Arabian society before Islam. Qutb considered the existing political order and all Western political ideologies as *jahiliyya*. On the other hand, a political system based on Islamic law he considered *hakimiyya* or *hakimiyyat Allah*—essentially, God's sovereignty on earth. *Hakimiyya* is itself intimately connected to the caliphate and the salafi movement in general. In his famous text, "Signposts Along the Road," Qutb idealizes the original salafi community, emphasizing that with the downfall of the caliphate, the Muslim community fell into *jahiliyya*, or ignorance. Once the community is spiritually restored to the status of the *salaf*, the rule of God on earth can be established and enshrined in the caliphate. See Sayyid Qutb, "Signposts Along the Road," in *Princeton Readings in Islamist Thought: Texts and Contexts from al-Banna to Bin Laden*, ed. Roxanne Euben and Muhammad Qasim Zaman (Princeton, NJ: Princeton University Press, 2009): 129–44.

12. Hassan al-Banna, the founder of the Muslim Brotherhood, advocated for a similar reorientation of the Muslim community in preparation for the establishment of an Islamic state.

13. Qutb's devotees included Muhammad Faraj, who was executed in 1982 for his role in the assassination of President Anwar Sadat. Faraj was an ideologue for Jama'at al-Jihad. Rather than viewing jihad as a progression from social "Islamization" to structural change, as Qutb did, Faraj instead argued that the first battlefield for jihad and the creation of an Islamic state is the "extermination of infidel rulers." See "Muhammad 'abd al-Salam Faraj," and "The Neglected Duty," in *Princeton Readings in Islamist Thought: Texts and Contexts from al-Banna to Bin Laden*, ed. Roxanne Euben and Muhammad Qasim Zaman (Princeton, NJ: Princeton University Press, 2009): 321–43.

14. Qutb also inspired the ideologies that drove the Gama'a Islamiyya, headed by Sheikh Omar Abdel Rahman, and the al-Jihad organization headed by Ayman al-Zawahiri. Like Qutb, Zawahiri spent time in prison; the experience helped to radicalize both men and influenced their approach toward jihad and violence. Also like Qutb, Zawahiri declared Arab regimes infidels for their repression of Islam and alliance with the West.

15. For a detailed account of how Arabs formed al Qaeda in Afghanistan, see Camille Tawil, *Brothers in Arms* (London: Saqi Books, 2010).

THE SEARCH FOR CONSENSUS

The jihad in Afghanistan against the Soviet Union brought together a diverse group of jihadi-salafists from across the Middle East and North Africa. The defeat of the Soviets, however, exposed deep strategic disagreements that had been subsumed by the common fight and shared experiences. Many of the Algerian, Libyan, and Egyptian fighters in Afghanistan returned to their home countries planning to fight their governments. Others, influenced partially by the Saudi regime and quietist or apolitical salafists, believed that violent jihad had ended and that a return to da'wa and proselytization was called for. Yet others were empowered by their victory and sought to refocus jihad against other enemies.

Even those who advocated continuing jihad disagreed about how to do so. Followers of Abdullah Azzam (a leading theorist on defensive jihad) argued that jihad can be waged only against non-Muslim invaders and should focus on anticolonial struggles in Palestine, the Caucuses, and elsewhere.[16] The Egyptian Ayman al-Zawahiri, who led the Egyptian al-Jihad organization and spent time in Egyptian prison, vehemently opposed Azzam's unwillingness to strike Arab governments. Zawahiri argued that authoritarian regimes in the Arab world had ceased to be Muslim. Therefore it was the duty of a (jihadi) vanguard to overthrow them.

During the 1990s, Zawahiri increasingly influenced Osama bin Laden, the scion of a wealthy and well-connected Saudi family who had made a name for himself financing and coordinating Arab fighters in Afghanistan. In 1996, bin Laden announced his intention to evict U.S. military forces stationed in Saudi Arabia following the 1991 U.S.-led war against Saddam

---

16. Abdullah Azzam, a Palestinian-born member of the Muslim Brotherhood, became one of the leading Arab figures in the jihad in Afghanistan. He was an early mentor and teacher of Osama bin Laden, though he opposed the influence of the Egyptian ideologues such as Zawahiri. He was assassinated, along with his two sons, in a car bomb near his home in Peshawar, Pakistan, on November 23, 1989. For an account of Azzam's early role in Afghanistan see Tawil, *Brothers in Arms*, 17–24.

Hussein.[17] In 1998, Zawahiri and bin Laden formally merged their operations to create al Qaeda. Bin Laden and Zawahiri were entrepreneurs and rebels within the jihadi-salafi movement. Al Qaeda represented a new model of jihad that focused on a global struggle against the "far enemy." The attacks against the U.S. embassies in Kenya and Tanzania in 1998 and later those of September 11, 2001, were not only a declaration of war against the United States, they were a rebellion against leading voices in the jihadi-salafi community who argued that war with the West would undermine their common goal of creating a new Islamic polity and society or caliphate.[18] The approach put al Qaeda on a collision course with Arab governments, some of which had provided institutional support for jihad in Afghanistan during the 1980s. Al Qaeda's new strategy revolutionized jihadi-salafists' struggle, and its attacks against the United States set a new standard for what could be achieved, silencing counterarguments and attracting fighters, supporters, and sympathizers to its cause.

Al Qaeda's approach to jihad was based on several strategic principles that distinguished it from other jihadi-salafi groups. First, al Qaeda prioritized global jihad against the United States and Europe (the "far enemy"). Targeting the "far enemy" that supported Arab regimes would make the "near enemy," those same local governments, crumble from within. Waging jihad in Syria, liberating Palestine, and fighting Shi'a were important causes, but distracted from the more immediate goal of fighting the far enemy.

Second, al Qaeda's focus on waging global jihad and attacking Western targets meant that it was less immediately concerned with theological questions, such as how and when to implement

---

17. Osama bin Laden, "Declaration of War against America," in *Princeton Readings in Islamist Thought: Texts and Contexts from al-Banna to Bin Laden*, ed. Roxanne Euben and Muhammad Qasim Zaman (Princeton, NJ: Princeton University Press, 2009): 436–59.
18. One of the leading salafi scholars opposing the global jihadi shift was Nasir al-Din al-Albani.

shari'a[19] and when to establish a caliphate. This focus contributed to its adoption of an evolutionary methodology or *manhaj* for reaching its ultimate objective—the caliphate. It used religious arguments when necessary to justify its policies, but it was not consumed by them, in part because such theological questions could be divisive. The territorial entities known as emirates, which had been established by al Qaeda's affiliates and by the Taliban in Afghanistan, were seen as a stage in the eventual establishment of a caliphate at a later time.

Third, al Qaeda emphasized the importance of building and maintaining a bond between the Muslim masses and the jihadi project. Al Qaeda's leadership saw Muslim populations as inherently ignorant of religion and unprepared to accept Islamic law without proper religious education and understanding. As a result, they believed that Muslim society must be properly prepared through education and da'wa before imposing Islamic law and establishing the caliphate.[20] When Abu Musab al-Zarqawi, then head of al Qaeda in Iraq (AQI), raised the issue of establishing a caliphate in 2004, al Qaeda's leadership explained that Muslims were not yet prepared, though leaders appeared to support efforts to establish an Islamic state in parts of Iraq in 2006–2007.[21] Zawahiri argued that an emirate or Islamic au-

---

19. Shari'a refers to a comprehensive set of regulations that govern every aspect of daily life, not just punishments for crimes.

20. Zawahiri writes that da'wa is an important part of the jihadi mission. It aims "to create awareness in the umma regarding the threat posed by the Crusader onslaught, clarify the true meaning of Tawheed in the sense that the rule and sovereignty belongs to Allah alone . . . by the permission of Allah, this will serve as a prelude to the establishment of the Caliphate according to the methodology of the Prophet." The propagational phase focuses on two fronts: educating the mujahid vanguard who will shoulder the responsibility of militarily confronting the "Crusaders and their proxies until the Caliphate is established," and "creating awareness within the masses, inciting them, and exerting efforts to mobilize them so they revolt against rulers and join the side of Islam and those working for its cause." See Ayman al-Zawahiri, "General Guidelines for Jihad," As-Sahab Media, 2013, https://azelin.files.wordpress.com/2013/09/dr-ayman-al-e1ba93awc481hirc4ab-22general-guidelines-for-the-work-of-a-jihc481dc4ab22-en.pdf.

21. For a study of al Qaeda in Iraq from 2006 to 2010, see Brian Fishman, "Redefining the Islamic State: The Fall and Rise of Al-Qaeda in Iraq," New America Foundation National Security Studies Program Policy Paper, August 2011, http://security.newamerica.net/sites/newamerica.net/files/policydocs/Fishman_Al_Qaeda_In_Iraq.pdf.

thority must be established first to prepare society for the caliphate through spiritual and religious education. In 2012, when al Qaeda in the Arabian Peninsula (AQAP) proposed an emirate in Yemen, al Qaeda cautioned that it was not the right time: if AQAP proved unable to provide sufficient services and function as a state, this failure might undermine the jihadi enterprise.[22] According to al Qaeda's strategy shari'a and proper Islamic governance could not be implemented if these basic needs were not met first.

Finally, al Qaeda was also concerned about not alienating Muslims through excessive violence against civilians, including Shi'a. In some cases it even advocated a form of détente with non-Muslim communities, including Shi'a and Christians.[23] While al Qaeda sees the Shi'a as misguided apostates, Zawahiri argues that at the current juncture al Qaeda should preach to them (and other deviant sects) rather than kill them, unless they attack Sunnis first.[24] At one point in 2005 Zawahiri counseled Zarqawi to slow his attacks against the Shi'a and their mosques in Iraq because such actions alienate the rest of the Muslim population. According to Zawahiri, the confrontation with the Shi'a is inevitable but need not take place immediately.[25] This sensitivity was a lesson learned from Algeria in the 1990s, when the insurgent Armed Islamic Group (GIA) lost popular support and legitimacy because of excessively violent tactics. Al Qaeda's central leadership has repeatedly invoked the Algerian experience to warn overzealous commanders to restrain themselves from excessive violence that could undermine popular support.

22. Nasir Abdel Karim al-Wuhayshi (Abu Basir), "Second Letter from Abu Basir to Emir of Al-Qaida in the Islamic Maghreb," in "Al-Qaida Papers," Associated Press, 2012, http://www.longwarjournal.org/images/al-qaida-papers-how-to-run-a-state.pdf.

23. Zawahiri, "General Guidelines for Jihad."

24. Ibid.; Ayman al-Zawahiri, "Acknowledging ISIS officially isn't part of AQ," February 3, 2014, http://justpaste.it/translt; see original Arabic here: http://justpaste.it/ea9k.

25. The Combating Terrorism Center at West Point, "Zawahiri's Letter to Zarqawi (English Translation)," July 2005, https://www.ctc.usma.edu/v2/wp-content/uploads/2013/10/Zawahiris-Letter-to-Zarqawi-Translation.pdf; see Arabic original here: https://www.ctc.usma.edu/v2/wp-content/uploads/2013/10/Zawahiris-Letter-to-Zarqawi-Original.pdf.

These tenets of al Qaeda's *manhaj* are presented clearly in the group's writings, correspondence, and statements. In another letter to Zarqawi in 2005, for example, Zawahiri gently warns the commander to temper his actions, and cites the importance of popular support in achieving al Qaeda's two short-term goals—removing U.S. troops from Iraq and establishing an Islamic entity in Iraq. The letter states: "We will see that the strongest weapon which the mujahadeen enjoy—after the help and granting of success by G-d—is popular support from the Muslim masses in Iraq, and the surrounding Muslim countries. So, we must maintain this support as best we can, and we should strive to increase it."[26] Zawahiri tells Zarqawi that public executions of prisoners and Shi'a have started to alienate people who do not understand the theological and ideological motivations behind such bloody actions. Abu Muhammad al-Maqdisi, a Jordanian-born jihadi-salafi thinker who shares al Qaeda's evolutionary strategy, has also weighed in repeatedly on the need to maintain public support.[27] He has accused the Islamic State of "distracting the people and diverting their attention from the Islamic project and burning any popular support and deterring any of the supporters across the Ummah from this current due to their bad practices..."[28]

Al Qaeda's cautious approach led it to navigate carefully local traditions, sensitivities, and practices. This caution, useful in

---

26. Ibid.
27. Jordanian born Abu Muhammad al-Maqdisi became a leading voice of al Qaeda on both theological and tactical matters. He has consistently criticized jihadists' public display of excessive violence, such as beheadings, for its negative impact on Islam and for undermining the salafi goal of creating an Islamic state. But his repudiation of Zarqawi, his former student, and al Qaeda in Iraq for its indiscriminate violence and targeting of Shi'a civilians made him a target for criticism among some Jordanian jihadi-salafists. For a more detailed analysis of Maqdisi's influence, see Joas Wagemakers, *A Quietist Jihad: The Ideology and Influence of Abu Muhammad al-Maqdisi* (New York: Cambridge University Press, 2012): 82–84, 244.
28. Abu Muhammad al-Maqdisi, "And Be Not Like Her Who Undoes the Thread which She has Spun, After it Became Strong," July 11, 2014, *pietervanostaeyen* (blog), http://pietervanostaeyen.wordpress.com/2014/07/14/and-be-not-like-her-who-undoes-the-thread-which-she-has-spun-after-it-has-become-strong-by-shaykh-abu-muhammad-al-maqdisi/.

building support networks among local populations out of necessity, also manifested itself in al Qaeda's gradual approach to implementing shari'a. Abdelmalek Droukdal, the emir of al Qaeda in the Islamic Maghreb (AQIM), sent a message of caution in mid-2012 to jihadists who controlled northern Mali: "One of the wrong policies that we think you carried out is the extreme speed in which you applied Shariah, not taking into consideration the gradual evolution that should be applied in an environment that is ignorant of religion."[29] AQIM shares Zawahiri's caution in forcing local populations to abide by shari'a before they are properly educated, for fear of alienating them.

As al Qaeda sought to unify, lead, and maintain a jihadi-salafi ideological and strategic consensus based on its *manhaj*, it repeatedly stressed the importance of *shura*, or consultation, in official statements and documents.[30] *Shura* was also an important factor in the group's hierarchical governing structure, which places an emir at the top and—as explained in a 2002 document entitled "Al-Qa'ida By-laws"—includes a *shura* or leadership council, executive council, regional councils, and military councils that are directly linked to the emir.[31] In the decade after September 11, 2001, jihadi-salafi groups across the Middle East and North Africa pledged their allegiance to bin Laden by swearing an oath of allegiance (*ba'ya*) which in turn must be accepted by al Qaeda. Al Qaeda's "brand" and presence grew through franchise or affiliate organizations such as AQIM, AQI, AQAP, and more recently its Syrian affiliate Jabhat al-Nusra. This bureaucracy and obsession with consensus was intended to strengthen the al Qaeda leader-

---

29. Letter from Abdelmalek Droukdal composed around July 2012, as published in "Mali-al-Qaida's Sahara Playbook," Associated Press, around July 2012, http://hosted.ap.org/specials/interactives/_international/_pdfs/al-qaida-manifesto.pdf.
30. See for example "'Al-Qa'ida By-laws (English Translation)' Harmony Document AFGP-2002-600048," Combating Terrorism Center at West Point Harmony Program, April 18, 2002, https://www.ctc.usma.edu/v2/wp-content/uploads/2013/10/Al-Qaida-Bylaws-Translation.pdf.
31. Ibid. The *shura* council is the most important body in that it oversees al Qaeda's strategy and considers crucial ideological and practical debates. The council plays an essential consultative role, but the emir has final decisionmaking authority. If he chooses, he can put issues to a vote and abide by the council's decision, but unless he opts for such a vote he is not bound by the council's suggestions.

ship's control and ensure that no decisions on tactics or strategy were taken without their approval. Al Qaeda's authority and the consensus it upheld were further bolstered by respected independent scholars who supported its relatively flexible theological and evolutionary approach, such as Abu Muhammad al-Maqdisi, Abu Qatada al-Filastini, and Abu Yahya al-Shinqiti. These figures collectively inspired and guided a generation of jihadi-salafi adherents in the decade after September 11, 2001.

Al Qaeda's senior leadership understood that it could never unify the many different jihadi-salafi groups. Instead it accepted differences as long as disparate groups demonstrated a vague commitment to jihad and accepted al Qaeda's leadership.[32] Al Qaeda was less concerned with dogma and theological debates than with managing a global network of affiliated groups that could build footholds across the region and beyond. Differences over strategy and priorities remained, but affiliates balanced pursuit of insurgencies against Arab governments with al Qaeda's global strategy of attacking Western targets. Moreover, the affiliates largely accepted al Qaeda's guidance when it came to theological and strategic issues such as engaging with Muslim populations, defining legitimate targets, and developing structures of Islamic government. After bin Laden's death in May 2011, many of these groups pledged allegiance to Zawahiri, bin Laden's successor. One of Zawahiri's key challenges was maintaining the unity of jihadi groups that were spread across a wide geographical area, faced different constraints, and operated in different political and security environments.

---

32. "As far as its relation with other groups is concerned, Al-Qa'ida is less selective: groups wishing to liaise with Al-Qa'ida or receive its support have to commit to jihad and, not to prove a commitment to a theological creed, but essentially to prove their jihadi—non nation-state—credentials. Beyond that, Al-Qa'ida is willing to work with or lend support to jihadi groups, even if they are more inflexible than necessary in matters of faith and practice, or even if they do not conceive of themselves as global jihadis, e.g., Egyptian Islamic Group, Egyptian Jihad Group and others." Nelly Lahoud, "Beware of Imitators: Al-Qa'ida through the Lens of its Confidential Secretary," Combating Terrorism Center at West Point Harmony Program, June 4, 2012, https://www.ctc.usma.edu/v2/wp-content/uploads/2012/06/CTC-Beware-of-Imitators-June2012.pdf.

A BROKEN CONSENSUS

Discord had tested jihadi-salafists in the past. This tension occasionally forced al Qaeda to reassert its leadership and strategy, and made affiliate groups reaffirm their loyalty to al Qaeda.[33] Moreover, disputes within al Qaeda affiliates such as AQIM broke the established chain of command, causing competition and divisions.[34] But nothing could have prepared the movement for what was about to transpire in Syria and Iraq in 2013–2014.

Syria provided a new battleground for jihad which helped reignite jihad in Iraq as well. Jihadists largely observed a basic division of labor throughout much of 2012 in Syria and Iraq:

---

33. In March 2008 Ayman al-Zawahiri released an online book reaffirming al Qaeda's strategy and priorities after criticism that it focused unduly on Iraq and Afghanistan while neglecting the Palestinian issue. See "Zawahiri Tries to Clear Name, Explain Strategy," Transnational Security Issue Report, International Research Center, April 21, 2008, http://fas.org/irp/eprint/zawahiri.pdf.

34. In December 2012 Mokhtar Belmokhtar, a local commander in AQIM's southern region, broke from AQIM and formed a new battalion called Those who Sign with Blood. Belmokhtar had an ongoing rivalry with AQIM head Abdelmalek Droukdal, which influenced the split. A letter by AQIM's Shura Council reprimanding Belmokhtar accused him of fragmenting the organization, and failing to commit any major attacks: "Any observer of armed action in the Sahara will notice clearly the failure of the Masked Brigade to carry out spectacular operations, despite the region's vast possibilities...moreover, you have received multiple directives and instructions from the Emirate of the organization urging you to carry out these acts. Despite all that, your brigade did not achieve a single spectacular operation targeting the crusader alliance." The letter continues: "...we consider it a dangerous attempt to secede from the community, fragment the being of the organization and tear it apart limb from limb." In January 2013, a few months after receiving the letter, Belmokhtar launched one of North Africa's boldest attacks ever, on Algeria's In Amenas gas processing facility, followed by two attacks in Niger against a French-owned uranium mine and a military base. For more complete correspondence between AQIM and Belmokhtar see "Letter from the Organization of al-Qaida in the Islamic Maghreb's Shura Council to our good brothers in the Shura Council of the Masked Brigade," in "Al-Qaida Papers," Associated Press, October 3, 2012, http://hosted.ap.org/specials/interactives/_international/_pdfs/al-qaida-belmoktar-letter-english.pdf; Christopher S. Chivvis and Andrew Liepman, "North Africa's Menace: AQIM's Evolution and the U.S. Policy Response," RAND Corporation, 2013, http://www.rand.org/content/dam/rand/pubs/research_reports/RR400/RR415/RAND_RR415.pdf.

For an account of the In Amenas attack see "The In Amenas Attack: Report of the Investigation into the Terrorist Attack on In Amenas," Statoil, September 2013, http://www.statoil.com/en/NewsAndMedia/News/2013/Downloads/In%20Amenas%20report.pdf.

Jabhat al-Nusra, commanded by Abu Mohammad al-Julani, operated in Syria while the Islamic State of Iraq (ISI), commanded by Abu Bakr al-Baghdadi, operated in Iraq. Baghdadi, however, had grander plans. In April 2013 he announced that both ISI and Jabhat al-Nusra were dissolved as independent organizations and instead would be reconstituted in one new organization known as the Islamic State of Iraq and al-Sham (ISIS).[35] The move sparked an immediate outcry from Julani and al Qaeda's leadership. Julani declared his allegiance to Ayman al-Zawahiri and al Qaeda rather than to Abu Bakr al-Baghdadi and what became ISIS.[36] While censuring the move, Zawahiri reminded

35. Baghdadi announced the dissolution of both the Islamic State of Iraq and Jabhat al-Nusra in favor of a united Islamic State in Iraq and al-Sham. He claimed that Jabhat al-Nusra is an "expansion for the Islamic State of Iraq and part of it" and that joining them together officially under the banner of the caliphate, once God wills its establishment, is an avoidance of "calamity," which is likely a reference to *fitna*, describing disunity and discord within the Muslim community. For an English translation of the original video message, see "'Give good news to the believers.' The declaration of the Islamic State in Iraq and al-Sham: An audio speech for Amir al-Muminin Abu Bakr al-Hussaini Al-Quraishi al-Baghdadi," Al-Manarah al-Bayda Foundation for Media Production, April 9, 2013, http://azelin.files.wordpress.com/2013/04/shaykh-abc5ab-bakr-al-e1b8a5ussaync4ab-al-qurayshc4ab-al-baghdc481dc4ab-e2809cannouncement-of-the-islamic-state-of-iraq-and-al-shc481m22-en.pdf.
36. What precipitated the rivalry and clash between ISIS and Jabhat al-Nusra is unclear. One view suggests strategic differences arose between Baghdadi and Jabhat al-Nusra commander Abu Mohammad al-Julani over the timing of declaring an Islamic state. Baghdadi called for doing so immediately while Julani followed al Qaeda's staged approach. Another view suggests that it resulted from a personal rivalry between the leaders of both groups. See Suhaib Anjarini, "The Evolution of ISIS," *Al Monitor*, November 1, 2013, http://www.al-monitor.com/pulse/security/2013/11/syria-islamic-state-iraq-sham-growth.html. In his response to Baghdadi's dissolution of Jabhat al-Nusra, Julani does not reject Baghdadi or his actions entirely: the question, rather is one of consultation and *ba'ya*—and Julani wants to clarify that he follows Zawahiri first. In Baghdadi's statement announcing the merger (see footnote 35), he himself acknowledges that scholars, or the ulema, do not support him—he knows he does not yet have consensus: "...as for the sincere Ulema we ask for your support to the religion and call you to join us hasn't time come to dust your feet with the soil of the land of jihad for the sake of Allah?... I swear by Allah you will find that fear for the sake of Allah is better from [than] the comfortable bed which you sleep in." For Julani's reaffirmation of support for Zawahiri, see "About the Fields of al-Sham," Al-Manarah al-Bayda Foundation for Media Production, April 2013, http://jihadology.net/2013/04/10/al-manarah-al-bay%E1%B8%8Da-foundation-for-media-production-presents-a-new-audio-message-from-jabhat-al-nu%E1%B9%A3rahs-abu-mu%E1%B8%A5ammad-

Baghdadi to focus his operations on Iraq, not Syria, which would remain under Jabhat al-Nusra's purview.[37] The split that ensued was more than just political competition for leadership, however: it was about the proper strategy to achieve jihadists' ultimate objectives.

While some jihadists called for reconciling the dispute, the split was about to deepen. In June 2014 Abu Bakr al-Baghdadi took an unprecedented step of declaring himself caliph of a new caliphate which would simply be called the Islamic State.[38] What was underway was nothing less than a rebellion against al Qaeda and an attempt to redefine jihadi strategy.

The split with al Qaeda was more immediately precipitated by Baghdadi's unilateral moves in Syria, but the decaying relationship between al Qaeda and the predecessors of the Islamic State long foretold this clash. What became the Islamic State in 2014 evolved from the Islamic State of Iraq (ISI) and al Qaeda in Iraq (AQI), which was formed in 2004 by Abu Musab al-Zarqawi.[39] From the beginning, al Qaeda had difficulty controlling Zarqawi and AQI. Though AQI pursued the "far enemy" by attacking U.S. forces in Iraq, it also intentionally deepened sectarian tensions by attacking Shi'a civilians and minority groups, a strategy that intensified Iraq's civil war and contradicted al Qaeda's approach

---

al-jawlani-al-golani-about-the-fields-of-al-sham.

37. Ayman al-Zawahiri, "Testimonial to preserve blood of the mujahideen in Sham," *pietervanostaeyen* (blog), May 2014, http://pietervanostaeyen.wordpress. com/2014/05/03/dr-ayman-az-zawahiri-testimonial-to-preserve-the-blood-of-mujahideen-in-as-sham/. In May 2014 Zawahiri lectures Baghdadi to "focus on Iraq, which needs more effort, empty yourself for it even if you see yourselves as wronged! To stop this massacre and to focus on the enemies of Islam and the Sunnis in Iraq." Baghdadi is accused here of overstepping his bounds, of ignoring Zawahiri's orders, and ignoring al Qaeda's strategy and plan. Specifically, he implores Baghdadi to "Come back to the Sam' wa Ta'ah (hearing & obedience) to your leaders. Come back to what your Shaykhs and leaders worked for and preceded you in it."
38. On the first day of Ramadan 2014, Abu Muhammad al-Adnani al-Shami, a spokesman for ISIS, declared Abu Bakr al-Baghdadi caliph of the "Islamic State" in an audio statement posted online. See Abu Muhammad al-Adnani al-Shami, "This is the Promise of Allah," Al Hayat Media Center, June 29, 2014, https://ia902505. us.archive.org/28/items/poa_25984/EN.pdf.
39. Prior to establishing Al Qaeda in Iraq Zarqawi led a group called Tawhid wal Jihad (Monotheism and Jihad).

regarding Shi'a.[40] AQI gained a reputation for brutal violence against Shi'a, minorities, and eventually against Sunni groups that opposed its actions. By late 2006 AQI adopted the name Islamic State of Iraq and announced the creation of a Sunni state in western Iraq.[41]

ISI's fortunes declined once Sunni tribes that had previously accepted its presence began confronting the group in cooperation with the U.S. military. Many of its top leaders were killed by U.S. forces and local Iraqi allies. The group was already badly wounded in 2010, when a mid-level bomb maker, Ibrahim Awad Bu Badri, later known as Abu Bakr al-Baghdadi, became ISI's emir.[42] Had there been no war in Syria, ISI would likely have remained a shadow of its former self. But the Syrian conflict's sectarian nature fed the extreme violence and tension that AQI and ISI had fostered and capitalized on in Iraq almost a decade earlier, and enabled jihadi-salafists to reemerge in both Syria and Iraq.

In contrast to al Qaeda, which held that conditions were not yet ripe for shari'a or the caliphate, the Islamic State expresses a sense of urgency about both. It understands the importance

---

40. In 2006 for example AQI bombed the golden-domed Shi'a al Askari Mosque in Samarra and in 2007 launched a series of bombings against the Yazidi community that killed nearly 800 people. See Andrew Wander, "How Suicide Bombings Shattered Iraq," *Al Jazeera*, October 24, 2010, http://www.aljazeera.com/secretiraqfiles/2010/10/2010102216102542862s.html; "Mastermind of Iraq Yazidi Attack Killed: U.S. Military," Reuters, September 9, 2007, http://www.reuters.com/article/2007/09/09/us-iraq-yazidis-idUSL0930932320070909.

41. Al Qaeda in Iraq created the Mujahideen Shura Council as a front to run the Islamic State of Iraq. See Fishman, "Redefining the Islamic State," 8.

42. Abu Bakr al-Baghdadi rose through the ranks of various jihadi-salafi groups in Iraq including the Islamic State of Iraq, though many details of his activities remain murky. According to some accounts he joined Zarqawi as a smuggler in 2003. He may have been imprisoned by U.S. forces in Iraq for a period of time. According to an "official" biography posted online by the Islamic State, Baghdadi earned degrees in Islamic studies and served on al Qaeda in Iraq and the Islamic State of Iraq's shari'a committees. He allegedly became emir of ISI in April 2010 after the reported death of its former emir. See Peter Beaumont, "Abu Bakr al-Baghdad: The Isis Chief with the Ambition to Overtake Al-Qaida," *Guardian*, June 12, 2014, http://www.theguardian.com/world/2014/jun/12/baghdadi-abu-bakr-iraq-isis-mosul-jihad. For the Islamic State's "official biography see "A Biography of Abu Bakr al-Baghdadi," SITE Intelligence Group, July 16, 2013, http://news.siteintelgroup.com/blog/index.php/entry/226-the-story-behind-abu-bakr-al-baghdadi.

of building popular support by providing social services and in-doctrinating young people, but it is less concerned than al Qaeda is with popular *approval* of its actions, and has little tolerance for dissent when it comes to its doctrine. The Islamic State believes that the caliphate must be established immediately. According to its key spokesman, Abu Muhammad al-Adnani al-Shami, it was the proper time to establish the caliphate because the Islamic State had fulfilled a series of conditions or prerequisites. If the conditions are ripe, it is a sin *not* to establish the caliph-ate.[43] "Running after crowds," as Islamic State leaders accuse al Qaeda of doing, undermines God's authority because it forces the jihadi movement to bend its rules—divinely-given rules, as they believe—to popular will, rather than abiding by God's law.

Not content to simply reject al Qaeda's advice to pursue change gradually and use violence selectively, the Islamic State has embraced rampant violence. It proudly displays, through so-cial media and other online platforms, photographs and videos of beheadings, crucifixions, and mass executions of prisoners, and it publicly administers other punishments such as flogging. Moreover, it has labeled anyone who opposes its doctrine as an infidel. This broad definition of *takfir* allows the Islamic State to justify killing a wide swath of civilians and opponents.

The Islamic State has marked Shi'a as a primary enemy, and has thus deepened the sectarian conflict in Iraq and Syria. In a departure from al Qaeda's measured approach toward Shi'a, Baghdadi has called on Muslim youth to carry out jihad against

---

43. Adnani lists a series of practices that the Islamic State must implement as a prelude to the caliphate: *hudud* or canonical Qur'anic punishment, demolition of grave markers and shrines, release of prisoners "by the edge of the sword," free-dom of movement, appointment of judges, collection of *jizyah* taxes on Christians, collection of *zakat*, and education of the population through religious classes and lessons in mosques. After describing the above prerequisites, he writes: "There only remained one matter, a wajib kifa'i (collective obligation) that the umma sins by abandoning. It is a forgotten obligation... It is the Khilafa (caliphate)... —the abandoned obligation of the era." Having met the requirements, the Islamic State has "gained the essentials necessary for Khilafah, which the Muslims are sinful for if they do not try to establish." See Adnani, "This is the Promise of Allah."

the "*Safavid rafida.*"⁴⁴ *Safavid* refers to the Safavid or Persian Empire, which adopted Shiʻa Islam in the early sixteenth century.⁴⁵ *Rafida* is a derogatory term used to describe Shiʻa; it means "those who refused" the correct succession of historical caliphs. Adnani has also explicitly criticized al Qaeda for its approach to the Shiʻa: "The difference between the [Islamic] State and Al-Aqʼidah...is a matter of crooked religion and deviated Manhaj... a Manhaj which believes...that the filty Rafidah polytheists are only but accused and they should be preached to, not fought!"⁴⁶ The Islamic State's position reflects Zarqawi's earlier views. In a 2004 letter, Zarqawi wrote that "if we succeed in dragging them [Shiʻa] into the arena of sectarian war, it will become possible to awaken the inattentive Sunnis as they feel imminent danger and annihilating death at the hands of these Sabeans."⁴⁷

The Islamic State uses its battlefield success to bolster its religious credentials and legitimacy while undermining its jihadi-salafi rivals. Adnani, for example, claims that God is rewarding the Islamic State with battlefield success because of its piety.⁴⁸

44. Al-Baghdadi, "Allah will not allow except that His Light should be perfected," Fursan al-Balagh Media, July 2012, http://azelin.files.wordpress.com/2012/07/shaykh-abc5ab-bakr-al-e1b8a5ussaync4ab-al-qurayshc4ab-al-baghdc481dc4ab-22but-god-will-not-allow-except-that-his-light-should-be22-en.pdf.
45. The Safavid dynasty ruled from 1501 to 1722 and adopted Shiʻite Islam as the official state religion in part to distinguish itself from the neighboring Ottoman Empire which followed Sunni Islam.
46. Abu Muhammad Al-Adnani al-Shami, "This is not our methodology nor will it ever be," Chabab Tawhid Media, April 2014, http://azelin.files.wordpress.com/2014/04/shaykh-abc5ab-mue1b8a5ammad-al-e28098adnc481nc4ab-al-shc481mc4ab-22this-is-not-our-manhaj-nor-will-it-ever-be22-en.pdf.
47. Sabeans, a pre-Islamic people living in Southern Arabia, are considered by Muslims as one of the three pre-Islamic monotheistic religions. Zarqawi likely equates them with people who rejected Islam. For the text of the letter, see "Zarqawi Letter: February 2004 Coalition Provisional Authority English Translation of Terrorist Musab al Zarqawi Letter Obtained by United States Government in Iraq," February 2004, U.S. Department of State, http://2001-2009.state.gov/p/nea/rls/31694.htm.
48. In "This is not our methodology," Adnani asks God to destroy the state and deny its victories if it is not fulfilling His will. "O Allah, if this State is a State of Khawarij then break its back, kill its leaders, forgo its banner and guide its soldiers to truth. O Allah, if this is an Islamic State, ruling by Your Book and the Sunnah of Your

He also belittles al Qaeda leaders like Zawahiri and Maqdisi for not actively engaging in battle: they "cannot handle jihad of the elite far away from hotels, conferences, offices, lights, and cameras."[49] The rebellion against al Qaeda and its strategy triggered a crisis of authority within jihadi-salafi ranks. As the Islamic State and al Qaeda compete to shape jihadi-salafi strategy—and to be seen as the legitimate shapers of that strategy—the groups have denounced one another, rebutted accusations, and leveled new criticisms. When Baghdadi announced ISIS's merger with Jabhat al-Nusra, Zawahiri responded by sharply criticizing Baghdadi for violating the principles of *shura*, claiming that ISIS "only consulted themselves" and Jabhat al-Nusra "says they were not consulted."[50] He levels the same criticism multiple times: "We were not informed about its [ISIS's] creation, nor counseled. Nor were we satisfied with it rather we ordered it to stop."[51] Zawahri takes the opportunity to reaffirm al Qaeda's evolutionary approach: "Rather the guidelines of the group is not to announce Emirates/States in this stage."[52]

Prophet, fighting Your enemies, then keep it firm, honour it and grant it victory, and establish it upon the earth, and make it as the Khilafah upon the Way of the Prophethood."

49. Adnani, "This is the Promise of Allah."

50. Ayman al-Zawahiri, "Testimonial to preserve blood of the mujahideen in Sham." This particular statement comes more than a year after Baghdadi's April 2013 announcement of the JN/ISIS merger. Here, Zawahiri condemns the infighting between Jabhat al-Nusra and ISIS over the past year, lamenting that their conflict has caused the shedding of innocent Muslim blood and caused *fitna* within the community. He urges them to stop fighting and instead, seek reconciliation. In this document, Zawahiri is reviewing the missteps taken by ISIS and its earlier iterations, noting that at each successive juncture it violated shura, failed to inform Al Qaeda Central of its plans, and disobeyed orders.

51. The same message is given on February 3, 2014, when Zawahiri officially disowns ISIS. "Firstly: Qae'dat al-Jihad (Al Qaeda) declares that it has no links to the ISIS group." He reiterates the importance of *shura* and the principle of consultation and affirms that AQ does not create states or emirates without consulting appropriate leaders and scholars. See Ayman al-Zawahiri, "Acknowledging ISIS officially isn't part of AQ," February 3, 2014, http://justpaste.it/translt: see original Arabic here: http://justpaste.it/ea9k.

52. Ibid.

In response to this criticism, the Islamic State launched a series of verbal assaults on al Qaeda's commitment to jihad, doctrinal purity, and authority to lead the umma and jihad. These claims go beyond earlier disagreements and constitute an unprecedented effort to delegitimize and displace al Qaeda's leadership. In April 2014 Islamic State spokesman Adnani harshly criticized al Qaeda and its *manhaj*: "The leaders of Al-Qa'idah deviated from the right manhaj... Al-Qa'idah today is no longer the Qa'idah of jihad, and so it is not the base of jihad."[53] The implication is that the proper *manhaj* is committed to immediately establishing a caliphate. Al Qaeda's *manhaj*, Adnani continued, "believes in pacifism and runs after majorities"; it shies away "from mentioning jihad and declaring tawhid" and instead mentions "revolution, popularity, uprising, striving, struggle, republicanism, secularism."[54]

Al Qaeda's broad response has been to suggest that the Islamic State's actions violate the principle of *shura* and creates discord or *fitna*.[55] More narrowly, it has attacked Baghdadi's religious credentials and implied that the group overall acts without the guidance of authoritative and respected religious scholars. According to Maqdisi, the Islamic State "has no consideration for the scholars of the Ummah and its prominent figures."[56] He added that "not even one scholar from the divine scholars supported them or trusted them or aligned with them."[57] Of the Islamic State's declaration of the caliphate, Maqdisi writes: "They abrogated their first pledge of allegiance to their leaders and rebelled against their emirs, and they transgressed against their senior figures when they declared the first state, and when they declared the second they shed protected blood and refused to be judged by the Shariah. Therefore, it is our right to ask: What will

53. Adnani, "This is not our methodology."
54. Ibid.
55. See Basma Atassi, "Iraqi al-Qaeda Chief Rejects Zawahiri Orders," *Al Jazeera*, June 15, 2013, http://www.aljazeera.com/news/middleeast/2013/06/201361517221782781o.html.
56. Maqdisi, "And Be Not Like Her Who Undoes the Thread."
57. Ibid.

they do after the declaration of the Caliphate?"[58] The implied answer is that the rebellious and violent acts will continue and in the process will distort both Islam and the jihadi project. Though the Islamic State rejects al Qaeda's leadership, it on occasion invokes the name of al Qaeda leaders, including bin Laden, who still commands respect in jihadi circles. "So be assured O soldiers of the Islamic State, for we are by Allah's will progressing upon the Manhaj of the Imam Shaykh Usamah [bin Laden], and the Amir of the martyrdom seekers Abu Mus'ab Az-Zarqawi, and the founder of the state Abu 'Umar Al-Baghdadi."[59] In this way the Islamic State seeks to build on bin Laden's legitimacy by claiming to be his authentic heir, even as the group turns its back on bin Laden's approach to jihad. By claiming to be bin Laden's heir, Baghdadi is explicitly claiming legitimacy over bin Laden's designated heir and successor, Zawahiri.

IMPLICATIONS

The struggle for authentic leadership has created confusion within jihadi-salafi circles, and it has important ramifications for the United States and other governments that share a common goal of fighting violent extremism.

First, competition for legitimacy, authority, and recruits will drive jihadi-salafi groups to more extreme measures and greater violence as groups seek to distinguish themselves from their rivals. Past experience demonstrates that internal tension and competition among violent extremists heightens the threat against Western and local targets. In December 2007, for example, Algerian militants attacked UN headquarters in Algiers, killing over 31 people. The attacks were carried out by the Salafi Group for Preaching and Combat (GSPC), which had changed

---

58. Ibid.

59. Adnani, "This is not our methodology." Abu Omar al-Baghdadi was the alleged former emir of the Islamic State of Iraq who was reportedly killed in April 2010. Adnani claims that Abu Bakr al-Baghdadi received *ba'ya* in Iraq from Islamic State leaders as the successor to Abu Omar al-Baghdadi. See "Who Was the Real Abu Omar al-Baghdadi," *Asharq al-Awsat*, April 20, 2010, http://www.aawsat. net/2010/04/article55251030.

its name to al Qaeda in the Islamic Maghreb as part of an official affiliation with al Qaeda in late 2006. Though Algerian militants had long targeted Western interests, the UN attack was AQIM's way of demonstrating to al Qaeda its commitment to global jihad, rather than to a narrow Algerian insurgency. Similarly, Mokhtar Belmokhtar launched the 2013 In Amenas attack in response to disagreements and criticism by AQIM's senior leadership. During the bold operation, 32 fighters attacked the Tiguentourine gas plant and took nearly 800 people from over 30 countries hostage for four days. In the end 40 civilians were killed. The attack was intended in part to undermine AQIM's leadership by demonstrating Belmokhtar's capability and primacy within North African jihadi-salafi circles.

Second, the rivalry is forcing jihadi-salafi groups across the Middle East and North Africa and beyond to choose sides in this internal struggle. Will jihadi groups continue swearing allegiance to al Qaeda's leadership and follow the jihadi strategy put forward by Zawahiri and others, or will they choose the strategy of violence against minorities and the immediate establishment of the caliphate? The Islamic State has called for jihadi-salafists to pledge their loyalty to the group and its goals and to launch attacks wherever possible. At first, some groups called for resolving the dispute. AQIM was one of the first to enter the debate, arguing that consultation and consensus were paramount to the broader movement's unity. In an official announcement, AQIM stated that "...It is obvious to all Muslims and Jihad organizations with a truthful approach that such an announcement (about the Caliphate) cannot come without Shura, in accordance with the command of Allah the Glorious to His believing slaves."[60] AQIM further reiterated its allegiance to Zawahiri and called on leading scholars to help resolve the dispute in order to

---

60. "AQIM New Statement: The Year of the Jama'ah . . . The Hope of the Ummah," *INCA News*, July 4, 2014, http://www.incanews.com/en/africa/596/aqim-new-statement-the-year-of-jamaah-the-hope-of-the-ummah.

avoid *fitna*. Abu Iyadh al-Tunsi, the leader of Tunisia's Ansar al Shari'a, also issued a statement calling for reconciliation.[61]

Some other groups, inspired by the Islamic State's example and call to action, have announced—and sought to demonstrate—their loyalty to the Islamic State. In September 2014, after Adnani called on Islamic State followers to kill Americans and Europeans "in any manner or way,"[62] an AQIM splinter group in Algeria known as Jund al-Khilafa swore allegiance to the Islamic State and responded by kidnapping and beheading a French citizen.[63] In eastern Libya, the Shura Council of Islamic Youth has reportedly sworn allegiance to the Islamic State. Reports also suggest that numerous other groups have pledged loyalty to the Islamic State including the Egyptian group Ansar Beit al-Maqdis, which operates in the Sinai Peninsula. In many

---

61. See Thomas Joscelyn, "Ansar al-Sharia Tunisia Leader Says Gains in Iraq Should Be Cause for Jihadist Reconciliation," *Long War Journal*, June 14, 2014, http://www. longwarjournal.org/archives/2014/06/ansar_al_sharia_tuni_8.php.

62. Adnani counsels the *muwahidun*—monotheists, or all believing Muslims—to kill non-believers. Notably, he tells Muslims to ignore advice or verdicts from others, once again reiterating the Islamic State's refusal to abide by *shura* or consultative decisions as al Qaeda prefers. He says, "If you can kill a disbelieving American or European—especially the spiteful and filthy French—or an Australian, or a Canadian, or any other disbeliever from the disbelievers waging war, including the citizens of the countries that entered into a coalition against the Islamic State, then rely upon Allah, and kill him in any manner or way however it may be. Do not ask for anyone's advice and do not seek anyone's verdict. Kill the disbeliever whether he is civilian or military, for they have the same ruling. Both of them are disbelievers." Abu Muhammad al-Adnani al-Shami, "Indeed Your Lord is Ever Watchful," *pietervanostaeyen* (blog), September 22, 2014, http://pietervanostaeyen.wordpress. com/2014/09/25/abu-muhammad-al-adnani-ash-shami-indeed-your-lord-is-ever-watchful/.

63. In July 2014, Algerian press reports claimed that Abu Abdullah Othman al-Asemi, an AQIM judge for the central region, declared his support for the Islamic State in an audio recording. On July 4, 2014, AQIM posted a statement reiterating its support for Zawahiri, despite Asemi's alleged declarations. Jund al-Khalifa, the Algerian AQIM breakaway, issued a statement in which AQIM central region commander Khaled Abu Suleimane (Gouri Abdelmalek) claimed leadership of the new group. See "Splinter Group Breaks from al Qaeda in North Africa," Reuters, September 14, 2014, http://in.reuters.com/article/2014/09/14/algeria-security-idINL-6N0RF0F020140914/; Atef Kadadra, "Al-Qaeda Group Divided on Islamic State," *Al Monitor*, July 21, 2014, http://www.al-monitor.com/pulse/security/2014/07/ separate-statements-highlight-possible-rift-in-aqim.html.

cases the validity of these pledges are questionable and statements are often contradicted, demonstrating either deliberate efforts to confuse or internal debates within jihadi-salafi groups over affiliation. The result will be a further fragmentation of jihadi-salafi groups.

Third, identifying with the Islamic State can boost the prestige of smaller militant groups by associating them with a recognized and feared brand name, just as smaller groups used the al Qaeda brand in the past. At the moment, operational links between these smaller groups and the Islamic State remain vague. Should the Islamic State continue growing, its networks could provide assistance and operational guidance to smaller associated groups beyond Iraq and Syria. Neither al Qaeda nor the Islamic State is likely to emerge as a clear winner in establishing a jihadi-salafi consensus. Instead, each will have its own following of affiliate groups and supporters, which will in turn create two competing blocs and strategies. This division will remain fluid, however, and internal disagreements and debate among affiliate groups will likely create ongoing confusion about allegiances among jihadi-salafi groups.

LOOKING FORWARD

The Islamic State's rebellion against al Qaeda has shaken the jihadi-salafi community. Just as bin Laden's decision to attack the United States signaled a dramatic shift in jihadi-salafi goals more than a decade ago, the Islamic State's disregard for al Qaeda's leadership, rejection of its strategy, and declaration of the caliphate is reshaping the jihadi-salafi landscape. Its creation of a quasi-state governing structure with territory, courts, infrastructure, and independent revenue streams has revolutionized jihad in that adherents can experience the goal of jihad—the caliphate—immediately. This self-declared caliphate has attracted thousands of people from around the region, Europe, and beyond.[64] In some cases foreigners have brought their children or

---

64. As of September 2014, U.S. government estimates suggest that Islamic State fighters in Iraq and Syria could total between 20,000 and 31,500. That number

families to live in the geographical entity that the Islamic State established. This allows people to experience jihad in a new way by actively participating in building a new society and political structure. The Islamic State's achievements to date have also inspired a new generation of young people who believe in the power of violence and the goal of immediately establishing a caliphate through direct action. Their battlefield successes (until now) have energized many fighters who interpret their military victories as proof of the movement's authenticity and adherence to God's will.

These successes, however, have also raised high expectations among those who have flocked to join the Islamic State. This means that the rulers of the Islamic State will have to demonstrate (rather than merely assert) that what they have created indeed resembles the state of the earliest Muslims. Controlling territory in Syria and Iraq and declaring a caliphate has allowed the Islamic State to distinguish itself from al Qaeda. It remains to be seen if holding territory will become the new currency of jihadism and whether the caliphate becomes a new rallying point for jihadi-salafists and other—nonviolent—salafists. The Islamic State's legitimacy and identity, unlike al Qaeda's, is defined partly by its territorial control. The loss of contiguous territory or of a stronghold such as Mosul would likely undermine the Islamic State's appeal and legitimacy given the centrality of geographical territory to the movement's identity.

Al Qaeda is now fighting for its legitimacy and leadership. It failed to adjust to the dramatic regional shifts under way in the region or reinvent itself. Yet, it remains a dangerous network and still commands loyalty from thousands of fighters and sym-

---

might include 15,000 fighting in Syria alone, among them 2,000 westerners. Ken Dilanian, "CIA: Islamic State group has up to 31,500 fighters," Associated Press, September 11, 2014, http://bigstory.ap.org/article/cia-islamic-state-group-has-31500-fighters; see also Scott Shane and Ben Hubbard, "ISIS Displaying a Deft Command of Varied Media,"*New York Times,* August 30, 2014, http://www.nytimes.com/2014/08/31/world/middleeast/isis-displaying-a-deft-command-of-varied-media.html.

pathizers around the world. It is unlikely to cede leadership of the jihadi-salafi project without a fight. The schism splitting the jihadi-salafi community is unlikely to be resolved in any conclusive way. Instead, for the foreseeable future pressure will mount for jihadi-salafists to choose sides in an increasingly polarized struggle that will define the movement for the next generation.

3. KEY ELEMENTS OF THE COUNTERTERRORISM CHALLENGE

Thomas M. Sanderson with Joshua Russakis and Michael Barber

Countering terrorism in the Middle East and North Africa (MENA) today is a complex endeavor. Heightened political turmoil combined with socioeconomic pressures creates conditions conducive to armed militant activity. Extremist groups are also taking advantage of a steady supply of weapons and foreign fighters, porous borders, social media tools, reliable revenue streams, and ungoverned space.

More than a decade of counterterrorism and counterinsurgency activity—both victories and losses—offers key lessons for the United States in today's struggle.[1] But violent extremists have also learned many lessons after years of parrying with local and foreign forces.[2] Today's counterterrorism coalition must understand the value and limits of recent experience as its members craft approaches to an adaptive, highly motivated adversary.

The MENA region offers several counterterrorism challenges. Egypt's Sinai, Libya, Yemen, and parts of Lebanon

---

1. Key lessons from over a decade of counterterrorism and counterinsurgency activity include among others, the importance of local partnerships, trusted security services (either local or international), human intelligence, counter messaging, economic development, and political inclusion.

2. These lessons include the importance of diversifying and localizing funding methods, of using social media, of exploiting corrupt government officials, and of carrying out effective governance in safe havens.

are experiencing a range of violent extremist activity. But the Syria-Iraq theater, where Western countries and local partners have undertaken an offensive against the Islamic State, offers the most significant test for counterterrorism strategies as they confront broad safe havens, robust funding portfolios, and a steady supply of motivated foreign fighters.

Each of these elements played a role in conflicts with Islamic State predecessors, and they continue to factor into counter-terrorism efforts against other militant groups. Complicating these efforts is that the Islamic State and other violent extremist groups in the region, such as Jabhat al-Nusra (also known as the al-Nusra Front) and al Qaeda in the Arabian Peninsula (AQAP), blend both insurgent and terrorist characteristics, a complicated hybrid that requires a new set of counterterrorism strategies.

Focusing broadly on the MENA region and more narrowly on the Islamic State, this chapter delves into three of the most confounding elements of battling violent extremists: the funding of extremist groups, their use of "foreign fighters," and their access to safe havens. This chapter begins with a look at terror financing and strategies to counter it over the past decade and the urgent need for adaptation in the face of the Islamic State's more locally-based funding. It also addresses the impact of Arab Gulf donors' efforts on a range of Syrian opposition groups. It then turns to the critical role of foreign fighters, including their motivations, recruitment, and battlefield experience—and perhaps most importantly, the fighters' potential return to the many countries from which they hail. Finally, the chapter reviews the role of terrorist safe havens and discusses the implications of the vast territory now dominated by the Islamic State, and which sits in the heart of the Middle East and next door to NATO member Turkey.

Although many groups present serious threats to regional and international security—including Jabhat al-Nusra in Syria, AQAP in Yemen, and local radicalized factions operating in Syria, Iraq, and across North Africa—the focus is on the Islamic

State because it has become the center of gravity for violent extremism in the Middle East.

COUNTERING THE FINANCING OF TERRORISM

As the Syrian conflict has unfolded since early 2011, the structure of terrorist financing has adapted. In the third year of this conflict, insurgent groups—especially the Islamic State—seem to have become less reliant on foreign funds as opportunities for "living off the land" have expanded, stabilized, and proven viable.

Over the last three years, the dynamics between Gulf Cooperation Council (GCC) governments and their donor-citizens created a dizzying array of funds that have fractured the Syrian moderate opposition, perhaps beyond repair. At the same time, these funds empowered the radical elements that constitute the current threat in Syria and Iraq. While donor fatigue and penalties against private donors degraded giving over time, neither seems to have significantly stemmed the flow or disrupted the full array of illicit terror financing. The U.S. Treasury Department's recent update to the Specially Designated Nationals (SDN) list[3] shows several additional designations of Qataris and Kuwaitis, suggesting there is still much work to do.[4]

But insurgent groups like Jabhat al-Nusra and the Islamic State do not rely only on external donors for funding. The groups' accumulation of territory has made new revenue options available to them. By looking to their immediate environment for resources, these groups have established a portfolio of assets offering durability and flexibility that is more difficult to attain when funding is dominated by external donations. Money-making activities arising from possession of territory include

---

3. The Specially Designated Nationals (SDN) list is published by OFAC and maintains a list of individuals and companies that are controlled by or act for or on the behalf of a sanctioned company. Additionally, the list bears the names of individuals, groups, and entities, such as terrorists and narcotics traffickers designated under U.S. sanction programs that are not country-specific.

4. U.S. Department of Treasury, "Counter Terrorism Designations: Specially Designated List Update," September 24, 2014, http://www.treasury.gov/resource-center/sanctions/OFAC-Enforcement/Pages/20140924.aspx.

taxing civilians under their control, extorting businesses, and kidnapping for ransom, as well as illicit trading of oil, government property, and antiquities. The Islamic State offers the best example of a group whose diverse local revenue generation—aided significantly by its control of a safe haven—lends resilience and capability for engaging a range of adversaries. The long-term viability of a robust "war economy" run by the Islamic State is uncertain, however, especially as pressure points on revenue streams and financial chokepoints begin to appear with the introduction of targeted U.S. and coalition strikes and more aggressive U.S. Treasury actions,

While this capacity to generate revenue locally is increasingly worrisome in the context of Syria and Iraq, the phenomenon is not limited to the Levant conflict. In recent years, the al Qaeda constellation of affiliates has also learned to extract value from territory and populations under its control. Ventures in kidnapping for ransom yielding tens of millions of dollars, smuggling and drug trafficking operations in Afghanistan and Pakistan, and money-laundering systems involving the exportation of charcoal and importation of sugar in Somalia demonstrate terrorist groups' attempts to localize their funding and rely less on foreign financing. With the U.S. Treasury unable to seize ill-gotten cash and slap banks with regulations to confront this hybrid model of terrorist funding,[5] the West must rethink its strategy for countering the financing of terror (CFT). The lessons learned from U.S. engagement in Syria will offer guidance for dislodging locally funded terrorist groups elsewhere.

Historically, terrorist groups have built both local and international funding networks. For example, Hamas finances its charities—and violent attacks—through da'wa committees, which are proselytization organizations that generate financial, popular, and logistical support locally and internationally.[6] Al

---

5. Juan C. Zarate and Thomas M. Sanderson, "How the Terrorists Got Rich: In Iraq and Syria, ISIS Militants Are Flush with Funds," *New York Times*, June 28, 2014, http://www.nytimes.com/2014/06/29/opinion/sunday/in-iraq-and-syria-isis-militants-are-flush-with-funds.html.

6. Juan C. Zarate, *Treasury's War: The Unleashing of a New Era of Financial Warfare* (New York: Public Affairs, 2014), 70–71.

Qaeda has solicited financial support from Gulf benefactors to fill its coffers in South Asia, using Islamic charities as a benevolent facade for the constant influx of money.[7]

In 1989—in other words, even before the attacks of September 11, 2001—the Group of Seven (G7) countries established the Financial Action Task Force (FATF), which sets standards and outlines measures that help governments combat money laundering, terrorist financing, and other threats to the integrity of the international financial system.[8] In the years since the attacks of September 11, 2001 the U.S. government has sharply refined its CFT strategy. Combining international partnerships, anti-terror-financing and anti-money-laundering laws, and interagency intelligence sharing to identify terrorist operatives and supporters, the United States has managed to disrupt some terrorist funding networks.

The drivers of CFT were Executive Order (EO) 13224, Title III of the Patriot Act,[9] and international cooperation via Financial Intelligence Units.[10] Signed into law by President George W. Bush on September 23, 2011, EO 13224 authorizes the U.S. Treasury, in coordination with other U.S. agencies, to freeze the assets and transactions of individuals and entities that it designates as offenders or supporters of terrorism. With these drivers and institutions in place the United States could work with foreign governments to lock terrorist groups and their financiers out of the global economy. Given the prevalence of al Qaeda sympathizers in GCC countries, increased coordination with Gulf state actors was crucial to creating an international system for combatting terrorist-financing institutions, banks, and individuals.

In addition to freezing assets and excluding actors accused of financing terrorism from the larger world economy, the United

---

7. Ibid.

8. "Who We Are," Financial Action Task Force, http://www.fatf-gafi.org/pages/aboutus/.

9. "Executive Order 13224," U.S. Department of State, September 23, 2001, http://www.state.gov/j/ct/rls/other/des/122570.htm.

10. International Monetary Fund, *Financial Intelligence Units: An Overview* (Washington, DC: International Monetary Fund, 2004), ix, http://www.imf.org/external/pubs/ft/FIU/.

States took other steps to impede funding sources and flows, including supporting military action by regional or state security missions to disable important funding sources for terrorist groups. To confront the al Qaeda affiliate al-Shabaab, for example, the United States provided financial support to regional security forces that dislodged the group from its revenue-generating ports.[11] A somewhat less successful effort is the U.S. Army's attempt to cripple the Taliban in Afghanistan by destroying the poppy fields upon which its opium trade revenues rely.[12] A more successful effort, jointly carried out by the Drug Enforcement Administration, U.S. Treasury Department, and U.S. military, was one that targeted the Taliban's financial infrastructure and managed to shut down the money exchange houses and *hawaladars* tied to the group.[13] After more than a decade of sustained counterterrorism efforts, al Qaeda core leadership in Pakistan is forced to rely on most of its financial support from its affiliates in Yemen and Somalia.[14]

However, the CFT strategies that have been successful against combat groups like al Qaeda, Hamas, and Hezbollah are not an option in Syria and Iraq today. There, bad banks, govern-

---

11. These ports, specifically Kismayo in southern Somalia, were essential to the group's maintenance and generated US$35 million to US$50 million in revenue per year. U.N. Security Council resolutions, specifically resolution 2036 (2012), attempted to ban U.N. member states from continuing to import charcoal from al-Shabaab–controlled ports. Despite this resolution, the U.N. found that Gulf Cooperation Council countries, notably Saudi Arabia and United Arab Emirates, were "slow to implement the ban." *Report of the Monitoring Group on Somalia and Eritrea pursuant to Security Council Resolution 2002 (2011)*, United Nations Security Council, UN document S/2012/544, June 27, 2012, 15, http://www.un.org/ga/search/view_doc.asp?symbol=S/2012/544.

12. Alissa J. Rubin and Matthew Rosenberg, "Drug Traffic Remains as U.S. Nears Afghanistan Exit," *New York Times*, May 26, 2012, http://www.nytimes.com/2012/05/27/world/asia/drug-traffic-remains-as-us-nears-afghanistan-exit.html.

13. Thomas M. Harrigan, statement before the Senate Caucus on International Narcotics Control, U.S. Senate, July 20, 2011, 5, http://www.justice.gov/dea/pr/speeches-testimony/2012-2009/110720_herrigan_hearing.PDF.

14. Clint Watts, "Assessing the Terrorist Threat 13 Years after 9/11: Old Guard Al Qaeda, Team Islamic State & the Upstarts," *War on the Rocks*, September 11, 2014, http://warontherocks.com/2014/09/assessing-the-terrorist-threat-13-years-after-911-old-guard-al-qaeda-team-isis-the-upstarts/.

ment support, and charitable fronts comprise only part of the problem. In addition to these illicit networks of finance, many of the armed groups now involved in the conflict have turned to criminal activity and profiteering to sustain their operations.

EARLY STAGE FUNDING FOR SYRIAN OPPOSITION GROUPS

Funding from the Gulf

As the Syrian conflict evolved, the whims of state and citizen actors led to the funding of various rebel groups. Without coordination, these multiple donors—state and non-state, with different interests and motivations—fomented the fracturing of the moderate opposition and in part fostered the expansion of extremist groups in Syria.[15] GCC states did supply funding to the conflict, but by failing to stop their citizens from funding multiple groups, they harmed the opposition; this was especially true of Qatar and Kuwait.

In a bid to project power into Syria, Qatar located individuals and rebel groups it thought to be "ideologically on the same wavelength"—political Islamists and salafists.[16] Seeking to promote the spread of radical ideologies and provide military support for opposition groups, the Qatari government invited radical Kuwaiti sheikhs like Hajjaj al-Ajmi, a U.S. Specially Designated National accused of providing financial backing to Jabhat al-Nusra, to speak to its citizens and establish collection campaigns parallel to those in Kuwait.[17] In spite of recent designations of Qatari citizens as financing terrorist organizations in

---

15. Ben Hubbard, "Private Donors' Funds Add Wild Card to War in Syria," *New York Times*, November 12, 2013, http://www.nytimes.com/2013/11/13/world/middleeast/private-donors-funds-add-wild-card-to-war-in-syria.html; Joby Warrick, "Private Money Pours into Syrian Conflict as Rich Donors Pick Sides," *Washington Post*, June 16, 2013, http://www.washingtonpost.com/world/national-security/private-money-pours-into-syrian-conflict-as-rich-donors-pick-sides/2013/06/15/67841656-cf8a-11e2-8845-d970ccb04497_story.html; William McCants, "Gulf Charities and Syrian Sectarianism," *Foreign Policy*, September 30, 2013, http://mideast.foreignpolicy.com/posts/2013/09/30/the_gulf_s_sectarian_syria_strategy.
16. Elizabeth Dickinson, "The Case Against Qatar," *Foreign Policy*, September 30, 2014, http://www.foreignpolicy.com/articles/2014/09/30/the_case_against_qatar_funding_extremists_salafi_syria_uae_jihad_muslim_brotherhood_taliban.
17. Ibid.

Syria,[18] Qatar's emir, Sheikh Tamim bin Hamad Al Thani, maintains that "we don't fund terrorists" and that fund-raising was orchestrated by individuals alone.[19] Despite the emir's claims, the Qatari government seems complicit in "outsourcing" fundraising roles to its private citizens. Using its citizens as proxy funders, Qatar is able to meddle in the Syrian conflict from the backseat, avoiding liability and acting as though it were incapable of monitoring its citizens' financing activities.[20]

Funding for Syrian opposition and extremist groups also came from the Kuwaiti government and its citizens. Private donations at the outset of the Syrian revolution, when protests were still localized, were made primarily by Syrian expatriates living in Kuwait, usually to family members in the form of remittances. As the revolutions derailed and civil war ensued, more Kuwaitis sought to contribute humanitarian aid. Then Syrians approached Kuwaitis for donations, outside of the closely-knit Kuwaiti charity networks.[21] This connection served both sides well: Syrian fundraisers could generate more aid, while Kuwaiti charities received current and accurate information to best direct their support. As the Syrian revolution gave way to the current broader conflict, the intentions of Kuwaiti funders began to shift as well.[22] Enabled in part by the government's lax terrorism financing laws and by freedom of speech and association, funder preferences and networks proliferated in Kuwaiti society.[23]

18. U.S. Department of Treasury, "Counter Terrorism Designations: Specially Designated List Update."

19. Mick Krever, "Qatar's Emir: We Don't Fund Terrorists," *CNN*, September 25, 2014, http://www.cnn.com/2014/09/25/world/meast/qatar-emir/index.html.

20. Dickinson, "Case against Qatar."

21. Tom Keatinge, "The Importance of Financing in Enabling and Sustaining the Conflict in Syria (and Beyond)," *Perspectives on Terrorism* 8, no. 4 (June 8, 2014): 56, http://www.terrorismanalysts.com/pt/index.php/pot/article/view/360.

22. Elizabeth Dickinson, "Playing with Fire: Why Private Gulf Financing for Syria's Extremist Rebels Risks Igniting Sectarian Conflict at Home," Center for Middle East Policy Analysis Paper 31, Brookings Institution, Washington, DC, 5, http://www.brookings.edu/research/papers/2013/12/06-private-gulf-financing-syria-extremist-rebels-sectarian-conflict-dickinson.

23. Despite the establishment of Kuwait's independent Financial Intelligence Unit in 2013, political appointments of alleged terrorism financiers do little to demonstrate that the country is serious about cracking down on terrorism financing.

The formation of armed groups in Syria in early 2012, documented in part by social media,[24] drew new funders and with them a new dynamic—not just in Kuwait but in the Gulf more broadly. Portraying the conflict as a jihad, social media campaigns solicited donations from funders who were invited to wage "financial jihad" by supporting "holy warriors" in Syria.[25] Fundraising campaigns like "Wage jihad with your money" and the "Ramadan Campaign" set donor goals, listed the types and amounts of ammunition that could be supplied to fighters with a certain dollar amount, or specified how much it would cost to equip and send one mujahid or "holy warrior" to Syria.[26] These fundraising tactics could be very lucrative, and a single evening might yield US$350,000 dollars.[27] Once in the hands of rebel groups, this money could be used to buy weapons on the black market.[28]

As the conflict dragged on, a combination of fatigue, disgust, and disillusionment diminished the number of donors who

---

24. "Tashkil katibat al shaykh Hajjaj al-'Ajmi fi reef Abu Kamal" [The creation of Sheikh Hajjaj al-Ajmi's battalion in the village of Bukamal], YouTube video, 1:48, posted by "Freesyriaali," June 14, 2012, https://www.youtube.com/watch?v=KN7pYgtgkak; "Inshiqaq kabir wa tashkil 'Amro bin al-'Aas" [A great split and the creation of Amro Bin Al-Aas Brigade], YouTube video, 1:12, posted by "Channel (qanaat) freedomaleppo," March 25, 2012, https://www.youtube.com/watch?v=mODXX88Sa9U.

25. On the use of social media, see "Fundraising Campaign in Kuwait for Designated Terrorist Group Jabhat Al-Nusra Using Facebook, Twitter, Skype, You-Tube," *The Cyber & Jihad Lab*, May 17, 2013, http://cjlab.memri.org/lab-projects/tracking-jihadi-terrorist-use-of-social-media/fundraising-campaign-in-kuwait-for-designated-terrorist-group-jabhat-al-nusra-using-facebook-twitter-skype-youtube/#!prettyPhoto. For the idea of "financial jihad," see Aimen Dean, Edwina Thompson, and Tom Keatinge, "Draining the Ocean to Catch One Type of Fish: Evaluating the Effectiveness of the Global Counter-Terrorism Financing Regime," *Perspectives on Terrorism* 7, no. 4 (August 27, 2013): 63, http://www.terrorismanalysts.com/pt/index.php/pot/article/view/282.

26. On these campaigns, see Thomas Joscelyn, "Popular Saudi Cleric Endorses Islamic Front, Calls for Cooperation with Al Qaeda," *Long War Journal*, December 14, 2013, http://www.longwarjournal.org/archives/2013/12/popular_saudi_sheikh.php; Dickinson, "Playing with Fire," 13, 15.

27. Estimates for the amount of money gathered this way are in the tens, if not hundreds, of millions, but the estimate repeated here is inferred from the public displays of fundraising via social media and transparent donors. The potential for more discreet financial networks is high, and there is no way to know how much money travels through them.

28. Warrick, "Private Money Pours into Syrian Conflict."

supported the moderate Syrian opposition.[29] The remaining donors were highly motivated, deeply ideological individuals whose funding followed their radical preferences. Radical donors funded only the most hard-line groups, which served to bolster extremist elements within the opposition and to fracture the opposition along ideological fault lines.[30] According to statements found on social media sites, radical donors directly funded Syrian al Qaeda affiliates or funded Syrian rebel groups that openly cooperated with them, like Ahrar al Sham.[31] In time, these groups rose to prominence in the conflict, with Jabhat al-Nusra drawing in fighters from the Free Syrian Army and other moderate groups because it could offer salaries and better organization.[32]

Funding from the Local War Economy

While international funding has extended the life of the conflict, it has simultaneously degraded Syria's economy.[33] This has

29. Keatinge, "Importance of Financing," 56.

30. McCants, "Gulf Charities and Syrian Sectarianism."

31. Dickinson, "Playing with Fire," 14. Dickinson specifies several Kuwaiti individuals (Shafi al-Ajmi and Mohammad Hayef al Mutairi) and donor foundations (Council of Supporters of the Syrian Revolution) that support al Qaeda's Syrian affiliate or the Syrian rebel groups that cooperate with it.

32. Hassan Hassan, "Influenced by Abu Musab Al Suri, Jabhat Al Nusra Has the Potential to Spread beyond Syria's Borders," *National*, March 4, 2014, http://www.thenational.ae/thenationalconversation/comment/a-jihadist-blueprint-for-hearts-and-minds-is-gaining-traction-in-syria.

33. It should be noted that private Gulf financing of Syria has been curved by a number of actions on behalf of the United States and the Kuwaiti government. In 2014, the Office *of Foreign Assets Control* of the U.S. Treasury designated three Kuwaiti-based financiers of terrorist organizations in Syria and Iraq as terrorist financers. Under article 16 of Law No. 106 of 2013, Kuwait has installed its first fully independent Financial Intelligence Unit. The law also stipulates tighter enforcement of anti-terror-finance legislation. It is hard to see Kuwait as serious about reforms, however, given the 2014 appointment of Nayef al-Ajmi, who openly calls Syria a legitimate jihad and appears to be linked to fund-raising for extremist rebels in Syria, to the post of justice minister.
On the degradation of Syria's economy, see Rabbie Nasser, Zaki Mehchy, and Khaled Abu Ismail, "Socioeconomic Roots and Impact of the Syrian Crisis," Syrian Center for Policy Research, January 2013, 41, http://scpr-syria.org/en/S34/%E2%80%9CSocioeconomic-Roots-and-Impact-of-the-Syrian-Crisis%E2%80%9D-2013.

created space for the emergence of a profitable war economy, built on illicit activities such like looting, smuggling, currency trading, and black market sales.[34] As different insurgent groups have expanded control in Syria and Iraq, they have further developed their revenue lines.[35] Control of border crossings and land routes around the Turkish frontier now offers insurgents lucrative revenue streams via taxation and extortion, as well as direct access to supply and distribution routes to traffic their own goods.[36] A portfolio of revenue-generating illicit activity, now in its third year, offers the core financial support that makes foreign funding less relevant.[37]

While a number of armed groups in the Syrian-Iraqi theater rely on local funding streams, the Islamic State offers perhaps the best example of a group with a diversified mix of revenue—an arrangement that potentially offers long-term viability for the organization. One study estimates that the revenue from extorted taxes in Mosul alone nets the group nearly US$8 million each month.[38]

The Islamic State's appropriation and sale of Syrian and Iraqi state infrastructure and equipment provide another source of funding. With the Islamic State's rapid advance through Iraq in June 2014, the group gained control of several small Iraqi oil fields.[39] In July, the Islamic State also consolidated its hold on

34. Abigail Fielding-Smith, "Profiteers Become Another Obstacle to Peace in Syria," *Financial Times*, December 1, 2013, http://www.ft.com/intl/cms/s/0/f4d8e1ba-5853-11e3-9da6-00144feabdc0.html?siteedition=intl#axzz2mLggRuxK.
35. Interview with Ahmed Assi, Suqqur al Sham spokesman, January 15, 2014, Turkey.
36. Samer Abboud, "Syria's War Economy," *Syria in Crisis* (blog), Carnegie Endowment for International Peace, January 9, 2014, http://carnegieendowment.org/syriaincrisis/?fa=54131. Northern Storm Brigade, a group linked to the Free Syrian Army, in 2012 seized control of the Bab al-Salam border crossing and later negotiated shared control of the border with and the Islamic Front's Tawhid Brigade.
37. Keatinge, "Importance of Financing," 57.
38. "Al-Qaeda in Iraq (a.k.a. Islamic State in Iraq and Greater Syria)," Council on Foreign Relations, http://www.cfr.org/iraq/al-qaeda-iraq-k-islamic-state-iraq-greater-syria/p14811.
39. Deborah Amos, "How The Islamic State Smuggles Oil To Fund Its Campaign," *NPR*, September 9, 2014, http://www.npr.org/blogs/parallels/2014/09/09/346844240/how-the-islamic-state-smuggles-oil-to-fund-its-campaign.

oil fields in the eastern Syrian province of Deir ez-Zor when it seized Syria's largest oil field from rival jihadi group Jabhat al-Nusra.[40] At the height of the Islamic State's oil production in July 2014, the group reportedly made an estimated US\$3 million each day on the black market.[41] Further territorial advances into Iraq and subsequent expansion inside of Syria have provided additional transportation options for the stolen oil.[42]

The Islamic State enjoys a variety of different avenues for selling its ill-gotten oil. While some reports have detailed the process by which the group sells oil to Turkish smugglers, evidence suggests that the bulk of the Islamic State's oil sales are within Syria and Iraq, and go through middlemen for various governments or to bootleg refineries in those countries.[43] Systemic disorder within Syria and Iraq has ensured steady demand for rebel-controlled oil.

Under heavy sanctions that have helped to decimate the Syrian economy,[44] the Assad regime has turned to several back channels to ensure that oil continues to flow and that the lights stay on.[45] The Assad regime reportedly relies on a middleman—Syrian businessman George Haswani—to make cash drops in Palmyra for the Islamic State's oil.[46]

40. "Islamic State 'Seizes Key Syria Oil Field,'" *Al Jazeera*, July 3, 2014, http://live. aljazeera.com/Event/Syria_Live_Blog.

41. Karen Leigh, "ISIS Makes Up To \$3 Million a Day Selling Oil, Analysts Say," *Syria Deeply*, July 28, 2014, http://www.syriadeeply.org/articles/2014/07/5856/isis-3-million-day-selling-oil-analysts/; Borzou Daragahi and Erika Solomon, "Fuelling Isis Inc," *Financial Times*, September 21, 2014, http://www.ft.com/intl/cms/s/2/34e874ac-3dad-11e4-b782-00144feabdco.html#axzz3ESzCXGmI.

42. Amos, "How the Islamic State Smuggles."

43. Daragahi and Solomon, "Fuelling Isis Inc."

44. U.S. Department of Treasury, "Syria Sanctions," May 2, 2014, http://www.treasury.gov/resource-center/sanctions/Programs/pages/syria.aspx.

45. Ghaith Abdul-Ahad, "Syria's Oilfields Create Surreal Battle Lines amid Chaos and Tribal Loyalties," *Guardian*, June 25, 2013, http://www.theguardian.com/world/2013/jun/25/syria-oil-assad-rebels-tribes.

46. Interview with Nick Blanford, journalist for the Christian Science Monitor, January 24, 2014, Turkey; Tony Badran, "Minority Report: Is the Link between Assad and the Islamic State a Christian One?" *Now Lebanon*, August 9, 2014, https://now.mmedia.me/lb/en/commentaryanalysis/562681-minority-report; "Man hua George Haswani al-l-athi yusahhil bay' wa shiraa' al naft bayn Da'ish wa-l -nitham al Suri?" [Who is George Haswani, who facilitates the sale and purchase of oil between the Islamic State and the Syrian Regime?], *all4Syria*, September 2, 2014, http://all4syria.info/Archive/165946.

In Iraq, the Islamic State has successfully tapped into a network of homegrown refineries, Kurdish businessmen, and smuggling routes developed over decades when sanctions were in place against Saddam Hussein's Iraq.[47] Continued disagreement between the Kurdistan Regional Government (KRG) and Baghdad over whether the KRG may export oil directly and over the distribution of government funds to the KRG contributed to the KRG's tendency to overlook the purchase and refining of oil from sources linked to the Islamic State.[48]

Between Syria and Iraq, the Islamic State controls a large network of border crossings, rivers, and trafficking routes that are used to transport the ill-gotten oil into Turkey.[49] Several reports describe how local merchants move oil via oil tanker trucks, mules, and underwater pipes from the Islamic State across the border, using unpatrolled roads as well as official border crossings into Turkey. Smugglers have also used the Orontes River, which separates northwestern Syria from Turkey, to float barrels of fuel across the border. Depending on the quality of crude oil, the Islamic State can make between US$26 and US$60 dollars a barrel.[50] Once in Turkey, the oil is sold by smugglers for as much as 30 percent less than legitimately processed oil.[51]

Under mounting international scrutiny, Turkey has begun to crack down on Turkish smugglers in the city of Hacipasa. Oil smuggling between Turkey and Syria has been a booming business there for decades,[52] and it has significantly expanded in the wake of the Syrian conflict. One oil smuggler admitted

47. Daragahi and Solomon, "Fuelling Isis Inc."
48. Ibid.
49. Benoît Faucon and Ayla Albayrak, "Islamic State Funds Push into Syria and Iraq with Labyrinthine Oil-Smuggling Operation," *Wall Street Journal*, September 16, 2014, http://online.wsj.com/articles/islamic-state-funds-push-into-syria-and-iraq-with-labyrinthine-oil-smuggling-operation-1410826325.
50. Nour Malas and Maria Abi-Habib, "Islamic State Economy Runs on Extortion, Oil Piracy in Syria, Iraq," *Wall Street Journal*, August 28, 2014, http://online.wsj.com/articles/islamic-state-fills-coffers-from-illicit-economy-in-syria-iraq-1409175458.
51. Ibid.
52. "Turkey Cracks Down on Oil Smuggling Linked to ISIS," *Al Arabiya*, October 6, 2014, http://english.alarabiya.net/en/business/energy/2014/10/06/Turkey-cracks-down-on-oil-smuggling-linked-to-ISIS.html.

in an interview that he could make as much as US$6,500 dollars for a single trip transporting smuggled oil to other towns in Turkey. In the first eight months of 2014, the Turkish government seized 20 million liters of smuggled oil at the border, four times as much as the amount intercepted in 2013.[53] Residents of Hacipasa say that the government's greater vigilance has eliminated 70–80 percent of the smuggling, but other measures could be taken to reduce smuggling still further.[54]

Given the fluctuating price of oil, U.S. and coalition air strikes on mobile refineries, a lack of access to Islamic State bookkeeping, and contradictory reports on the value of the black market oil trade, it remains difficult to discern how much of the group's funding network comes from oil revenues.[55] But at the very least, the Islamic State's oil revenues appear critical to the organization's balance sheet, and their removal or sharp reduction would very likely damage the organization's fortunes. The recent escape of oil engineers (needed to run the refineries) from Islamic State control has in fact halved the group's oil revenues.[56] In the wake of this development, the group has reemphasized its smuggling operations at the expense of some local populations now experiencing fuel shortages.[57] Although running a robust oil trade generates at least US$1 million dollars of funding each day for the group,[58] it also creates dependencies

53. Ibid.
54. Ibid.
55. Ibid.; Steven Mufson, "Islamic State Fighters Drawing on Oil Assets for Funding and Fuel," *Washington Post*, September 15, 2014, http://www.washingtonpost.com/business/economy/islamic-state-fighters-are-drawing-on-oil-assets-for-funding-and-fuel/2014/09/15/a2927d02-39bd-11e4-8601-97ba88884ffd_story.html; Erika Solomon, "US Strikes at Isis Oil Sites in Syria," *Financial Times*, September 25, 2014, http://www.ft.com/intl/cms/s/0/5a2d2f04-44a2-11e4-ab0c-00144feabdc0.html#axzz3ESzCXGmI.
56. Hugh Tomlinson and Tom Coghlan, "Isis Oil Bonanza Cut by Half as Engineers Flee Caliphate," *Times* (London), September 13, 2014, http://www.thetimes.co.uk/tto/news/world/middleeast/article4205141.ece.
57. Ibid.
58. Matthew Olson, "A National Counterterrorism Center Threat Assessment of ISIL and Al-Qaeda in Iraq, Syria and Beyond," discussion, Brookings Institution, Washington, DC, September 3, 2014, http://www.brookings.edu/events/2014/09/03-national-counterterrorism-center-threat-assessment-isil-al-qaeda-iraq-syria-beyond.

that can be exploited when the Islamic State leaves citizens with a shortfall.

Other Sources of Funding

As a consequence of poor border control and Ankara's support of forces opposed to the Assad regime, criminal activity has flourished across the Syria-Turkey frontier. CSIS field research at the Syria border crossing of Bab al-Salam found a robust trafficking in passports procured from fallen fighters or sold by those entering Syria for battle—presumably on a one-way ticket to a suicide attack.[59] The recycled passports—some from "visa waiver" countries in Europe—represent a security threat, given that purchasers could use them to carry out violent acts in Europe or the United States.

Antiquities smuggling has further bolstered Islamic State coffers. Although this type of profiteering is not a new phenomenon, its adoption by the Islamic State demonstrates the group's ability to tap into preestablished criminal trades to turn a profit.[60] Since late 2012, the Islamic State and other insurgent groups have capitalized on the unrest to pillage priceless antiquities from archaeological sites.[61] In Syria's al-Nabuk—an area in the Qalamoun Mountains west of Damascus where antiquities are up to 8,000 years old—the Islamic State is believed to have smuggled US$36 million worth of artifacts.[62] Some sources speculate that the group's revenue— generated from the 20 percent "plunder tax" they charge for permitting antiquities traffickers to continue their activities—is one of the organization's

59. Interview with Turkish passport trafficker, January 14, 2014, in Turkey at the Syrian border gate of Bab al-Salam.
60. Kathleen Caulderwood, "How ISIS Pillages, Traffics And Sells Ancient Artifacts On Global Black Market," *International Business Times*, June 18, 2014, http://www.ibtimes.com/how-isis-pillages-traffics-sells-ancient-artifacts-global-black-market-1605044.
61. Mark V. Vlasic, "Islamic State Sells 'Blood Antiquities' from Iraq and Syria to Raise Money," *Washington Post*, September 14, 2014, http://www.washingtonpost.com/opinions/islamic-state-sells-blood-antiquities-from-iraq-and-syria-to-raise-money/2014/09/14/49663c98-3a7e-11e4-9c9f-ebb47272e40e_story.html?tid=HP_opinion.
62. Martin Chulov, "How an Arrest in Iraq Revealed Islamic State's $2bn Jihadist Network," *Guardian*, June 15, 2014, http://www.theguardian.com/world/2014/jun/15/iraq-Islamic State-arrest-jihadists-wealth-power.

major sources of revenue.[63] The result is not only funding for terrorist activity, but damage to future generations dependent on the nation's cultural heritage for the tourism industry.

In Iraq, the Islamic State's control of approximately 40 percent of the wheat supply offers yet another reliable revenue source while also enabling the group—through managing bread production and subsidization—to act as a "state" that provides for its people. (The Islamic State also uses wheat as a weapon by withholding the staple from religious minorities.[64]) The group has forced farmers and silo workers to continue working and operating equipment under its watch. Freeing them could cripple the Islamic State's ability to provide wheat beyond that already harvested, and destroying wheat silos could create problems throughout Iraq. With the Islamic State controlling all nine of Nineveh Province's wheat silos, the Iraqi government has already lost a large input for a major source of food.[65]

In amassing a plethora of local funding sources, the Islamic State has proven, at least for the time being, that it is able to sustain a war economy.[66] As long as the group is able to gain more territory and revenue sources, it can carry on paying local Sunnis and ex-Ba'athists for their loyalty, while also subsidizing goods and providing services to citizens. Given the variety of revenue sources described here—and given recent reports claiming that private outside donations comprise only 5 percent of the Islamic

63. Cem Erciyes, "Islamic State Makes Millions from Stolen Antiquities," *Al Monitor*, September 2, 2014, http://www.al-monitor.com/pulse/security/2014/09/turkey-syria-iraq-isis-artifacts-smuggling.html.

64. Maggie Fick, "Special Report: Islamic State Uses Grain to Tighten Grip in Iraq," Reuters, September 30, 2014, http://www.reuters.com/article/2014/09/30/us-mideast-crisis-wheat-idUSKCN0HP12J20140930; Filipa Ioannou, "ISIS's Latest Weapon: Wheat," *Slate*, September 30, 2014, http://www.slate.com/blogs/the_slatest/2014/09/30/isis_wheat_financing_legitimacy_for_militant_group.html. The Islamic State is also using water as an instrument of control; see Erin Cunningham, "Islamic State Jihadists Are Using Water as a Weapon in Iraq," *Washington Post*, October 7, 2014, http://www.washingtonpost.com/world/middle_east/islamic-state-jihadists-are-using-water-as-a-weapon-in-iraq/2014/10/06/aead6792-79ec-4c7c-8f2f-fd7b95765d09_story.html.

65. Maggie Fick, "Special Report: Islamic State Uses Grain to Tighter Grip in Iraq."

66. "Can the U.S. Cut off ISIS from Its Funding?" CBS News, August 14, 2014, http://www.cbsnews.com/news/can-the-u-s-cut-off-isis-from-its-funding/.

State's operating budget[67]—traditional U.S. CFT approaches will be challenged.

For now, some of those living under the Islamic State have acknowledged the apparent efficiency and stability of its governance, as evidenced by a proportionate tax regime, the issuing of receipts, and subsidization of food.[68] But changing revenue conditions could undermine the Islamic State's strategy and present a potential opportunity in any CFT strategy.

Implications
The accumulation of territory, and with it the assumption of control over such reliable funding sources as oil fields and wheat supplies, has allowed the Islamic State to become increasingly self-sufficient. Moreover, its diverse local financing methods enable it to evade most Western restrictions. The revenue streams on which it now relies, however, may be less durable than once was thought. Geographic setbacks, in which the group is dislodged from a town, oil field, or border crossing, clearly reduce its potential revenue. So do difficulties in keeping oil fields staffed and operating. Less clear is whether the Islamic State's funding portfolio is sufficiently diversified so as to withstand the loss of one revenue stream. But if funding is hobbled or eliminated, the group risks potential collapse.

Running a state is also expensive. Despite its reported millions of dollars in daily oil revenues, the Islamic State must spend this money to maintain control of its territory and the allies living there. The group has responsibility for governance

---

67. Hannah Allam, "Records Show How Iraqi Extremists Withstood U.S. Anti-Terror Efforts," *McClatchy*, June 23, 2014, http://www.mcclatchydc.com/2014/06/23/231223/records-show-how-iraqi-extremists.html?sp=/99/100/&ihp=1.
68. A Raqqa goldsmith, for example, said of the Islamic State's rule in the group's self-declared capital: "I feel like I am dealing with a respected state, not thugs." Quoted in Anne Barnard, "Hezbollah Takes Risks by Fighting Rebels in Syria," *New York Times*, May 7, 2013, http://www.nytimes.com/2013/05/08/world/middleeast/hezbollah-takes-risks-by-fighting-rebels-in-syria.html. See also Ben Hubbard, "In a Syrian City, Islamic State Puts Its Vision into Practice," *New York Times*, July 23, 2014, http://www.nytimes.com/2014/07/24/world/middleeast/islamic-state-controls-raqqa-syria.html.

measures, from shari'a courts to basic sanitation,[69] and must pay salaries to jihadi commanders—and, increasingly, foreign fighters—which range from US$400 to thousands of dollars per month. Nor do alliances with local tribesmen come cheap.[70] As this group continues to operate as a local government, CFT strategies need to exploit these linkages and dependencies on revenue flows.

Response
In light of today's formidable challenges in Syria and Iraq, and indeed across the MENA region wherever instability and violence reign, CFT responses must target havens where insurgents and terrorists establish or participate in a war economy. Eliminating havens will force groups to spend more time raising funds than conducting operations. It will also interrupt important insurgent-partner relationships and provide an opening for coalition forces.

An effective response to the present threat must include dislodging the Islamic State from towns and border crossings it now controls. Given the role that these key nodes play in transport and communication—essential components to the war economy—strikes on these revenue generators will weaken the group. However, carrying out strikes in a comprehensive fashion will likely require a physical presence on the ground, an option that does not yet appear viable.

CFT measures must also focus on the black market trade in the many illicit goods keeping insurgent groups afloat. Cooperation with regional actors is essential on this front, especially in Turkey, where substantial amounts of oil end up heading to market.

Finally, authorities need to map the funding networks that facilitate the black market trade and smuggling upon which the Islamic State relies. They must then interrupt the facilitators,

---

69. Aaron Zelin, "The Islamic State of Iraq and Syria Has a Consumer Protection Office," *Atlantic*, June 13, 2014, http://www.theatlantic.com/international/archive/2014/06/the-isis-guide-to-building-an-islamic-state/372769/.

70. Wassim Bassem, "Money, Power Draw Young Iraqis to IS," *Al Monitor*, August 12, 2014, http://www.al-monitor.com/pulse/originals/2014/08/iraq-jurf-al-sakhar-men-join-islamic-state.html.

nodes of money exchange, and points of entry into the formal financial system. Once it becomes harder and costlier for the Islamic State to do business and access outside donors, charities, and financial facilities, the international coalition can begin to constrict and degrade the group's financial underpinning and ultimately its global reach.

FOREIGN FIGHTERS

Conflict across the MENA region—in particular in Syria and Iraq—demonstrates the deep impact of Sunni "foreign fighters" on the battlefield. According to Matthew Olsen, the director of the U.S. National Counterterrorism Center, total foreign fighters in Syria and Iraq exceeded 12,000 individuals as of July 2014.[71] This estimate includes as many as 3,000 Europeans and upwards of 100 Americans.[72] By mid-September 2014, the Central Intelligence Agency had dramatically revised that number upward, estimating that the Islamic State alone might have as many as 15,000 total foreign fighters.[73]

Hailing from nearly 80 different countries—including Saudi Arabia, France, Indonesia, Russia, Pakistan, and the United States[74]—these men (and some women) join a wide spectrum of insurgent militias, including the Free Syrian Army, Jabhat al-Nusra, and the Islamic State. Foreign fighters serve in many roles and can be formidable combatants.[75] Understanding this

71. Kevin Baron, "The Number of Foreign Fighters in Syria Now Exceeds 12,000 and Rising" *Defense One*, July 25, 2014, http://www.defenseone.com/threats/2014/07/the-number-of-foreign-fighters-in-Syria-now-exceeds-12000-rising/89732/.

72. Brian Bennett and Richard A. Serrano. "More Western Fighters Joining Militants in Iraq and Syria," *Los Angeles Times*, July 19, 2014, http://www.latimes.com/world/middleeast/la-fg-foreign-fighters-20140720-story.html#page=1.

73. "CIA Says IS Numbers Underestimated," *Al Jazeera*, September 12, 2014, http://www.aljazeera.com/news/middleeast/2014/09/cia-triples-number-islamic-state-fighters-201491232912623733.html.

74. Ed Pilkington, "UN Unanimously Passes Resolution to Combat 'Foreign Terrorist Fighters,'" *Guardian*, September 24, 2014, http://www.theguardian.com/world/2014/sep/24/un-security-council-resolution-terror-threat-obama.

75. Though significant numbers of Shi'ite fighters have also traveled to Syria and Iraq to battle violent Sunni extremists, this section focuses exclusively on the more visible and wider Sunni phenomenon, which was in large part propelled by the Syrian civil war and later fuelled by the Islamic State push into Iraq.

large component of the overall body of violent extremists is critical to degrading groups such as the Islamic State and potentially to preventing terrorism on the home front.

Aspiring fighters find relatively easy access to the battle zone. Porous borders, such as Turkey's 500-mile frontier with Syria, offer a two-way channel for fighters moving between operations and recuperation. The fighters, most of them young men, have diverse motivations. Some come to defend civilians from "apostate" Shi'ite government forces and their militias. Others pursue fulfillment absent back home: a sense of self-worth, respect, empowerment, purpose, and jihadi "street cred." Some fighters joining the Islamic State seek to defend the caliphate declared by the group's leader Abu Bakr al-Baghdadi on June 29, 2014.[76]

With violence in Syria and surrounding areas unlikely to abate in the next few years, the influential role of foreign fighters promises to continue. As the fighting advances, these individuals sharpen the skills and networks that make them a potential threat when they return home or move on to other nations.

Historical Context
Foreign fighters are a long-standing problem in the Syria-Iraq region. During the most intense years of the Iraq War, spanning 2005 to 2007,[77] roughly 4,000 foreign fighters flocked to Iraq via Syria and other nations to fight Western and local Shi'ite forces.[78] The fighters came from within the MENA region and further afield.

Documentation and analysis of foreign fighters by the West Point Combating Terrorism Center sheds light on the number and origins of fighters present during one of the more dangerous periods of the Iraqi insurgency, from August 2006 to

---

76. Vera Mironaova and Sam Whitt, "A Glimpse into the Mind of Four Foreign Fighters in Syria," *CTC Sentinel* 7, no. 6 (June 2014): 5, https://www.ctc.usma.edu/posts/a-glimpse-into-the-minds-of-four-foreign-fighters-in-syria; Matt Bradley, "ISIS Declares New Islamist Caliphate," *Wall Street Journal*, June 29, 2014, http://online.wsj.com/articles/isis-declares-new-islamist-caliphate-1404065263.
77. U.S. and international forces withdrew from Iraq in 2010.
78. Aaron Y. Zelin, "Sunni Foreign Fighters in Syria: Background, Facilitating Factors and Select Responses," PfPC Background Paper 1, Partnership for Peace Consortium of Defense Academies and Security Studies Institutes, May 21, 2014, 1–4, http://www.pfpconsortium.com/#!policy-recommendations/c2ab.

August 2007. The biographical data, which was discovered by U.S. forces in October 2007, was gathered by precursors of to-day's Islamic State group, known then as the Islamic State of Iraq (ISI).[79] These revealing records detail the backgrounds of roughly 700 foreign fighters arriving over a 12-month period. The three largest sources of these fighters were Saudi Arabia (41 percent), Libya (18.8 percent), and Syria (8.2 percent).[80] The fighters often served as suicide bombers directed against U.S. forces, adversarial Sunni tribes, and Shi'ite targets.

Though this one-year snapshot provides evidence of sub-stantial numbers of foreign fighters, the lack of available data for all insurgent groups deploying these motivated combatants throughout the war precludes a comprehensive assessment of their impact.[81] Nonetheless, it is clear that foreign fighters did remain a threat—one that would have been higher had the Is-lamic State of Iraq enjoyed a bona fide safe haven. Among other advantages, a sanctuary would have made it possible to obscure foreign fighters whose "accents and lack of local knowledge" re-sulted in negative exposure for the al Qaeda affiliate.[82]

With the departure of U.S. and other allied forces from Iraq in December 2011, violence persisted as both Sunni and Shi'ite attacks continued along sectarian lines. Both Sunni (al Qaeda in Iraq, Ansar al Islam) and Shi'ite (Jaysh al Mahdi) militias and insurgent groups failed to disarm after the U.S. withdrawal, and instead accounted for the majority of the ensuing violence.[83] ISI also conducted a campaign to free fighters from prisons across

79. Joseph Felter and Brian Fishman, "Al-Qa'ida's Foreign Fighters in Iraq: A First Look at the Sinjar Records," Combating Terrorism Center at U.S. Military Academy, December 2007, https://www.ctc.usma.edu/v2/wp-content/uploads/2010/06/aqs-foreign-fighters-in-iraq.pdf, 3.

80. Ibid, 7.

81. Anthony Cordesman, *Iraq's Sunni Insurgents: Looking Beyond Al Qa'ida*, Center for Strategic and International Studies, 2007, 8.

82. Brian Fishman, "Syria Proving More Fertile than Iraq to Al-Qa'ida's Opera-tions," *CTC Sentinel* 6, no. 11-12, (November 2013): 2.

83. Anthony Cordesman, *Iraq After US Withdrawal: US Policy and the Iraqi Search for Security and Stability*, Center for Strategic and International Studies, July 3, 2012, http://csis.org/files/publication/120702_Iraq_After_US_Withdrawal.pdf, 30.

Iraq, releasing individuals who now fill the ranks of a growing menace.[84]

As 2012 began, the civil war in Syria was already at a full boil. Massacres of Sunni civilians and home-grown opposition forces drew both ISI and foreign fighters to Syria, which had recently served as a way station for international jihadists heading for Iraq. Then, in a reversal, the Assad government became the target of violent Sunni extremists. Syria's territory "provided a haven for the Qaeda affiliate to reconstitute itself with an influx of foreign fighters," who would soon play a key role in future operations.[85]

Motivated in part by Sunni ideologues portraying Syria as a legitimate jihad to defend Sunni Muslims against despotic Shi'ite forces, foreign mujahideen flocked to Syria.[86] Radical groups like Jabhat al-Nusra and the Islamic State likewise attempted to entice foreign volunteers.[87] In a video entitled "Those Who Believed, Migrated, and Waged Jihad," the Islamic State calls attention to the presence of foreign mujahideen within the group's ranks and calls for the migration of more foreign fighters to Syria.[88] One account by a Dutch fighter reveals that appeals from a fellow countryman already in Syria encouraged others to make the journey.[89]

---

84. "Iraq Jailbreaks: Hundreds Escape in Taji and Abu Ghraib," BBC News, July 22, 2013, http://www.bbc.com/news/world-middle-east-23403564.

85. Peter Baker and Eric Schmitt, "Many Missteps in Assessment of ISIS threat," *New York Times*, September 29, 2014, http://www.nytimes.com/2014/09/30/world/middleeast/obama-fault-is-shared-in-misjudging-of-isis-threat.html.

86. "Top Cleric Qaradawi Calls for Jihad against Hezbollah, Assad in Syria," *Al Arabiya*, June 2, 2013, http://english.alarabiya.net/en/News/middle-east/2013/06/02/Top-cleric-Qaradawi-calls-for-Jihad-against-Hezbollah-Assad-in-Syria.html.

87. Bill Roggio, "Tunisian Jihadist Calls for Clerics, Youth to Fight in Syria," *Long War Journal*, July 20, 2013, http://www.longwarjournal.org/archives/2013/07/tunisian_jihadist_ca.php.

88. "Al-l-atheen aamanu wa hajiru wa jahadu," [Al-Furqan Media Presents a New Video Message from the Islamic State of Iraq and Al-Sham: "Those Who Believed and Migrated"], *Jihadology*, July 9, 2013, http://jihadology.net/2013/07/09/al-furqan-media-presents-a-new-video-message-from-the-islamic-state-of-iraq-and-al-sham-those-who-believed-and-migrated/.

89. For a translation of the account see Pieter Van Ostaeyen, "Guest Post: Dutch Foreign Fighters—Some Testimonials from the Syrian Front," *Jihadology*, October 13, 2013, http://jihadology.net/2013/10/13/guest-post-dutch-foreign-fighters-some-testimonials-from-the-syrian-front/.

Foreign Fighters' Role in the Conflict

Foreign jihadists are key factors in the Syrian conflict. While some have embedded with preexisting radical groups like Jabhat al-Nusra and the Islamic State,[90] others have formed distinctly non-Syrian battalions like Jaysh al Muhajireen wal Ansar (JMA)—a predominantly Chechen jihadi group linked to the Islamic Caucasus Emirate.[91] In addition to serving as foot soldiers, foreign militants have also acted as suicide bombers and executioners in publicized videos. The suicide operations carried out by British national Abdul Waheed Majid,[92] American Moner Mohammad Abusalha,[93] and Malaysian Ahmad Tarmimi Maliki[94] serve as chilling examples of the radicalization of foreigners in the Syrian conflict.

Foreign fighters even ascend to the upper echelons of leadership within their groups. Tarkhan Tayumurazovich Batirashvili (nom de guerre Omar al Shishani) is an ethnic Chechen with an extensive portfolio in the Syrian conflict, which he joined in March 2012.[95] Known to be a military commander for the Islamic State's Syrian operations, he is referred to in a recent

---

90. Joseph Chinyong Liow, "ISIS Goes to Asia," *Foreign Affairs*, September 21, 2014, http://www.foreignaffairs.com/articles/142004/joseph-chinyong-liow/isis-goes-to-asia.

91. Bill Roggio, "Chechen Commander Leads Muhajireen Brigade in Syria," *Long War Journal*, February 20, 2013, http://www.longwarjournal.org/archives/2013/02/chechen_commander_le.php. JMA merged with three other groups to form the Helpers of Islam Front in July 2014. As reported by the blog Chechnensinsyria.com, the new merger includes several other battalions that were primarily composed of foreign fighters from Saudi Arabia, Turkey, and Morocco.

92. Darshna Soni, "Relaxed and Smiling: Suspected British Bomber in Syria," *Channel 4 News*, February 14, 2014, http://www.channel4.com/news/syria-abdul-waheed-majeed-suspected-suicide-bomber.

93. Thomas Joscelyn, "US Officials Have Identified American Suicide Bomber in Syria," *Long War Journal*, May 31, 2014, http://www.longwarjournal.org/archives/2014/05/officials_have_ident.php.

94. "ISIS and the First Malaysian Suicide Bomber," *Star Online*, June 14, 2014, http://www.thestar.com.my/News/Nation/2014/06/14/ISIS-and-the-first-Malaysian-suicide-bomber/.

95. U.S. Department of Treasury, "Treasury Designates Twelve Foreign Terrorist Fighter Facilitators," September 24, 2014, http://www.treasury.gov/press-center/press-releases/Pages/jl2651.aspx.

video simply as "Military Commander,"[96] suggesting his position as the group's overall military leader in both Syria and Iraq. This suggestion is supported by further video evidence as well as by a list of specific military operations attributed to him.[97]

As Abu Bakr al-Baghdadi's July 2014 audio message indicates, foreigners are needed for maintenance of his group's territory. Appealing to those who can help build communities, Baghdadi implores Muslim "scholars," "medical doctors," and "engineers of all different specializations and fields" to fulfill their *wajib 'ayni*, or individual religious duty, by moving to the Islamic State.[98]

Although they were actively encouraged to stay home in the early days of the conflict, women also serve the Islamic State.[99] They may serve as fighters' wives, run sex-slave brothels full of captured Iraqi and Syrian women, or enforce shari'a law restrictions on female dress and activity.[100] Women also work as doctors, nurses, and engineers in Islamic State hospitals.[101] Exact numbers of women supporting the Islamic State are unknown, but London's International Centre for the Study of Radicalisation (ICSR) estimates that about 10–15 percent of the total num-

96. "Al-I'tiṣām Media Presents a New Video Message from the Islamic State of Iraq and Al-Shām: 'Breaking of the Border,'" *Jihadology*, October 13, 2013, http://jihadology.net/2014/06/29/al-iti%e1%b9%a3am-media-presents-a-new-video-message-from-the-islamic-state-of-iraq-and-al-sham-breaking-of-the-border/.

97. For video evidence, see Bassem Mroue, "Omar Al-Shishani, Chechen in Syria, Rising Star in ISIS Leadership," *Christian Science Monitor*, July 3, 2014, http://www.csmonitor.com/World/Latest-News-Wires/2014/0703/Omar-al-Shishani-Chechen-in-Syria-rising-star-in-ISIS-leadership. For the list of military operations, see U.S. Department of Treasury, "Treasury Designates Twelve Foreign Terrorist Fighter Facilitators."
As of September 24, 2014, al Shishani has been added to the U.S. list of Specially Designated Global Terrorists under Executive Order 13224.

98. Abu Bakr al-Baghdadi, "A Message to the Mujahidin and the Muslim Ummah in the Month of Ramadan," Al-Hayat Media Center, July 4, 2014, https://ia902501.us.archive.org/2/items/hym3_22aw/english.pdf.

99. Aryn Baker, "How ISIS Is Recruiting Women from around the World," *TIME*, September 6, 2014, http://time.com/3276567/how-isis-is-recruiting-women-from-around-the-world/.

100. "UK Female Jihadists Run ISIS Sex-Slave Brothels," *Al Arabiya*, September 12, 2014, http://english.alarabiya.net/en/variety/2014/09/12/UK-female-jihadists-run-ISIS-sex-slave-brothels.html.

101. Baker, "How ISIS Is Recruiting Women from around the World."

bers of foreigners traveling to Syria are female, with at least 30 women traveling from Sweden alone.[102]

Reasons and Motivations for Coming

Aaron Zelin, a leading American authority on foreign fighters in Syria, identifies seven primary factors that help draw people to battle: the simplicity of reaching Syria; the existence of established transit and facilitation networks; social media as a multifaceted enabler; sympathy for Syrian suffering; Syria's "cool" and relatively comfortable appeal (in contrast to hardship locations such as Yemen, Mali, and Afghanistan); the conflict's "religious-historical and millenarian pull;" and the sectarian drive of anti-Shi'ism.[103]

Another motivating factor that often combines with those just listed is the personal hardship that fighters may face in their home countries. Difficult socioeconomic conditions make the decision to fight in Syria an easy one for many aspiring soldiers. A life of marginalization and deprivation and lacking in personal dignity (frequently the result of harsh treatment by local security services) motivates young men to seek empowerment and fulfillment in battle. Such young men are also inspired by witnessing powerful popular movements overthrow oppressive governments across the MENA region.

There are in addition sectarian reasons why fighters go to Syria. Indeed, as the conflict has worsened, fighters, funders, and clerics, both Sunni and Shi'ite, have relied more heavily on a "vocabulary of sectarianism" that appeals to religious loyalties.[104] In response to Shi'ite Hezbollah leader Hassan Nasrallah's vow of unwavering military support to the Assad regime,[105]

102. "It Ain't Half Hot Here, Mum," *Economist*, August 30, 2014, http://www.economist.com/news/middle-east-and-africa/21614226-why-and-how-westerners-go-fight-syria-and-iraq-it-aint-half-hot-here-mum?fsrc=scn/tw/te/pe/ed/itaintshalfhotheremum.

103. Zelin, "Sunni Foreign Fighters in Syria."

104. Dickinson, "Playing with Fire," 16; Aaron Y. Zelin and Phillip Smyth, "The Vocabulary of Sectarianism," *Foreign Policy*, January 29, 2014, http://mideastafrica.foreignpolicy.com/posts/2014/01/29/the_vocabulary_of_sectarianism.

105. Dominic Evans, "Hezbollah Will Stay in Syria as Long as Needed: Nasrallah," Reuters, November 14, 2013, http://www.reuters.com/article/2013/11/14/us-syria-crisis-hezbollah-idUSBRE9AD0D820131114.

several prominent Sunni clerics rallied together to incite Sunnis to pursue jihad against the Shi'ite forces.[106] Anti-Shi'ite rhetoric permeates the appeals made to Sunni fighters from around the world to wage jihad in defense of innocent Muslims in Syria. Both radical extremist groups and the moderate opposition use anti-Shi'ite slurs like "Nusayri" and "Safawi" in reference to the Syrian Army or Hezbollah.[107] This sectarian rhetoric seeks to capitalize on a historic division among the sects and at worst attempts to portray the Syrian conflict in terms of a prophesized apocalyptic battle.

At the same time, recruiters also paint a picture of an orderly, pious life with friendship and conveniences fighters may lack in their home country. In a conversation recorded several years ago, an American in Somalia contrasts the religious lifestyle of fighters to the secular morality of home as he seeks to recruit a young American in Boston to join al-Shabaab in Somalia and wage jihad. The Somali tells his Boston contact, Tarek Mehanna, in 2006, "Akhi (brother), pray five times a day. Do you know where I am? You can't even smoke cigarettes. It is illegal." He adds, "I will set you up with everything. I'll have people pick you up, a place for you to stay and, heck, if you want, I can have a wife waiting for you."[108] Eight years later, the rhetoric used to recruit foreigners for jihad is very similar and significantly more accessible.

Syria, or the "land of Sham," is central to the Islamic account of the coming apocalypse. Specifically, the region is the supposed location for the final struggle between the antichrist and

---

106. "Sunni Clerics Make Joint Call for Jihad in Syria," *Al Arabiya*, June 13, 2013, http://english.alarabiya.net/en/News/middle-east/2013/06/13/Sunni-clerics-make-joint-call-for-Jihad-in-Syria.html.

107. See "Sa'udi yusharik ma' al Jaysh al Hor fi qital al Nusayriyya" [A Saudi participates with the Free Syrian Army in the killing of Nusayri], YouTube video, 0:40, posted by "Vitamin Com," August 22, 2012, http://www.youtube.com/watch?v=kZ7BXC2H_MY&feature=youtube_gdata_player; "(7) Dimn silsilat ghazwat al ayn bi-l-ayn; and "(8) Qasf masakin dubat al jaysh al Nusayri fi Dara'a" [(7) In the series of raids 'an eye for an eye' and (8) Bombing the houses of Nusayri army officers with rockets and mortars in Dara'a], *Jihadology*, August 30, 2013, http://jihadology.net/2013/08/30/two-new-statements-from-jabhat-al-nu%e1%b9%a3rah-12/.

108. "ISIS Operates Sophisticated Propaganda Machine," *CNN*, September 17, 2014, http://edition.cnn.com/TRANSCRIPTS/1409/17/lvab.02.html.

Jesus, who "will come down to the white minaret on the east side of Damascus (Dimashq)."[109] This narrative is exploited by jihadi publications seeking recruits. Jabhat al-Nusra's media wing, Al Minara Al Bayda, is named after the minaret central to the apocalypse mythos. The Islamic State's English-language magazine publication is titled *Dabiq*, named after a town north of Aleppo in Syria in which a sixteenth-century battle ending in Ottoman victory placed the entirety of modern Syria under Muslim control.

In multiple issues of *Dabiq*, Islamic State propagandists use religious rhetoric and historical references to draw in potential fighters and reinvigorate those already in place. Published in English, the magazine is directly aimed at a Western Muslim audience. With its inclusion of a quotation from deceased al Qaeda in Iraq leader Abu Musab Zarqawi, the second issue of the magazine makes clear its intention to target potential foreign fighters:

> The first priority is to perform hijrah from wherever you are to the Islamic State . . . Rush to the shade of the Islamic State with your parents, siblings, spouses, and children. There are homes for you and your families. You can be a major contributor towards the liberation of Makkah, Medinah, and al-Quds. Would you not like to reach Judgment Day with these grand deeds in your scales.[110]

The issue ends with a quotation from "Allah's Messenger" emblazoned on a photograph of Islamic State fighters:

> "You will invade the Arabian Peninsula, and Allah will enable you to conquer it. You will then invade Persia, and Allah will enable you to conquer it. You will then invade Rome, and Allah will enable you to conquer it. Then you will fight the Dajjal, and Allah will enable you to conquer him."[111]

109. Jean-Pierre Filiu, *Apocalypse in Islam,* trans. M. B. DeBevoise (Berkeley: University of California Press, 2011), 18.

110. "The Flood," *Dabiq* (Al Hayat Media Center), 2014, https://azelin.files.wordpress.com/2014/07/islamic-state-e2809cdc481biq-magazine-2e280b3.pdf.

111. Ibid. "Dajjal" is an evil figure, or antichrist, in Islamic theology. A common Arabic word, "dajjal" has roots in the words "lie" or deceit" and references the Islamic belief that a future antichrist will appear pretending to be the messiah.

The religious language is intended to portray the Islamic State as the rightful leader of the Islamic empire's restoration.

While the pathos of Pan-Islamism may draw some to Syria, the reasons for which foreigners flock to Syria are innumerable and individually based. For some foreign fighters, leaving their homes means choosing "a glorious life" over an "animalistic" one.[112] Others leave situations of relative wealth and comfort to engage in holy war.[113] For Muslims who are not well integrated in the Western countries where they live, and who may be subject to anti-Muslim sentiment, jihad in Syria may hold particular appeal.[114] To the marginalized, Syria and Iraq offer excitement, purpose, and commitment to a larger goal. Recruiters increase incentives for individuals who are unsure about going to Syria, selling the rewards and personal fulfillment of waging jihad.[115]

Once someone is determined to join the fight, the relative ease of getting into Syria facilitates matters. Marc Pierini, former European Union ambassador to Turkey, called Turkey's lax borders "an open door policy to jihadists in Turkey. So much so that the flight from Istanbul to Gaziantep has been called . . . jihad express."[116] Although many countries border Syria, foreign jihadists' stories cite Turkey's southern border as their point of entry into Syria.[117] In an interview, a French foreign jihadist who had entered Syria in 2013 described how easily he passed into Syria via Turkey, lying about his intent to do "commercial business" and "philanthropic work."[118]

---

112. Mironaova and Whitt, "Glimpse into the Mind," 18.
113. Van Ostaeyen, "Guest Post: Dutch Foreign Fighters."
114. Pieter Van Ostaeyen, "Guest Post: Belgian Jihadis in Syria," *Jihadology*, September 5, 2013, http://jihadology.net/2013/09/05/guest-post-belgian-jihadis-in-syria/; "Islamophobia: Understanding Anti-Muslim Sentiment in the West" Gallup, December 2011, http://www.gallup.com/poll/157082/islamophobia-understanding-anti-muslim-sentiment-west.aspx; Nadim Roberts, "The Life of a Jihadi Wife: Why One Canadian Woman Joined ISIS's Islamic State," CBC News, July 7, 2014, http://www.cbc.ca/1.2696385.
115. Nick Paton Walsh, "Syrian Jihadists Using Twitter to Recruit Foreign Fighters," CNN, June 4, 2014, http://www.cnn.com/2014/06/03/world/meast/syria-defector-recruits-westerners/index.html.
116. John Vandiver, "Europe's Fear: Turkey's Porous Border Serves as Gateway for ISIL's Spread," *Stars and Stripes*, July 5, 2014, http://www.stripes.com/news/europes-fear-turkey-s-porous-border-serves-as-gateway-for-isil-s-spread-1.291646.
117. Mironaova and Whitt, "Glimpse into the Mind," 5.
118. Ibid.

Virtual Recruitment
Widely available social media applications allow non-Syrians in the conflict to document their activity, while creating a certain mythos of heroism, righteousness, and noble sacrifice.[119] Extremist groups, most notably the Islamic State, run highly sophisticated social media platforms to reach potential jihadists from foreign lands and to broadcast messages of brutality, militarism, religious fanaticism, and humanitarian aid.[120] The ever-expanding range of social media options offers extremists wide avenues for recruiting foreigners, organizing travel arrangements, and distributing propaganda to their attentive audience.

To help potential fighters arrange their travel to Syria and to directly contact individual fighters in a more private manner, many Islamic State recruiters employ the popular online and smartphone messenger apps Kik, Skype Messenger, and Surespot.[121] If recruits want to ask extremists on the ground more in-depth questions behind anonymous usernames, they can use websites like Ask.fm to find personalized information on topics ranging from grooming to packing lists for jihad.[122]

Extremists in Syria and Iraq are active on many social media platforms, but they have used Twitter and video-sharing sites most successfully. The Islamic State's media department, Al Hayat Media Center, is in control of video production and various official social media accounts for the group. At its height in June, the group used more than one dozen official provincial

---

119. Richard Barrett, *Foreign Fighters in Syria* (New York: Soufan Group, 2014), 17, http://soufangroup.com/wp-content/uploads/2014/06/TSG-Foreign-Fighters-in-Syria.pdf.
120. Rita Katz, "Air Strikes Won't Disrupt Islamic State's Real Safe Haven: Social Media," Reuters, September 24, 2014, http://blogs.reuters.com/great-debate/2014/09/24/beware-of-the-online-caliphate-is-wants-more-than-syria-and-iraq/.
121. Jarret Brachman, "Transcending Organization: Individuals and 'The Islamic State'" START Analytical Brief, National Consortium for the Study of Terrorism and Responses to Terrorism, June 2014, http://www.start.umd.edu/pubs/START_TranscendingOrganizationIndividualsandtheIslamicState_Analytical-Brief_June2014.pdf.
122. Ibid.

accounts spread across the territory it controls to post official releases followed by as many as 50,000 people per account.[123]

The Islamic State often uses simple "bait and switch" tactics in which links to gruesome videos of beheadings are embedded between popular hashtags like #Brazil during the World Cup, and #ScotlandDecides during the Scottish vote for independence.[124] Numerous rebel and extremist factions in Syria, including Jabhat al-Nusra and the Islamic State, use Twitter accounts to post photos and videos of battle action, images of stolen materiel, scenes of daily life, pro-Islamist rants, and messages of support to other extremist groups.[125]

Video messages from foreign fighters already in Iraq and Syria represent a major motivating factor for jihadists flowing to the region. In these videos, which are used mainly by the Islamic State, combatants act as spokesmen for the group and issue impassioned appeals to recruits. In an Islamic State video produced in late June 2014, fighters who claimed to hail from the UK and the United States spoke in English and called on fellow Muslims to join them: "You can either be here in these golden times, or you can be on the sidelines commentating."[126] In a mid-July 2014 video, also produced by the Islamic State, Canadian foreign fighter Andre Poulin was portrayed in a prerecorded clip released after his death on the battlefield. After describing his

123. Rita Katz, "Follow ISIS on Twitter: A Special Report on the Use of Social Media by Jihadists," *Insite Blog: On Terrorism and Extremism*, June 26, 2014, http://news.siteintelgroup.com/blog/index.php/entry/192-follow-isis-on-twitter-a-special-report-on-the-use-of-social-media-by-jihadists.

124. Lorraine Ali, "Islamic State's Soft Weapon of Choice: Social Media," *Los Angeles Times*, September 22, 2014, http://www.latimes.com/entertainment/la-et-islamic-state-media-20140922-story.html.

125. "My Beloved Brothers in Dawlah, Know That Every Time You Get Bombed It Feels like We of JN Get Bombed, Your Blood Is Our Blood!!!," Abu Rayan, Twitter post, October 1, 2014, https://twitter.com/AbuRayanMuhajir/status/517249359717867520.

126. Al-Hayat Media Center, "There Is No Life Without Jihad," video, 13:26, 2014, http://jihadology.net/2014/06/19/al-%E1%B8%A5ayat-media-center-presents-a-new-video-message-from-the-islamic-state-of-iraq-and-al-sham-there-is-no-life-without-jihad/.
The video shows foreign fighters from a variety of regions, including the United States, Europe, and Southeast Asia—and includes some who are portrayed as martyrs following their deaths.

life in Canada as a regular citizen, Poulin called for other Cana-
dians and Westerners to carry out jihad—emphasizing the many
roles that foreigners can have within the Islamic State: "We need
the engineers, we need doctors, we need professionals, we need
volunteers . . . there is a role for everybody."[127]
Foreigners from non-Western nations have also appeared
in passionate video messages. In a late July 2014 video titled
"Join the Ranks," an Indonesian Islamic State fighter called on
Indonesian Muslims to leave their homelands and join him in
Syria.[128]
A decade removed from the days of terrorist rhetoric disseminated through slow-moving jihadist forums, Islamic State
propaganda is almost impossible to eliminate entirely.[129] Each
time Twitter has cracked down on individual or provincial accounts, the militant group has quickly moved to other social
media platforms such as Diaspora,[130] which functions through
decentralized private servers and is unable to suspend individual accounts.[131] (The group has even called for so-called lone
wolves to kill Twitter corporation employees in retaliation for
removal of Islamic State accounts.[132]) Videos removed from You-
Tube are re-posted on forums and websites like the public access video-sharing site LiveLeak. For a short time, Islamic State

---

127. "Canadian Andre Poulin, killed in Syria appears in IS video," YouTube video,
2:19, posted by "LoneWolf Sager," July 16, 2014, https://www.youtube.com/
watch?v=GX4jTdnVtao.
128. Al-Hayat Media Center, "Join the Ranks," video, 8:27, 2014, http://jihadology.
net/2014/07/22/al-%E1%B8%A5ayat-media-center-presents-a-new-video-mes-
sage-from-the-islamic-state-join-the-ranks/.
129. Rita Katz, "Air Strikes Won't Disrupt Islamic State's Real Safe Haven:
Social Media," Reuters, September 24, 2014, http://blogs.reuters.com/great-de-
bate/2014/09/24/beware-of-the-online-caliphate-is-wants-more-than-syria-and-
iraq/.
130. Aaron Mamiit, "ISIS Turns to Diaspora after Getting Booted by Twitter," *Tech
Times*, August 26, 2014, http://www.techtimes.com/articles/13888/20140826/isis-
turns-to-diaspora-after-getting-booted-by-twitter.htm.
131. "Islamic State Fighters on Diaspora," *The Diaspora* Blog, August 20, 2014,
https://blog.diasporafoundation.org/4-islamic-state-fighters-on-diaspora.
132. Rita Katz, "The Islamic State Has a New Target: Twitter, and Its San Francisco
Employees," *Washington Post*, September 18, 2014, http://www.washingtonpost.
com/posteverything/wp/2014/09/18/the-islamic-state-has-a-new-target-twitter-
and-its-san-francisco-employees/.

organizers created their own Android application, called "The Dawn of Glad Tidings," that allowed users to collect extremist tweets in one place.[133]

Facing Reality

The reality on the ground, however, can be disappointing for some. Many foreigners who traveled to Syria or Iraq and joined hard-line groups have become disillusioned with the experience—unhappy with their individual role, the enemy, and the quality of life. Unmet expectations are not uncommon, and some fighters have already returned home. According to the Danish Security Service (PET), some foreigners even returned home after just a few days.[134]

Fuelling disillusionment is the frequent scenario where fighters—having traveled with hopes of battling the regime of Bashar al-Assad—instead fight other rebel and extremist factions.[135] A British citizen who traveled to Syria "pumped up with the propaganda" told a researcher at ICSR in London that the situation on the ground had changed: "Now it's just Muslims fighting Muslims. We didn't come here for this."[136] The phenomenon is not new—one Jabhat al-Nusra coordinator claimed in February 2014 that "hundreds, if not more than two thousand, went back to their home countries."[137]

Further, the quality of life in Syria or Iraq is almost certainly worse than what most foreign fighters were led to expect by

133. J. M. Berger, "How ISIS Games Twitter," *Atlantic*, June 16, 2014, http://www.theatlantic.com/international/archive/2014/06/isis-iraq-twitter-social-media-strategy/372856/?utm_source=Sailthru&utm_medium=email&utm_term=%2AMideast%20Brief&utm_campaign=2014_The%20Middle%20East%20Daily_6.17.14.

134. Barrett, *Foreign Fighters in Syria*.

135. Erika Solomon and Sam Jones, "Disillusioned Foreign Fighters Abandon Rebel Ranks in Syria," *Financial Times*, March 18, 2014, http://www.ft.com/intl/cms/s/0/a26ffc5c-adfc-11e3-bc07-00144feab7de.html#axzz3EoBoUFUY.

136. Shiraz Maher and Peter Neumann, "Borin Johnson's Proposal for British Fighters in Syria and Iraq is Dangerous and Counterproductive," *Independent*, August 26, 2014, http://www.independent.co.uk/voices/comment/boris-johnsons-proposal-for-british-fighters-in-syria-and-iraq-is-dangerous-and-counterproductive-9692303.html.

137. Solomon and Jones, "Disillusioned Foreign Fighters Abandon Rebel Ranks in Syria."

recruiters, and may be worse than what they left back home. According to Hilal Khashan, a political science professor at the American University of Beirut, "After spending time fighting for Daesh [Islamic State] in Iraq and Syria, they came to a conclusion that no matter how bad in their opinion life was in the West, it still remains much better [than] what they are currently encountering."[138]

Regardless of how long they stay in the region, foreign fighters who travel to Syria and Iraq gain valuable battle experience and training. In many cases, their radicalized ideals are reinforced by extremist groups, which also transfer new values to them. With this experience and potentially increased level of radicalization, foreign fighters could return to their countries of origin and carry out or plan attacks. Fighters in Syria and Iraq have threatened their countries of origin directly,[139] though it can be difficult to separate threatening extremist rhetoric and serious plans for action.

But the same disillusionment that sends foreign fighters back to their home countries as an increased threat also presents an exploitable weakness. In his testimony to the Foreign Affairs Subcommittee on Europe, Eurasia, and Emerging Threats, expert Thomas Joscelyn pointed out that "disillusioned foreign fighters can be a good source of intelligence concerning which jihadists are the most capable and committed."[140] Attempting to capitalize on the potential for disillusionment, the U.S. Department of State created a video that seeks to dissuade aspiring fighters before they go.[141]

---

138. Quoted in Paul Crompton, "Fed-up Foreign ISIS Fighters 'Likely to Struggle' When Returning Home," *Al Arabiya*, September 13, 2014, http://english.alarabiya. net/en/perspective/analysis/2014/09/13/Fed-up-foreign-ISIS-fighters-likely-to-struggle-when-returning-home.html.

139. Al-Hayat Media Center, "Flames of War," video, 55:14, 2014, http://www.live-leak.com/view?i=22f_1411220248.

140. Thomas Joscelyn, "Islamist Foreign Fighters Returning Home and the Threat to Europe," *Long War Journal*, September 19, 2014, http://www.longwarjournal.org/archives/2014/09/islamist_foreign_fig.php.

141. "Welcome to the "Islamic State" Land (ISIS/ISIL)," YouTube video, 1:09, posted by "ThinkAgain TurnAway," August 22, 2014, http://www.youtube.com/watch?v=-wmdEFvsYoE.

Implications

Despite dramatic extremist rhetoric—the threat to "paint the White House black," for example[142]—it is difficult to discern what threats real and what are for show. Many groups, and the Islamic State in particular, rely on propaganda to induce fear. The infamous passport burning video,[143] while made to communicate a specific message about the invalidity of borders and secular states' sovereignty, illustrates a point made by Thomas Hegghammer in early 2013: "Most foreign fighters do not 'come home to roost.'"[144] Rather, fighters engage in their jihad away from home with no designs to return. While no hard figures about this trend are yet available, anecdotal accounts of men and women making *hijrah* (or permanent migration) to the Islamic State with the intention of establishing families and lives there are on the rise.[145]

At the same time, as the number of transnational fighters increases, so does the number of those attempting to return to their home nation. If the flow of foreign fighters to extremist groups in the Iraq and Syria battle space continues unabated, a return attack on fighters' home nations grows more likely.

This trend draws attention to national intelligence agencies' inability to accurately track all individuals suspected of travelling to Syria and Iraq to fight. The directors of the Federal Bureau of Investigation (FBI), the U.S. Department of Homeland Security (DHS), and the U.S. National Counterterrorism Center—the agencies tasked with tracking the movement of Americans to foreign battlefields—acknowledged the challenges that they

142. "Exclusive: Islamic State Member Warns of NYC Attack In VICE News Interview," YouTube Video, 8:09, posted by "VICE News," September 25, 2014, http://www.youtube.com/watch?v=j8TLu514EgU&feature=youtube_gdata_player.

143. Al Furqan Media, "Mu'asisat Al Furqan Taqdim 'Huwa Samaakum Al Muslimin' Al Dawla Al Islamiyya Fi Al Iraq Wa as Sham" [Al Furqan Media presents 'He Named You Muslims' the Islamic State in Iraq and Sham"], video , 12:31, " April 13, 2014, http://jihadology.net/2014/04/13/al-furqan-media-presents-a-new-video-message-from-the-islamic-state-of-iraq-and-al-sham-the-muslims-he-hears-you/.

144. Thomas Hegghammer, "Should I Stay or Should I Go? Explaining Variation in Western Jihadists' Choice between Domestic and Foreign Fighting," *American Political Science Review* 107, no. 1 (February 2013): 15, doi:10.1017/S0003055412000615.

145. Mironaova and Whitt, "Glimpse into the Mind," 5; Roberts, "Life of a Jihadi Wife."

face in this process. In the words of FBI director James Comey, there are "thousands of ways to get from the United States to Syria and there are tens of thousands of Americans who travel for legitimate purposes every single day . . . Once in Syria, it's very difficult to discern what happens there."[146] For the thousands of fighters who enter Syria and Iraq from European countries, the threat of a return attack extends to other nations that participate in the visa waiver program, including the United States. European Union officials have also voiced their concern about potential return attacks on European soil, which they have called nearly "inevitable."[147]

In fact, one such attack has already taken place. On May 24, 2014, a lone French gunman named Mehdi Nemmouche allegedly killed four people in the Jewish Museum in Brussels, Belgium.[148] Nemmouche reportedly spent a year fighting in Syria before returning to Germany in March 2014.[149] His car was found to contain an AK-47, a handgun, and a makeshift Islamic State flag.[150] At least one other possible attack has been averted, moreover. In January 2014 Greek border police arrested Ibrahim Boudina, a Frenchman who had fought for Jabhat al-Nusra and the Islamic State in Syria for over a year. He had a USB drive with bomb-making instructions in his possession; a handgun and homemade explosives were found in an apartment complex in Cannes where Boudina had been hiding.[151]

---

146. House Committee on Homeland Security, "FBI, DHS, NCTC Heads Agree: ISIS Recruitment and Radicalization of Americans Dangerous and Difficult to Track," press release, September 17, 2014, http://homeland.house.gov/press-release/fbi-dhs-nctc-heads-agree-isis-recruitment-and-radicalization-americans-dangerous-and.

147. Ian Traynor, "Major Terrorist Attack Is 'inevitable' as Isis Fighters Return, Say EU Officials," *Guardian*, September 25, 2014, http://www.theguardian.com/world/2014/sep/25/major-terrorist-attack-inevitable-isis-eu.

148. Frances Robinson, "French Suspect in Brussels Jewish Museum Killings Charged," *Wall Street Journal*, July 30, 2014, http://online.wsj.com/articles/french-suspect-in-brussels-jewish-museum-killings-charged-1406725425.

149. Evan Kohlmann and Laith Alkhouri, "Profiles of Foreign Fighters in Syria and Iraq," *CTC Sentinel* 7, no. 9 (September 2014): 4, https://www.ctc.usma.edu/v2/wp-content/uploads/2014/09/CTCSentinel-Vol7Iss91.pdf.

150. Ibid.

151. Ibid., 5.

Foreign fighters represent a core capability for the Islamic State and other extremist groups. Highly motivated and numerous, foreign fighters offer a ready-made international network that could be activated for attacks. Even if fighters do not return to their homelands to carry out attacks, they are willing messengers who encourage others to join them by appearing in recruitment and propaganda videos.

But inherent in their status as foreigners is an exploitable weakness. Restricting the flow of these aspiring jihadists to foreign battlefields could weaken the extremist groups that are so dependent on them for personnel replenishment. For now though, impeding the movement of these fighters remains very difficult.

Responses

The growth of the foreign fighter phenomenon in Syria and Iraq presents a dynamic threat to the United States, the West in general, and various countries around the world. In response to this threat, members of the international community have sought to block the movement of foreign fighters and counter the ideology pulling them overseas.

The United States pursues a very strong program of engagement and information sharing with dozens of international partners. Among other efforts, it has appointed a senior adviser for "partner engagement on Syria foreign fighters," requested DHS assistance with porous borders and the movement of foreign fighters, shared information on foreign fighter trends gathered by the U.S. intelligence community, implemented anti-recruitment messaging through the Center for Strategic Counterterrorism Communications of the U.S. State Department, engaged in best-practice exchanges with Europe on laws and tools for investigation and prosecution through the Justice Department, and entered into international information-sharing agreements focused on identifying "terrorist travel activity" through the FBI.[152]

---

152. White House, "Comprehensive U.S. Government Approach to Foreign Terrorist Fighters in Syria and the Broader Region," press release, September 24, 2014, http://www.whitehouse.gov/the-press-office/2014/09/24/fact-sheet-comprehensive-us-government-approach-foreign-terrorist-fighte. ISIL—Islamic State of

These international efforts to counter violent extremist ideology and the flow of foreign fighters were highlighted in President Obama's September 24, 2014, speech to the UN General
Assembly. President Obama called on the world in general and
Muslim communities in particular to "explicitly, forcefully, and
consistently reject the ideology of organizations like al Qaeda
and ISIL [and] to stop the flow of fighters into and out of the region," at the same time noting that more than 40 countries were
joining the coalition to confront the Islamic State.[153]

Broad measures already in place to thwart the flow of foreign
fighters include United Nations Security Council Resolution
2178, passed on September 24, 2014, which requires member
states to "prevent and suppress the recruiting, organizing,
transporting, or equipping of individuals" who seek to participate in jihadist movements and terrorist activities in foreign
countries.[154] This legally binding resolution specifically targets
fighters with aspirations of traveling and conducting terrorist
operations in conflict zones, such as Syria and Iraq.

In attempts to reduce the effectiveness of extremist recruiting through social media, international companies—including Twitter, YouTube, and Facebook—move quickly to
remove graphic videos and individual accounts linked to suspected terrorist groups. In late September, Twitter removed over
400 Islamic State–linked accounts in one day.[155] Individual users
of social media are also acting to counter recruitment efforts.
Hashtag campaigns, both serious and satirical, have included
trending topics like #NotInMyName and #MuslimApologies.
Such campaigns have raised awareness about jihadists' use of
Twitter, though they have also spurred charges of Islamopho-

Iraq and the Levant—is another name for ISIS—Islamic State of Iraq and al-Sham
or Islamic State of Iraq and Syria.

153. Barack H. Obama, "Remarks by President Obama in Address to the United
Nations General Assembly," White House, September 24, 2014, http://www.
whitehouse.gov/the-press-office/2014/09/24/remarks-president-obama-address-
united-nations-general-assembly.

154. Ed Pilkington, "UN Unanimously Passes Resolution to Combat 'Foreign
Terrorist Fighters,'" *Guardian*, September 24,2014, http://www.theguardian.com/
world/2014/sep/24/un-security-council-resolution-terror-threat-obama.

155. J. M. Berger, Twitter post, September 29, 2014, 8:20 pm, https://twitter.com/
intelwire/status/516789689106579457.

bia.[156] Certainly the actions of Twitter alone, without direct Western government intervention, will not eliminate extremist use of social media entirely, and many jihadists claim it is an endless game of whack-a-mole.[157] At the same time, continued deliberate, targeted action from social media companies has been shown to slow and limit the propagation of extremist ideology.[158]

Reinforcing these international efforts are national measures to inhibit aspiring fighters from traveling abroad. In early September 2014, UK Prime Minister David Cameron gave British law enforcement the power to seize the passports of suspected Islamist militants seeking passage to conflict zones in the Middle East.[159] In Southeast Asia—home to numerous violent extremist groups such as Jemaah Islamiya and the Abu Sayyaf Group—Singapore's Internal Security Act specifically targets nationals who travel to fight in conflict zones. The act enables Singapore to issue both detention orders and restriction orders to ban known and potentially threatening individuals, respectively, from leaving the country.[160] Saudi Arabia, possessing a 500-mile border with Iraq and home to a large number of foreign fighters already in Syria, took the important and rare step of issuing a royal decree on February 3, 2014, banning the travel of its citizens to fight in Syria or anywhere abroad. Violations of

156. Hannah Gais, "Fight Against Islamic State Group Hits Twitter and Social Media," *US News and World Report*, October 3, 2014, http://www.usnews.com/opinion/blogs/world-report/2014/10/03/fight-against-islamic-state-group-hits-twitter-and-social-media.

157. Ben Makuch, "Banning Islamic State Jihadists from Twitter Is Like Playing Whack-a-Mole," *Motherboard-VICE*, August 21, 2014, http://motherboard.vice.com/en_uk/read/isis-twitter-whack-a-mole.

158. J. M. Berger, "Resistible Force Meets Movable Object," *Intel Wire*, October 2, 2014, http://news.intelwire.com/2014/10/resistable-force-meets-movable-object.html.

159. William James and Kylie MaClellan, "Britain Unveils Powers to Strip Suspected Islamist Fighters of Passports," Reuters, September 1, 2014, http://uk.reuters.com/article/2014/09/01/uk-syria-crisis-britain-idUKKBN0GW1Z920140901.

160. Government of Singapore, Internal Security Act, http://statutes.agc.gov.sg/aol/search/display/view.w3p;page=0;query=DocId%3A%225ba26ddb-fd4c-4e2e-8071-478c08941758%22%20Status%3Ainforce%20Depth%3A0;rec=0.

the law carry punishment of up to 20 years in prison.[161] Leading Islamic clergy have also advised against joining extremist groups and traveling to Syria and Iraq. In June 2012, Sheikh Ali al-Hikmi of the Saudi Council of Senior Scholars, Saudi Arabia's highest religious authority, issued a fatwa prohibiting any acts of jihad in Syria.[162] To further undermine the efforts of jihadi groups in Syria and Iraq, the council later issued a statement denouncing terrorism as "contrary to the purposes of the great religion of Islam" and calling it "nothing more than corruption and criminality rejected by Islamic shari'a law and common sense."[163] The National Imams Consultative Forum of Australia also echoed this sentiment, issuing a statement advising Australians not to travel to Syria and Iraq to fight, but instead to provide humanitarian support for the Syrian people through legal and acceptable channels.[164]

Law enforcement at the national level has also been extremely active in disrupting channels of support to fighters hoping to move to the battlefield. French law enforcement arrested five people on suspicion of recruiting young women to join Islamist groups in Syria in September 2014.[165] Police in Bangladesh arrested Samiun Rahman, a young Muslim from London, who ran recruitment operations in Bangladesh for both the Islamic State and Jabhat al-Nusra.[166] And in September 2014, Australian

161. Angus McDowall, "Saudi Arabia to Jail Citizens Who Fight Abroad," Reuters, February 3, 2014, http://in.reuters.com/article/2014/02/03/saudi-law-syria-assad-idINDEEA120A620140203.

162. "Saudi Religious Authority Forbids 'Jihad' in Syria," *Al-Akhbar,* June 7, 2012, http://english.al-akhbar.com/node/8198.

163. Ian Black, "Saudi Clerics Declare Isis Terrorism a 'Heinous Crime' under Sharia Law," *Guardian,* September 17, 2014, http://www.theguardian.com/world/2014/sep/17/saudi-clerics-fatwa-declares-terrorism-heinous-crime-sharia-law.

164. Shahram Akbarzadeh, "Imams Accept Syrian War Risk Is a Reality," *Herald Sun,* March 19, 2014, http://www.heraldsun.com.au/news/opinion/imams-accept-syrian-war-risk-is-a-reality/story-fni0ffsx-1226859520193?nk=cf9cd2846b4948ca 373c9ae3b67de3f9.

165. Hannah Strange, "France Arrests Five People for Allegedly Recruiting Young Women for Jihad in Syria," *VICE News,* September 17, 2014, https://news.vice.com/article/france-arrests-five-people-for-allegedly-recruiting-young-women-for-jihad-in-syria.

166. Shiv Malik, Aisha Gani, and Saad Hammadi, "Briton Arrested in Bangladesh

authorities raided homes in Sydney and Brisbane, thwarting a planned terrorist attack by Islamic State sympathizers to perform "public killings," detaining 15 people.[167] With no slowdown in sight for foreign fighters seeking to join violent extremist groups in Syria, Iraq, and across the MENA region, adaptive multinational efforts to prevent this flow remain a top priority. Should the Islamic State and Jabhat al-Nusra encourage some of these foreign fighters to return home and engage in violent acts, the battle will open up a new and unwelcome front in counterterrorism.

SAFE HAVENS

Today, U.S. military officials identify more terrorist and insurgent sanctuaries in the MENA region than at any time since the attacks of September 11, 2001.[168] These safe havens offer a range of benefits: refuge from government forces; space to train fighters and launch operations; and opportunities to raise revenue, build coalitions, threaten adversaries, and—especially in the case of the Islamic State—control territory where the group can govern and claim legitimacy. Painful experience with groups like AQAP in Yemen has shown that these terrorist safe havens are very difficult to eliminate and can pose a direct threat to the United States and other nations.

Safe havens occur in countries where the established government is unwilling or unable to confront terrorist organizations on their territory, and where these organizations sometimes provide services not offered by corrupt, weak, or inept rulers. In nations experiencing severe internal strife, such as Yemen or Afghanistan, government authority does not extend to all regions, and these conditions offer room for violent extremists to operate.

'Confessed to Recruiting' for Isis," *Guardian*, September 29, 2014, http://www.theguardian.com/world/2014/sep/29/briton-arrested-bangladesh-recruiting-islamic-state.

167. "Australia Police Raids Foil 'Beheading Plot,'" *Al Jazeera*, September 18, 2014, http://www.aljazeera.com/news/asia-pacific/2014/09/australia-makes-raids-foil-violent-acts-201491834852407966.html.

168. Interview with senior U.S. Defense Department official, April 29, 2014, Washington, D.C.

Some states are devoid of any government capacity or presence, a situation that further enables the free movement of violent extremists. Somalia since 1991 and today's Libya are stark examples. Insurgent, terrorist, and criminal groups operate from these areas, threaten vulnerable populations, and plot attacks against their neighbors and more distant targets. Al Qaeda and other violent extremists continue to operate in safe havens in Afghanistan, Somalia, Yemen, Mali, the Philippines, Pakistan, and elsewhere. All these areas remain of great concern, but it is the sprawling, two-state safe haven dominated by the Islamic State that causes such apprehension today.

The Islamic State's capture and control of key areas and resources across large parts of Syria and Iraq affords them a highly prized operational base in the heart of the Middle East. By early fall 2014, the Islamic State controlled key supply routes, cities, and border crossings that connect territory from the northern Syrian city of Raqqa east through Deir ez-Zor, across to Iraq's northern city of Mosul, and southward along the Tigris River.

Though not all the area between these points are directly in Islamic State hands, tightly networked control of important nodes enables the group to regulate travel, trade, communication, and populations. This capacity offers the Islamic State the advantage of either permitting or impeding most activities, thus extending its influence between and beyond areas where the group is physically present. This situation will continue to favor the Islamic State until coalition forces can reduce or eliminate the sanctuary.

An All-Too-Familiar Problem

Ungoverned territory and safe havens have long been features of many states with large landmasses, rugged and remote terrain, and an inability or unwillingness to extend authority to all corners of their nation. Indeed, some officials have even welcomed violent extremists into their country for political and ideological purposes, enabling them to openly establish a base of operations.

Osama bin Laden enjoyed a safe haven in Sudan from 1991 to 1996; he was welcomed as a guest of Sudanese president Omar al-Bashir and the hard-line Islamist ideologue Hassan Abdallah al-Turabi.[169] Taking advantage of his personal wealth and heroic status, bin Laden used his new base in Sudan to network with other violent extremists and plan strikes against the United States. Both Saudi Arabia and the United States (along with Egypt) pressured Sudan into ejecting bin Laden in 1996.[170]

Afghanistan and Pakistan served as al Qaeda's next sanctuary, and the site where the group trained for and executed major terror attacks. These included the 1998 bombings of U.S. embassies in Nairobi, Kenya, and Dar es Salaam, Tanzania;[171] the 2000 attack on the USS Cole in Yemen; and most notably, the September 11, 2001, attacks in the United States. Bin Laden remained in Afghanistan until mid-December 2001, at which point he fled U.S. forces for sanctuary in Pakistan.[172]

The Afghanistan-Pakistan region quickly became the archetype for a lethal terrorist safe haven where an accommodating government allowed its remote territory to serve as a base of extremist operations. It merits noting that Faisal Shahzad was trained in Pakistan by the Tehrik i Taliban Pakistan before attempting to set off a car bomb in New York's Times Square in 2010.

Despite (or, perhaps, partly as a result of) NATO's 2011 intervention in Libya, the North African country has evolved into a safe haven for a range of Islamist groups and militias. Initially

169. *The 9/11 Commission Report: Final Report of the National Commission on Terrorist Attacks upon the United States (9/11 Report)* (Washington, DC: National Commission on Terrorist Attacks upon the United States, 2004), 57, http://govinfo.library.unt.edu/911/report/index.htm.

170. "Timeline: Life of Osama Bin Laden," Reuters, May 2, 2011, http://www.reuters.com/article/2011/05/02/us-binladen-events-idUSTRE7411F920110502.

171. Early planning stages for the East Africa embassy bombings also took place in Sudan.

172. John Kerry, *Tora Bora Revisited: How We Failed to Get Bin Laden and Why It Matters Today,* report to members of the Committee on Foreign Relations, United States Senate, John Kerry, Chairman, 111th Congress (Washington, DC: Government Printing Office, 2009), 2, http://catalog.hathitrust.org/Record/007384189.

hailed as a success,[173] the NATO air campaign created a new security and power void that rival militias quickly filled. Spurred on by intractable political disputes, many militias have gained strength over time; estimates put the number of militias operating in Libya in the low hundreds.[174] These non-state groups pursue nationalist, sectarian, and tribal goals while engaging in various criminal activities, including extortion, smuggling, and kidnapping.[175] The safe haven and deteriorating security situation in Libya offer important lessons for future action in Iraq and Syria—suggesting that the U.S.-led coalition should be an enduring one, and that it should seek political inclusion, economic development, and militia demobilization.

Yemen, a focal point in the United States' ongoing counterterrorism campaign, exemplifies how a terrorist group can manipulate terrain, political strife, and a host of other domestic issues to carve out a safe haven, in spite of a central government's opposition. Al Qaeda in the Arabian Peninsula, since 2009 a sworn affiliate of the al Qaeda organization, has taken advantage of a nation riven by years of insurrection, sectarianism, and tribal animosities to fashion space for sophisticated operations against the United States and the Yemeni government. Pitched antigovernment violence in Yemen between January and September 2011 further destabilized the country and strengthened AQAP.[176]

---

173. Ivo H. Daalder and James G. Stavridis, "NATO's Victory in Libya: The Right Way to Run an Intervention," *Foreign Affairs* 91, no. 2 (March/April 2012): 2–7, http://www.foreignaffairs.com/articles/137073/ivo-h-daalder-and-james-g-stavridis/natos-victory-in-libya.

174. Christopher S. Chivvis and Jeffrey Martini, *Libya After Qaddafi: Lessons and Implications for the Future* (Santa Monica, CA: RAND National Security Research, 2014), http://www.rand.org/content/dam/rand/pubs/research_reports/RR500/RR577/RAND_RR577.pdf.
Estimates for the number of militias operating in Libya range from the low hundreds across the entire country, to hundreds operating in single cities. The variation arises from different definitions of 'militias' and 'armed groups.'

175. Mieczyslaw P. Boduszynski and Kristin Fabbe, "What Libya's Militia Problem Means for the Middle East, and the U.S .," *Los Angeles Times*, September 23, 2014, http://www.latimes.com/opinion/op-ed/la-oe-0923-boduszynski-libya-lessons-20140924-story.html.

176. "Arab Uprising Country by Country: Yemen (Yemen Timeline)," BBC News, http://www.bbc.com/news/world-12482293.

The terrorist activity that AQAP planned and executed from the Yemen sanctuary is notable for its sophistication and ambition. It includes the nearly successful December 25, 2009, attack against the Northwest Airlines flight over Detroit, Michigan, and the October 2010 and May 2012 attempts to destroy U.S.-bound aircraft.

Across the Gulf of Aden from Yemen lies Somalia, one of the most persistent and emblematic terrorist safe havens on the globe. The nation has experienced nothing short of anarchy since President Siad Barre was toppled in 1991. Fighting in 2006 between the fundamentalist Islamic Courts Union (at the time considered "the most powerful force in Somalia"[177]) and a feeble Transitional Federal Government backed by U.S.-supported Ethiopian forces gave rise in 2007–2008 to a splinter group called al-Shabaab.[178] Al-Shabaab established a formal, if fitful, relationship with the al Qaeda network in February 2012.[179]

From its founding through today, al-Shabaab has perpetrated acts of extreme violence against civilians and local and regional government forces inside lawless Somalia. From 2007 to 2012, al-Shabaab killed more than 1,600 people and wounded more than 2,100 through nearly 500 separate terrorist attacks.[180] Al-Shabaab's two most notable attacks were executed in Uganda and Kenya. A July 2010 bombing in Kampala—one of the countries with forces taking part in the African Union Mission in Somalia (AMISOM)—killed 74 people.[181] An attack on the Westgate

177. United Nations Monitoring Group on Somalia, "Report of the Monitoring Group on Somalia pursuant to Security Council Resolution 1676 (2006)," United Nations, 2006, 39, http://www.un.org/ga/search/view_doc.asp?symbol=S/2006/913.
178. Ken Menkhaus, "Al-Shabaab's Capabilities Post-Westgate," *CTC Sentinel*, 7, no. 2 (February 2014): 4.
179. U.S. National Counterterrorism Center, "Al-Shabaab Group Profile," http://www.nctc.gov/site/groups/al_shabaab.html.
180. Erin Miller, "Al-Shabaab Attack on Westgate Mall in Kenya," START Background Report, National Consortium for the Study of Terrorism and Responses to Terrorism, September 2013, http://www.start.umd.edu/sites/default/files/publications/local_attachments/STARTBackgroundReport_alShabaabKenya_Sept2013.pdf.
181. Max Fisher, "Why al-Shabaab Would Attack in Uganda," *Atlantic*, July 12, 2010, http://www.theatlantic.com/international/archive/2010/07/why-al-shabaab-

Mall in Nairobi—planned and launched from the Somali safe haven—killed 67 people between September 21 and 24, 2013.[182] Al-Shabaab indicated that the latter attack was revenge for the actions of Kenya's armed forces inside Somalia.[183]

Terrorist safe havens look different in various contexts and therefore require tailored responses. In general, however, they require the constant threat of lethal force, blockage of funding, and control over the flow of foreign fighters. Without these, safe havens have proven to be a national and international security threat that remain very difficult to manage.

Recent Actions against Safe Havens
Safe havens are a cornerstone of terrorist capability and durability. The United States targets them and those who use them with a combination of direct action by Special Operations Forces (SOF), manned and unmanned aircraft, missiles, CFT measures, nation building, and other forms of technical support.

Strikes by drones—armed, pilotless aircraft—are probably the best-known manifestation of "kinetic" counterterrorism activity in safe havens. Drones are exceptionally important for striking terrorist targets deep in sanctuaries, where using SOF teams is too risky, or in situations where a foreign government is unable or unwilling to pursue and confront violent extremists.

U.S. drone strikes have made some progress against AQAP in Yemen. Cooperation with the government of President Abdurrahman Mansour Hadi and with former president Ali Abdullah Saleh has been key to this relative success. Yet despite approximately 115 drone strikes (killing upwards of 670 militants),[184] AQAP was still considered the most significant threat to the U.S. homeland by the Office of the Director of National In-

would-attack-in-uganda/59551/.
182. New York City Police Department, "Analysis of al-Shabaab's Attack at the Westgate Mall in Nairobi, Kenya," November 1, 2013, 3, http://www.scribd.com/doc/190795929/NYPD-Westgate-Report.
183. Ibid., 13.
184. Bill Roggio, "US Drone Strike Kills 3 AQAP Fighters in Central Yemen," *Long War Journal*, August 9, 2014, http://www.longwarjournal.org/archives/2014/08/us_drone_strike_kill_30.php.

telligence as of January 2014.[185] An indispensable part of U.S. counterterrorism strategy in recent years, drone strikes as a counterterrorism measure have inherent limitations, including intelligence challenges and frequent public outrage over questions of state sovereignty and civilian deaths. Even so, the Obama administration looks to efforts in Yemen as a partial model for host-nation cooperation as U.S. and partner forces attack the Islamic State in its Iraq-Syria safe haven.[186]

U.S. SOF engages militants operating out of safe havens in the Horn of Africa. In September 2009, helicopter-borne SOF pursued and killed Saleh Ali Nabhan.[187] Nabhan was wanted for his role in the 1998 al Qaeda attacks on U.S. embassies in Kenya and Tanzania. In September of 2014, the U.S. dealt a serious blow to al-Shabaab after a drone missile struck and killed the group's leader, Ahmed Abdi Godane, along with other senior members of the group, inside of Somalia.[188]

Targeted actions to diminish safe havens include, importantly, nonmilitary forms of assistance. Safe havens rely on ungoverned territory in nations with porous land, sea, and air borders, and fester in the absence of good governance and economic opportunity. Violent extremists occupying safe havens also depend on financial resources to sustain their activity. Impeding the movement of individuals and resources while helping to rebuild economies is a vital means of reducing terrorist sanctuaries.

185. "Transcript: Senate Intelligence Hearing on National Security Threats," *Washington Post*, January 29, 2014, http://www.washingtonpost.com/world/national-security/transcript-senate-intelligence-hearing-on-national-security-threats/2014/01/29/b5913184-8912-11e3-833c-33098f9e5267_story.html; "Drone Wars Yemen: Analysis," New America Foundation International Security Program, http://securitydata.newamerica.net/drones/yemen/analysis?utm_source=Sailthru&utm_medium=email&utm_term=%2ASituation%20Report&utm_campaign=SitRep_0801.

186. Barack H. Obama, "Remarks by the President on the Situation in Iraq" White House, June 19, 2014, http://www.whitehouse.gov/the-press-office/2014/06/19/remarks-president-situation-iraq.

187. "Recent Highlights in Terrorist Activity," *CTC Sentinel*, 2, no. 10 (October 2009): 20, https://www.ctc.usma.edu/v2/wp-content/uploads/2010/08/CTCSentinel-Vol2Iss10-Art8.pdf.

188. Jon Lee Anderson, "Killing Godone, Chasing ISIS," *New Yorker*, September 6, 2014.

The U.S. State Department's Regional Strategic Initiative (RSI) pursues efforts "in a regional context with the goal of shrinking the space in which terrorists operate."[189] This includes East Africa, Central Asia, the Eastern Mediterranean, Africa's Sahel region, and in Middle Eastern nations such as Iraq. The RSI program offers border security workshops[190] and conducts anti-kidnapping for ransom (KFR) workshops[191] as part of the Trans-Sahara Counterterrorism Partnership (TSCTP) in Africa.[192] These efforts are designed to better protect the local partners as well as reduce the chances that their territory will be used to launch attacks on other nations, including the United States.

A lack of economic opportunity in both urban and rural areas of developing countries provides opportunities for terrorist groups to recruit and radicalize individuals. Where a government is unable or unwilling to generate economic activity or provide services for citizens, especially young men, these forces are able to offer both licit and illicit opportunities, for example participation in trafficking or KFR operations.[193]

Afghanistan represents a case in which effective counterinsurgency strategies have reduced the threat posed by extremist groups, and it may offer some instructive lessons for combatting the hybrid insurgent-terrorist groups in the MENA region. Large areas in Afghanistan are outside of government control, and violent extremists hold sway over segments of the population. Groups such as the Afghan Taliban and the Haqqani Net-

---

189. U.S. Department of State, "Bureau of Counterterrorism, Regional Strategic Initiative," http://www.state.gov/j/ct/programs/index.htm#RSI.

190. U.S. Department of State, Bureau of Counterterrorism, "Terrorist Safe Haven," in *Country Reports on Terrorism 2013*, April 2014, 8, http://www.state.gov/j/ct/rls/crt/2013/224828.htm.

191. U.S. Department of State, *Annual Report on Assistance Related to International Terrorism: Fiscal Year 2013*, February 11, 2014, 1, http://www.state.gov/j/ct/rls/other/rpt/221544.htm.

192. TSCTP partner nations include Algeria, Burkina Faso, Chad, Cameroon, Mali, Mauritania, Morocco, Niger, Nigeria, Senegal, and Tunisia. See Trans-Sahara Counter-Terror Partnership, http://www.foreignassistance.gov/web/OU.aspx?OUID=373.

193. Interview with "Abu Khalid," illicit businessman and trader, January 14, 2014, Turkey. The subject exposed drug trafficking by extremists in Syria, particularly from the city of Al Bab.

work (a group associated with the Taliban) target vulnerable, often unemployed young men in an effort to weaken the regime in Kabul and retain control over parts of the country and lucrative trading routes. These insurgent, terrorist, and criminal groups are there to offer options—reinforced with threats—to vulnerable populations, whether they are unemployed lumbermen in the Korengal Valley or drought-stricken farmers in Helmand Province.[194]

Over the course of the U.S. war in Afghanistan, Provincial Reconstruction Teams combined military and civilian programs to provide international aid to citizens across the country.[195] An important component of the teams is the U.S. Agency for International Development (USAID), which provides economic and community development, good governance programming, and monitored U.S. reconstruction efforts in areas that might otherwise become a part of a terrorist or insurgent safe haven.[196]

The centrality of development to these approaches cannot be overstated. David Kilcullen, one of the world's leading authorities on counterinsurgency, argues for strategies that include economic development as a tool to "extend government control over the population and the environment while marginalizing the enemy in a physical and political sense."[197] Shrinking the space available to violent extremists reduces opportunities for revenue generation, recruitment, training, and operations against counterterrorism forces and civilians.

---

194. Afghanistan's 2014 United Nations Human Development Index (HDI) ranks the destitute nation 169 out of 187 countries, with 2013 annual per capita income registering a meager US$700. This rugged, inaccessible country is 78 percent rural, putting major stretches of its territory out of the reach of government security, health, education, and economic services. The similarly poor economic and social circumstances in Syria and Iraq have facilitated the recruitment of young men into extremist factions.

195. United States Agency for International Development, "Provincial Reconstruction Teams," October, 27, 2014, http://www.usaid.gov/provincial-reconstruction-teams.

196. Ibid.

197. David Kilcullen, *The Accidental Guerilla: Fighting Small Wars in the Midst of a Big One* (New York: Oxford University Press, 2009), 106.

The Islamic State Sanctuary

Beginning in March 2011 with the "Day of Dignity" protests, the conflict in Syria rapidly engulfed the nation and by August 2014 had claimed roughly 200,000 lives.[198] More than 1,000 militias and opposition groups battle one another as well as Syrian government forces, Shi'ite militias, and Lebanon's Hezbollah.[199] As a result of this turmoil and violence, vast areas of Syria have fallen outside of the Assad regime's direct or indirect control. The Syrian Observatory for Human Rights estimated in mid-July 2014 that the Islamic State controlled 35 percent of Syrian territory.[200] However, it is clear that some of this space remains contested by a combination of Syrian government forces and antiregime opposition forces that have regularly battled with the Islamic State.

Partly due to an ethnically exclusive Iraqi government under former Prime Minister Nouri al-Maliki and a near-constant political stalemate, the Islamic State was able to expand its large safe haven from Syria into Iraq. In the first half of 2014, the Islamic State forces stepped up attacks against Iraqi military forces. On January 3, 2014, they captured the Iraqi city of Fallujah on their way to taking much of Sunni-dominated western Iraq.[201] On June 10, the Islamic State captured Mosul, Iraq's second largest city. U.S. airstrikes in August combined with increased support to Kurdish Pesh Merga forces rolled back some Islamic State gains,[202] but as of October 2014, Islamic State–controlled areas

---

198. Megan Price, Anita Gohdes, and Patrick Ball, "Updated Statistical Analysis of Documentation of Killings in the Syrian Arab Republic," Human Rights Data Analysis Group, August 2014, 1, https://hrdag.org/wp-content/uploads/2014/08/HRDAG-SY-UpdatedReportAug2014.pdf\.
199. "Syria Crisis: Guide to Armed and Political Opposition," BBC News, December 13, 2013, http://www.bbc.com/news/world-middle-east-24403003.
200. Jennifer Cafarella, "ISIS Connects Strongholds in Deir Ez-Zour and Ar-Raqqa," *Institute for the Study of War Updates (blog)*, July 19, 2014, http://iswsyria.blogspot.com/2014/07/isis-connects-strongholds-in-deir-ez.html.
201. Liz Sly, "Al-Qaeda force captures Fallujah amid Rise in Violence in Iraq," *Washington Post*, January 3, 2014, http://www.washingtonpost.com/world/al-qaeda-force-captures-fallujah-amid-rise-in-violence-in-iraq/2014/01/03/8abaeb2a-74aa-11e3-8def-a33011492df2_story.html.
202. "Back to Iraq," *Economist*, August 16, 2014, http://www.economist.com/news/leaders/21612229-combining-military-force-political-brinkmanship-america-making-some-headway-back.

stretched from its Syrian headquarters in Raqqa well into Iraq's Anbar Province—and beyond.

Islamic State control of key Syrian and Iraqi cities represents a calculated plan to link cities, rivers, and border crossings to enable training, resupply, population management, revenue generation, and the movement of fighters. Importantly, it also offers the Islamic State the ability to highlight their control and governance of a re-established caliphate. The Islamic State reinforces its claim of a caliphate by refusing to acknowledge international borders—a refusal that is itself a threat to neighboring states.

During 2014, the safe haven that the Islamic State controls has expanded from secluded training grounds in rural settings to include major urban centers. Indeed, the Islamic State safe haven provides the most recognizable example of a mixture of urban and rural holdings. The fusion of these two environments gives the group greater flexibility to train and equip fighters for different circumstances and employ more versatile weaponry, and it improves the group's recruiting pitch to foreign fighters by offering them not just combat, but an opportunity to defend and nurture the only territory truly governed Islamically. Controlling both urban and rural areas also widens funding opportunities. Urban areas offer opportunities for taxation, extortion, and control of local economies, while rural areas enable exploitation of resources such as oil and agricultural products.

As of late September 2014, just prior to coalition air strikes that targeted oil refineries controlled by the Islamic State, the group reportedly held 10 refineries across Syria and Iraq, which produced a combined 80,000 barrels of oil per day to be sold on the black market for millions of dollars.[203] As noted earlier in this chapter, controlling and selling oil plays a significant role in the Islamic State's ability to sustain its operations.

As the Islamic State gained control of Iraqi and Syrian territory in 2013 and 2014, it effectively assumed responsibility for

---

203. Daragahi and Solomon, "Fuelling Isis Inc."
The figure of 80,000 combined barrels of oil reflects a reported 50,000 barrels a day from Syria and 30,000 from Iraq.

governance functions such as waste management and tax collection.[204] The precarious nature of Islamic State governance—dependent on many uncertain factors (e.g., reliable revenues to pay tribal and sectarian partners) along with discipline across a large organization—remains a potentially exploitable weakness.[205] This possible opening for forces seeking to dismantle and destroy the Islamic State is discussed above, in the section that discusses CFT strategies.

The Implications of and Possible Remedies for the Islamic State Safe Haven

Across Iraq, Afghanistan, Pakistan, Yemen, the Philippines, and other conflict areas, terrorist safe havens offer exceptional advantages to violent extremists. Rural and urban sanctuaries fester in the midst of conflict and where governments are too weak or too inept to provide citizens with services and economic opportunity. Terrorists plan, train, and operate from these areas with few reliable measures to interdict their activities. Even with concerted outside military, economic, and other forms of assistance, sovereign countries may be ineffective in reclaiming their territory, and safe havens remain a tremendous problem.

The Islamic State safe haven in Syria and Iraq—possessed of tens of thousands of foreign fighters, skilled bomb makers, attack plotters, weapons, money, and passports from visa waiver countries—represents a very serious threat to the integrity of Syria and Iraq, to nearby states, and to those beyond. As the safe haven has expanded throughout 2014, more young men have been brought into the ranks of Islamic State fighters. And as the declared Islamic caliphate solidifies, it stimulates and motivates thousands more to travel to the region and defend sacred territory. Those same fighters may possibly be deployed against local, regional, and more distant targets at the direction of the Islamic State's leadership.

---

204. Jenna Lefler, "Life under ISIS in Mosul," Institute for the Study of War, July 28, 2014, http://iswiraq.blogspot.com/2014/07/life-under-isis-in-mosul.html.
205. Keith Johnson, "The Islamic State Is the Newest Petrostate," *Foreign Policy,* July 28, 2014, http://www.foreignpolicy.com/articles/2014/07/28/baghdadis_hillbillies_isis_iraq_syria_oil_terrorism_islamic_state.

As discussed earlier, the presence of European foreign fighters in the conflict poses a serious threat to Western security. The proximity of the Islamic State's safe haven to Europe presents an especially serious problem for that continent and for the United States. At least 3,000 European fighters engaged in Syria and Iraq are only a short distance from home.[206] With several European nations now actively supporting efforts to weaken and destroy the Islamic State, there is a heightened possibility that some fighters will return home and engage in violence. And of the 38 countries participating in the Department of State's visa waiver program, 30 are European. This ability to board a plane from one of those 30 nations to the United States without a personal interview at a local U.S. embassy reduces opportunities for detecting threatening travelers.[207]

The return of radicalized, trained, and highly motivated foreign fighters is also a potential threat to dozens of other nations that have seen their citizens rush to the battle in Syria. Indonesia is believed to have between 50 and 100 fighters in Syria,[208] with many supporting the Islamic State.[209] With a recent history of terrorist violence by groups such as Jemaah Islamiya, there is fear in Indonesia, Singapore, Malaysia, and the Philippines that these fighters may return to rejuvenate Jemaah Islamiya, initiate their own terrorist group, and incite violence.

The central location of the Islamic State sanctuary—close to several energy-rich nations, vulnerable populations, plentiful weapons and finances, and U.S. and Western facilities—pres-

---

206. Sources estimate 3,000 to well over 4,000 European foreign fighters are currently in Iraq and Syria. See "It Ain't Half Hot Here, Mum," *Economist*; and "Foreign Fighters in Iraq and Syria: Where Do They Come From?" Radio Free Europe/Radio Liberty, October 2, 2014, http://www.rferl.org/contentinfographics/infographics/26584940.html.

207. U.S. Department of State, "Visa Waiver Program Participant Country List," http://travel.state.gov/content/visas/english/visit/visa-waiver-program.html.

208. Sidney Jones, "Indonesians and the Syrian Conflict," IPAC Report 6, Institute for Policy Analysis of Conflict, January 30, 2014, 1–12.

209. "Indonesia Fears Terror Backlash as Jihadist Fighters Head to Syria, Iraq," Agence-France Presse, June 20, 2014, http://www.scmp.com/news/asia/article/1536804/indonesia-fears-terror-backlash-jihadist-fighters-head-syria-iraq.

ents many potential targets for the group. With Lebanon already experiencing high levels of violence associated with the Syrian civil war—for which Lebanese Hezbollah bears some responsibility—the Islamic State's redoubt suggests greater violence and instability for Lebanon in the months and years ahead.

Jordan and Turkey border Syria and have reason to be concerned. Both states are U.S. allies, and attacks on them could push the United States into a wider commitment of military forces and other resources in the Middle East, despite the Obama administration's desire to avoid broader involvement. A further complication is the perception that U.S. actions against the Sunni extremist Islamic State are supporting the goals of Shi'ite Iran and Syria—a perception that may further sharpen the region's sectarian divide and hobble the counterterrorism coalition.

The centrality of Iraq to the global energy supply is yet another reason why a well-armed group occupying large parts of that turbulent nation, as well as its neighbor Syria, is of serious concern. At the beginning of 2013, Iraq boasted the world's fifth-largest crude oil reserves while ranking second in OPEC production at slightly more than 3 million barrels per day.[210] In early 2013, Jabhat al-Nusra reportedly received close to US$1.8 million per month from the Syrian regime to guarantee the continuation of oil production from oil fields controlled by the group.[211] While the control of some Iraqi and Syrian oil exports by extremist groups in the region constitutes a small amount of the countries' total output, the concern is Iraq's longer-term integrity and whether the nation can increase production in parallel to projected growth in worldwide consumer demand.[212]

---

210. U.S. Department of Energy Information Administration, "Iraq Country Overview and Analysis Brief," April 2013, http://www.eia.gov/countries/country-data.cfm?fips=iz.

211. Operatives from the Al-Nusra Front, Al-Qaeda's Branch in Syria, Together with Other Rebel Organizations, Have Taken over the Large Oil Field in Deir Ez-Zor," Meir Amit Intelligence and Terrorism Information Center, March 12, 2013, http://www.terrorism-info.org.il/en/article/20599.

212. Keith Johnson, "ISIS and the Long-Term Threat to Iraqi Oil," *Foreign Policy*, June 17, 2014, http://www.foreignpolicy.com/articles/2014/06/17/isis_and_the_long_term_threat_to_iraqi_oil.

Failing to do so could lead to higher prices and economic shocks. There is little doubt that the Islamic State safe haven facilitates an active and building threat to regional stability, and that it offers opportunities to strike beyond the confines of Iraq and Syria—into Europe, Southeast Asia, and North America. This sanctuary offers financial resources as well as space to network, train, and deploy fighters from around the world; launch attacks; recuperate after battle; claim legitimacy; and threaten adversaries.

From this safe haven, the Islamic State threatened the integrity of Iraq and threatens the United States back to battle in the region—a remarkable development by any measure. Though the center of gravity for this threat is the Islamic State safe haven, it is evident that other sanctuaries in the region could rise to the level of Syria and Iraq. Given the ongoing, unsettled regional landscape, new safe havens could easily emerge, and existing terrorist sanctuaries could be expanded.

U.S. policy should focus on continued work with coalition partners to shrink the safe haven through a combination of cutting Islamic State resource extraction and closing borders to foreign fighters and black-market oil trafficking. Additionally, the United States should help counter the Islamic State's claims of legitimacy by supporting credible Muslim voices, should strike Islamic State and Jabhat al-Nusra forces, and should stress the importance of progress on political reform in Iraq in an effort to separate extremist groups from Sunni communities sympathetic to its message of empowerment and revenge. Building and leading a coalition to "degrade and destroy" violent extremists in MENA safe havens demands all of these measures and more that will inevitably arise as the political and security landscape continues to change.

CONCLUSION

More than 15 years after the bombing of U.S. embassies in Kenya and Tanzania, countering terrorists such as al Qaeda, insurgencies such as the Islamic State and the Taliban, and a range of other violent extremists has yielded victories and setbacks. Adaptations and initiative by the adversary almost always outpace countermeasures, a disadvantage unlikely to end given states' slow and reactive nature.

With their large safe haven, robust funding schemes, and dependable supply of fighters from more than one-third of the world's countries, violent extremists in Syria and Iraq pose serious counterterrorism challenges. The threat from these extremists appears on many fronts: al Qaeda fighters from Afghanistan and Pakistan, identified as the Khorasan Group, are also present in Syria to plot attacks, while the local Syrian al Qaeda affiliate, Jabhat al-Nusra, has continued with its violent advance, to include taking over a Golan Heights border crossing with Israel.

When the United States and its partners began to respond in full to the Islamic State's rapid moves across Iraq in the summer of 2014, the group was steps ahead, pursuing a violent and successful agenda. After it captured large areas of Syria and Iraq and declared a caliphate, the West and its local allies scrambled to catch up.

The Islamic State's seasoned leadership and disciplined structure position it well to remain the center of gravity in Syria and Iraq. The group planned ahead and built a portfolio of renewable, diverse income sources that will lend it durability and insulation in the months and years ahead. A broad safe haven and the service provision the group conducts within it afford the Islamic State the legitimacy it claims in the caliphate declaration—while also allowing plenty of space to plan and execute operations. The high numbers of foreign fighters rushing to join the local fight are yet another potential tool against far-flung enemies now engaged in battle against the Islamic State. With a sophisticated social media capability to advertise and facilitate its goals and actions, the former al Qaeda affiliate appears to be at the vanguard of the global jihadi movement.

In each of these Islamic State advantages, however, can be found a weakness. As political change slowly moves forward in

Iraq, certain Sunni enablers and allies of the Islamic State could fall off or even turn against the group. Air strikes and other measures targeting the heart of the group's sources of funds—oil extraction, refining, and black market sales—have taken a serious toll. A drop in revenues and fewer allies will shrink the safe haven in which the Islamic State operates. It will also affect the insurgency's ability to support foreign fighters, a development that could come about in parallel with measures to keep the fighters home and to make crossing the Turkish border more difficult when they do manage to travel.

Counterterrorism forces have never witnessed such a significant challenge before, and success will demand no letup in commitment, creativity, and speed—for on the other side of the chessboard are organizations with equal drive to prevail. Opportunities for disruption and dismantlement may be short-lived, but they must be pursued.

4. TUNISIA: CONFRONTING EXTREMISM

Haim Malka[1]

Jihadi-salafi groups thrived in Tunisia after the government of Zine El-Abidine Ben Ali fell in January 2011. They swiftly took advantage of political uncertainty, ideological freedom, and porous borders to expand both their capabilities and area of operations. By the end of 2012 two strains of jihadi-salafism had emerged in the country. The first, which grew directly out of the revolutionary fervor and political openings of the Arab uprisings, prioritized and promoted religious outreach to mainstream audiences, often through social activism.[2] Ansar al Shari'a in Tunisia was the largest and most organized group taking this approach. The second strain followed al Qaeda's traditional method, with organized bands of underground fighters who emerged periodically to launch violent attacks against security forces and the government. This strain was represented by Tunisian jihadi-salafists calling themselves the Okba ibn Nafaa Brigade who established a base in Tunisia's Chaambi Mountains

---

1. Sections of this chapter are drawn from two previously published papers: Haim Malka and William Lawrence, "Jihadi-Salafism's Next Generation," Center for Strategic and International Studies, October 2013, http://csis.org/publication/jihadi-salafisms-next-generation; and Haim Malka, "The Struggle for Religious Identity in Tunisia and the Maghreb," Center for Strategic and International Studies, May 2014, http://csis.org/publication/struggle-religious-identity-tunisia-and-maghreb.
2. For a detailed analysis of hybrid jihadi-salafism and efforts to combine extremist ideology with social and political activism, see Malka and Lawrence, "Jihadi-Salafism's Next Generation."

on the Tunisian-Algerian border and launched numerous attacks against security forces.[3] The first model was primarily a political threat, while the second represented a security threat. Both models overlapped in that they shared the common goal of replacing the existing political order with an Islamic state and were guided by jihadi-salafi ideology, though each pursued a different strategy.

Jihadi-salafi activism of both types poses particular challenges to Tunisia as the country transitions to a competitive political system after decades of authoritarian rule. Until the 2011 revolution, Tunisia had largely been shielded from the extremist violence that had plagued neighboring Algeria and the rest of the region over the last few decades. But as Tunisia wrote its new constitution and moved toward new parliamentary and presidential elections, extremist violence heightened tensions between secularists and political Islamists in the debate over the role of religion in society[4] and deepened fissures between Tunisia's different Islamist streams.

The evolution of these two distinct yet overlapping models represented a debate over jihadi-salafi strategy in Tunisia after the fall of Ben Ali. Was Tunisia a land of da'wa (spiritual outreach and proselytization) or a land of jihad—in practical terms, should jihadi-salafists use direct violence against the state, or slowly build support through political and social activity in order to further their goals? The debate was complicated by the raging conflict in Syria against the Assad regime, which attracted hundreds and then thousands of young Tunisian men.[5] The rural insurgency in Tunisia that pursued al Qaeda's tradi-

---

3. The Okba ibn Nafaa Brigade was officially recognized by Tunisian authorities in December 2012 following the shooting death of a Tunisian National Guard member in the city of Kasserine.

4. The role of religion in society and Tunisian identity dominated much of the constitutional debate. The constitution was approved in January 2014, and Article 6 lays out the government's broad understanding of the role of religion.

5. Estimates as of November 2014 suggest approximately 3,000 Tunisian citizens fighting in Syria, making Tunisians one of the largest national groups participating in the conflict. See David D. Kirkpatrick, "New Freedoms in Tunisia Drive Support for ISIS," *New York Times*, October 21, 2014, http://www.nytimes.com/2014/10/22/world/africa/new-freedoms-in-tunisia-drive-support-for-isis.html?_r=0.

tional strategy was clearly violent. In the more politically active urban areas, developments were more ambiguous: jihadi-salafists took advantage of political freedom to organize, preach, and build constituencies. For them this was an important stage in creating a new social and political order based on Islamic law. Even as many urged jihad in Syria, local jihadi-salafi leaders counseled caution at home. Despite their predilection for vigilante violence and intimidation, they avoided confronting security forces or the state directly. For a time, Tunisia became a test case for jihadi-salafi experiments with political openings.

Tunisia's Ennahda-led government responded slowly at first to the growing jihadi-salafi threat. The Ennahda-led government's ambivalence was shaped by a combination of politics and ideology. After decades of repression, a wide range of Islamist ideas flourished following the fall of Ben Ali: political Islamists, salafists, traditional Tunisian religious leaders, and jihadi-salafists all competed in an open market of ideas. As the strongest and most organized political and social force, Ennahda sought to own this new political space by representing all Islamists. Yet a deepening political crisis reinforced by two assassinations in 2013 and rising violence against security forces changed Ennahda's calculations. The group outlawed Ansar al Shari'a, made personnel changes at the Ministry of the Interior, allowed security forces to pursue more aggressive tactics against militants, and eventually agreed to hand over power to a technocratic interim government—one that made security one of its top priorities after taking control in January 2014.

In the ensuing months these different threats and models of jihad evolved, intersected and became increasingly indistinguishable. The government has tackled jihadi-salafism in different yet complementary ways. First, it has boosted security force capabilities and pursued more aggressive and coherent law enforcement and counterterrorism operations. Security forces increased operations against militant individuals, safe houses, and bases while devoting additional resources and manpower to the fight. Second, the government has sought to fight extremist ideology and its appeal by redefining and promoting a Tunisian national Islamic identity, a process it has begun by centralizing control of mosques and religious space. While the security track is based on police and military action, the struggle against violent extremist ideology is more complicated and subject to intense debate within Tunisian society. Tunisia's new government and future governments will face the challenge of addressing the hard security threat jihadi-salafists pose both tactically and ideologically while avoiding the overly broad repression of religious expression that was a hallmark of past authoritarian regimes.

SALAFISM AND JIHADI-SALAFISM IN TUNISIA

Salafism, in both its violent and nonviolent forms, represents a rebellion against local Islamic traditions and practices. It challenges both the authority and legitimacy of local Islamic interpretations. Though salafism has competed with North African Islamic traditions for centuries, this struggle has intensified since the Arab uprisings of 2011, which created public space for both nonviolent salafism and violent extremist ideology to spread.

For centuries Tunisia boasted some of Islam's most important seats of religious education, in particular the Zaytouna Mosque. Local ulema played an important political as well as religious role into the late years of Ottoman control of Tunisia, opposing many modernizing reforms and the penetration of European influence into Tunisia.[6] The decline of the Ottoman Empire in North Africa and the advent of European colonization undermined Tunisia's traditional religious institutions, though the ulema continued to play an important social and educational role in Tunisian society and, on occasion, sided with the French protectorate authorities to check the power of local reformers. Tunisia was also one of the centers of the Islamic modernist movement—which sought to embrace modernity while maintaining the cultural centrality of Islam and Arabic—around the turn of the twentieth century.[7]

---

6. Kenneth Perkins, *A History of Modern Tunisia* (Cambridge: Cambridge University Press, 2004), 20–24.

7. Ibid., 64–65. The reformers in this camp were known in Arabic as *salafiyya* and, like contemporary salafists, advocated returning to Islamic source texts to overcome the Muslim world's stagnation; but they interpreted the Qur'an and Hadith in light of modern conditions and did not seek a puritanical return to past culture

It was the independence movement led by the country's first president, Habib Bourguiba, in the 1950s that imposed state secularism and broke the power and influence of Zaytouna. Bourguiba overhauled Tunisia's religious institutions, weakened the ulema (in part by confiscating all land endowments, or *habous* property, controlled by religious institutions[8]), and watered down the content of Islamic education and practice. Mosques were locked except during prayer times, and libraries were emptied or shuttered. Most importantly, Bourguiba's government dismantled Tunisia's prestigious seat of learning and transferred Zaytouna's educational functions to the University of Tunis.[9] Religious education was transformed into an academic discipline. For the next half century, the state security apparatus tightly controlled Tunisian Islam and religious education.[10]

Both Bourguiba and his successor, Ben Ali, also harshly repressed efforts by their opponents to advance an Islamist political project in Tunisia. Bourguiba saw himself as the enlightened, modernizing father of modern Tunisia, and he began his tenure by forcing Salah Ben Youssef, the leader of a faction that advocated a more Islamic, pan-Arab orientation for the country, into exile,[11] and putting many of his associates in prison. Remnants

---

and practices.

8. *Habous* is referred to as *waqf* or *awqaf* in other parts of the Muslim world. A debate over reviving *habous* in Tunisia will have a major impact on how mosques and religious institutions are funded. In 2013, some members of Ennahda tried to force through a new *habous* law that would have allowed the establishment of new endowments. The bill did not pass, but the issue will likely remain contentious.

9. Religious studies once administered by the Zaytouna Mosque were incorporated into the Higher Institute of Theology and the Higher Institute of Islamic Civilizations, both part of the University of Tunis.

10. After a broad crackdown against Islamists across Tunisia in the 1990s, salafi proselytism largely went underground, though some nonpolitical salafi preaching was tolerated.

11. Ben Youssef was from a family of merchants in Djerba and had closer ties to the religious establishment than Bourguiba. He espoused an uncompromising opposition to colonialism, grounded in Arab-Islamic values and a commitment to solidarity with other Middle Eastern and North African countries. He argued that Bourguiba was an agent of France and the West in general. Ali Mahjoubi, "Habib Bourguiba et Le Choix Occidental," in *Habib Bourguiba et l'établissement de l'Etat National*, ed. Abdeljalil Temimi (Zaghouan, Tunisia: Fondation Temimi Pour La Recherche Scientifique et l'Information, 2000), 105.

of the "Youssefists," along with religious authorities stripped of much of their power and other disaffected Tunisians, regrouped to found the Mouvement de la Tendence Islamique (MTI) in the 1970s. The MTI successfully supported some candidates for parliamentary elections in the 1980s, even as its leaders were arrested for defaming the president and speaking out against the state's stronghold on religious institutions and expression.[12] Bourguiba's hatred of this movement was so fierce that in 1987, after terrorist bombings in Sousse and Monastir for which the MTI denied responsibility, Ben Ali had to talk Bourguiba down from permitting the execution of top Islamist leaders—including Rachid al-Ghannouchi.[13]

When Ben Ali came to power in November 1987, it appeared at first that the political process might be opened to allow Islamists to participate. In the lead-up to the 1990 elections, the MTI changed its name to Ennahda and lobbied for legalization along with other political parties. Opinion among Tunisian elites shifted against this political opening, however, when it became clear that Ennahda would do well in the elections. Ben Ali shifted course and eventually repressed the Islamist movement as harshly as Bourguiba had, seeing it as an existential threat to Tunisian politics and society.[14]

Despite this strict regulation, Tunisia and other Maghreb countries were not immune from salafism and other external ideological influences. In the 1970s and 1980s, workers who returned from the Gulf with savings also brought back stricter Islamic practices and ideas after exposure to Wahhabism. Wealthy Gulf donors supported local charities, mosques, and schools that promoted salafi teachings. Arabization policies in education during the 1980s also attracted teachers from Egypt, the Levant, and the Gulf who often brought salafi and Islamist ideology. With the introduction of satellite television and then

---

12. Perkins, *History*, 168.

13. Ibid., 175. In August 1987, when the bombings occurred, Ben Ali served as interior minister. In October 1987 he was appointed prime minister.

14. Neil Hicks, *Promises Unfulfilled: Human Rights in Tunisia Since 1987* (New York: Lawyers Committee for Human Rights, 1993), 9–10, 46.

the Internet, charismatic sheikhs from Egypt and the Gulf could take their more puritanical and occasionally violent messages directly into people's homes.

These ideological seeds sprouted numerous salafi groups, which included some violent salafists committed to over-throwing governments across the Maghreb. As Algeria's civil war raged throughout the 1990s and Muammar el-Qaddafi sought to maintain his grip on power in Libya—and as fighters began to return to both countries from the conflict in Afghanistan—state security forces in Tunisia, Libya, Morocco, and Algeria imprisoned or killed thousands. Others fled to Afghanistan and Europe, where they formed various groups. The largest network of Tunisian jihadi-salafists formed the Tunisian Combatant Group, which cooperated with al Qaeda in Afghanistan and later al Qaeda in the Islamic Maghreb (AQIM).[15] Prior to the 2011 uprising, the Ben Ali government kept a tight grip on the country's security. The most serious attack in the preceding decade occurred in April 2002, when a suicide bomber affiliated with al Qaeda blew up a truck outside of an historic synagogue in Djerba, killing 21 people, most of them foreign tourists.[16]

When the Ben Ali regime collapsed in 2011, nonviolent salafi and jihadi-salafi ideologies had been percolating in Tunisia for decades. Salafists presented people with a coherent set of ideas and actions amidst political and economic uncertainty. They were motivated and forceful, and they quickly established themselves in mosques across the country where they could spread their message. In contrast, Tunisia's traditional state-sponsored ulema had long been neglected and discredited for their subservience to the Bourguiba and Ben Ali regimes and were unequipped for the ideological struggle that would ensue.

---

15. Two Tunisians associated with the Tunisian Combatant Group (also known as the Tunisian Islamic Fighting Group) assassinated Ahmed Shah Massoud, the head of Afghanistan's anti-Taliban Northern Alliance, two days before the September 11, 2001, attacks.

16. "German Terror Link: Djerba Bombing Trial Begins in Paris," *Der Spiegel*, January 5, 2009, http://www.spiegel.de/international/europe/german-terror-link-djerba-bombing-trial-begins-in-paris-a-599485.html.

JIHADI-SALAFISM AFTER THE UPRISINGS

Throughout most of 2011–2012, both jihadi-salafi streams focused on organization and recruitment. Without a security-minded autocrat in power, they suddenly enjoyed unprecedented freedom to organize and propagate their message. Their efforts were further aided by several local and regional circumstances.

First, a postrevolution prison amnesty released thousands of prisoners, many of whom had been arrested under Tunisia's 2003 antiterrorism law and further radicalized in prison.[17] This provided a stream of potential new recruits. Many former leaders were also released from prison or returned from exile. Seifallah Ben Hassine, also known as Abu Iyadh al-Tunsi, a former leader of the Tunisian Combatant Group, was released from prison in 2011 and shortly thereafter founded Ansar al Shari'a with Tarek Maaroufi, another former Tunisian Combatant Group leader, who returned to Tunisia in March 2012 after spending time in a Belgian prison.[18] Second, ongoing war and the disintegration of state authority in neighboring Libya provided a steady stream of weapons, while porous borders to the east (Libya) and west (Algeria) allowed fighters to move with fewer restrictions.[19]

---

17. According to a United Nations Human Rights Council report, "A total of 8,700 people benefited from this amnesty law either by being released from prison or—in the broad majority of cases—by being restored their political rights." See "Report of the Special Rapporteur on the Promotion and Protection of Human Rights and Fundamental Freedoms While Countering Terrorism, Martin Scheinin: Mission to Tunisia," UN document A/HRC/20/14/Add, March 14, 2012, 1, http://www.ohchr.org/Documents/HRBodies/HRCouncil/RegularSession/Session20/A-HRC-20-14-Add1_en.pdf.

18. Tunsi fought in Afghanistan and was arrested in Turkey in 2003, when he was extradited to Tunisia. He was sentenced to 68 years in prison under the 2003 Terrorism Law. See Synda Tajine, "A Jihadist Comes Home and Tunisia Cracks Down," *Al Monitor*, September 20, 2012, http://www.al-monitor.com/pulse/politics/2012/09/has-tunisias-government-turned-against-the-salafists.html#.

19. The border crossings with Libya at Jefara and Ben Guerdane are connected to the thriving arms markets that have been supplying jihadi-salafists as well as tribes and clans in southern Tunisia. Libyan militants have also been arrested for planning attacks against Tunisian security officials and government institutions. See Sam Kimball, "A Leaky Border Threatens Tunisia's Transition," *Foreign Policy*, May 27, 2014, http://transitions.foreignpolicy.com/posts/2014/05/27/a_leaky_border_threatens_tunisias_transition; "Tunisia Arrests Islamists from Libya, Says Were Planning Attacks," Reuters, May 21, 2014, http://www.reuters.com/article/2014/05/22/us-tunisia-islamists-idUSBREA4L0020140522.

Third, the expanding conflict in Syria heightened extremist rhetoric and provided an even greater motive for young men to join militant organizations either in Tunisia, elsewhere in the Maghreb, or in Syria. Politics also had an impact in two important ways. First, Tunisia's political polarization prevented effective cooperation between the Ennahda-led government and security forces dominated by personnel associated with the Ben Ali regime.[20] Anger at the role security forces played in upholding the Ben Ali regime and attempting to suppress the revolution against him was strong in the final days of the revolution and after it. The military's reputation was bolstered by its refusal to confront Tunisian demonstrators at the outset of the revolution, but the military was a small institution that Ben Ali had deliberately marginalized, and following the revolution its senior officer corps preferred to remain depoliticized. Following the National Constituent Assembly elections, the Ennahda-appointed interior minister, who had been imprisoned by the Ben Ali regime, clashed repeatedly with the police and security forces and dismantled key internal security branches. Ennahda also appointed its members and loyalists to key security positions within the Ministry of the Interior, causing friction with the ministry's rank and file, most of whom had been appointed under the previous regime. This tension undermined cooperation between the security services, weakened and divided the security apparatus, and prevented a clear national counterterrorism policy.

Second, the Ennahda-led government was ambivalent about religious extremism, for a combination of political and ideological reasons. As an Islamist organization that had previously been repressed, it had difficulty restricting other Islamists, and it failed to sufficiently condemn or act against the growing vigilante violence and incitement in 2011–2012. As a broad movement, Ennahda includes a conservative salafi faction that sympathized with and sought to protect young salafi and jihadi-

---

20. Ben Ali himself had emerged from the security services and had been head of the country's military security apparatus before taking over as president in 1987.

salafi activists.[21] Many of these comparatively conservative leaders viewed more militant young activists, including members of Ansar al Shari'a, as wayward or rebellious children who needed to be protected. Finally, Ennahda resisted confronting jihadi-salafists for political purposes. It sought to represent a wide tent of Islamist views and co-opt salafists, in part to gain future votes.

In the first year after the revolution, jihadi-salafists largely avoided a head-on confrontation with the security services. Ansar al Shari'a focused on social hegemony, which it sought through demonstrations and intimidation of academics, artists, and liberal activists. It restricted its use of violence to vigilante attacks against individuals and property, which destroyed Sufi shrines and mausoleums that the group considers elements of *shirk*, or polytheism.[22] Ansar al Shari'a's founding conference, held in 2011, attracted about 1,000 people. The following year the number of attendees grew to approximately 10,000. At its peak in 2012 it likely included 10,000 to 20,000 followers.[23] In addition to its active followers, Ansar al Shari'a attracted many sympathizers, who shared an ideological affinity with the movement and often benefited from the services it provided.

Though some within Ansar al Shari'a encouraged a subset of young people to abandon society for the Syrian front lines,

---

21. Among Ennahda members of the national constituent assembly who embraced salafi positions, Habib Ellouz and Sadeq Chorou were the most outspoken.

22. In January 2013, for example, salafists were accused of setting fire to the mausoleum of Sidi Bou Said, a Sufi sheikh buried near Tunis. See Roua Seghaier, "Thirty-Four Mausoleums in Tunisia Vandalized Since the Revolution," *Tunisia Live*, January 24, 2013, http://www.tunisia-live.net/2013/01/24/thirty-four-mausoleums-in-tunisia-vandalized-since-the-revolution/#sthash.WJM2homQ.dpuf.

23. *The Economist*, quoting a member of Ansar al Shari'a, claims the movement has 70,000 members, but that is likely a gross exaggeration. See "Dispatch from Tunisia: The Salafist Struggle," *Economist*, January 1, 2014, http://www.economist.com/blogs/pomegranate/2014/01/dispatch-tunisia. According to Tunisian press reports, Abu Iyadh al-Tunsi (the leader of Ansar al Shari'a in Tunisia) ordered 600 Tunisian followers currently in Syria back to Tunisia. But there is no clear evidence to support this claim or the assertion that Ansar al Shari'a controls Tunisian jihadi-salafists in Syria. See Anna Boyd, "Salafists' Desire to Attack Tunisian Government Grows as Jihadists Returning from Syria Likely to Boost their Capability," IHS Global Insight, December 6, 2013.

this new model of jihadi-salafism primarily sought to create mainstream networks that built local communities. Its leaders, such as Tunsi and Maaroufi, had previous al Qaeda affiliations, and its leading scholarly influences, such as Abu Muhammad al-Maqdisi, were prominent in al Qaeda circles. Yet, rather than focus on jihad against foreign "occupiers" or the state, these jihadi-salafi entrepreneurs sought local opportunities to spread their message through da'wa. They did not reject violence as a necessary tool or in principle; instead, they advocated carefully planned and targeted violence that helped to build popular support and advance their goals, rather than indiscriminate violence against civilians or security forces that could undermine popular support.[24] Like the nonviolent salafists, they sought to promote their values through preaching and persuasion in the first instance, with the ultimate goal being the implementation of a strict version of Islamic law within an Islamic state.

What differentiated Ansar al Shari'a during this period from armed groups such as the Okba ibn Nafaa Brigade—and made them more of a strategic threat—is that they were a part of Tunisian society.[25] Their leaders and activists were shopkeepers, teachers, construction workers, and (very often) well-networked informal economic sector actors, and this helped them recruit others. Unlike al Qaeda's jihadi-salafists, who withdraw from their communities to wage jihad, the new movement has sought

---

24. See Aaron Zelin, "Maqdisi's Disciples in Libya and Tunisia," *Foreign Policy*, November 14, 2012, http://mideast.foreignpolicy.com/posts/2012/11/14/maqdisi_s_disciples_in_libya_and_tunisia. See also Stefano M. Torelli, Fabio Merone, and Francesco Cavatorta, "Salafism in Tunisia: Challenges and Opportunities for Democratization," *Middle East Policy* 19, no. 4 (2012): 140–54, http://www.mepc.org/journal/middle-east-policy-archives/salafism-tunisia-challenges-and-opportunities-democratization.

25. Social activism and charity have long been central to the Islamist project and to Islamism's popularity. Islamist organizations across the Middle East and North Africa, whether primarily Sufi-oriented, salafi-oriented, or resistance-oriented, have successfully exploited the combination of militancy and social activity over many decades. Hamas, Hezbollah, and other organizations emerged in different contexts, but they also harnessed this combination successfully, in part due to weaker local political infrastructures in the Palestinian Territories and war-wracked Lebanon. In all cases local populations initially tolerate, participate in, and even come to depend on these social activities.

to wage jihad from within while remaining a part of society. This approach has given them the opportunity to directly interact with and potentially influence a much wider audience than al Qaeda and its affiliates ever could.

Even as scrutiny mounted, the leaders and guiding theorists of Ansar al Shari'a tried to avoid a confrontation with security forces and the state and preferred to take advantage of political openings to promote their cause. In November 2012 Tunsi declared that Tunisia was a "land of da'wa," or proselytization, not a "land of jihad."[26] He further explained that the revolutions had created new opportunities for da'wa and "more space to practice the rituals or religion and promote . . . virtue and prevent . . . vice."[27] Ansar al Shari'a and others who wanted to appeal to wider audiences argued that jihadi-salafists needed to build public support through charity and outreach before moving to open confrontation with the state. They sought to exploit political instability and freedom of expression to strengthen their numbers, influence, and capabilities. They would move from the da'wa phase to the confrontation phase once they had created a stronger base of popular support, fighters, training facilities, and weapons.[28]

Meanwhile, jihadi-salafists operating on the Algerian border were stockpiling weapons and entrenching themselves in the Chaambi Mountains. They pursued a very different strategy,

---

26. "Abu Iyadh: Tunis laysat ardan lil-jihad" [Abu Iyadh: Tunisia is not a land of jihad], *Attunisia*, November 3, 2012, http://www.attounissia.com.tn/details_article.php?a=73547&t=41&lang=ar&temp=1.

27. The full quote reads: "Also the youth of Tunisia and others not to leave the arena for the secularists and others to spread corruption on earth, rather it is obligatory on who is capable of them to stay in his place, and make jihad against the enemy of Allah and his enemy by evidence and clarification. Especially since that is easy with the revolutions that had a good impact in changing the reality, and turning the balances, which gave—Alhamdulillah—a wide space of Dawah to Allah Almighty, and gave the committed Muslim more space to practice the rituals or religion and promote of virtue and prevent of vice." See AQIM, "An Appeal to the Youth of Islam Who Are Eager to Hijrah for the Sake of Allah in the Islamic Maghrib and Tunisia," Fursan al-Balagh Media, March 2013, https://azelin.files.wordpress.com/2013/03/al-qc481_idah-in-the-islamic-maghrib-22call-to-the-youth-of-islam-to-those-who-aspire-to-hijrah-in-the-way-of-god-in-the-islamic-maghrib-in-general-and-tunisia-in-particular22-en.pdf.

28. This strategy is known as *tamkeen*, which means enabled or empowered.

one aimed at derailing Tunisia's fragile political transition by launching violent attacks and directly confronting security forces. Most of this activity was attributed to the Okba ibn Nafaa Brigade, which has ties to AQIM's northern emirate and includes both Tunisians and Algerians.[29] The group's attacks escalated from mine laying and ambushes to bolder attacks against security forces and specific targets. By mid-2013 the group had become a direct security challenge and was contributing to a growing sense of insecurity in the country. In July 2013, an attack in the Chaambi area killed eight soldiers—up to that point the largest loss of forces in a single attack—and violence continued escalating.[30] A year later, in July 2014, 14 soldiers were killed by gunmen at a checkpoint in the Chaambi area.[31] The attacks created a wave of public sympathy for the security forces in some sectors of society and greater public tolerance for more aggressive counterterrorism operations. Some media outlets sought to portray the fallen soldiers as sons of Tunisia and media campaigns toward the end of 2013 helped raise money for the families of security personnel killed in the line of duty.[32] This also contributed to growing opposition and frustration with the Ennahda-led government.

While rural violence and clashes with the Okba ibn Nafaa Brigade expanded in the west and north, urban violence by jihadi-salafists affiliated with Ansar al Shari'a also intensified. In September 2012 a mob of several hundred people attacked the U.S. embassy in Tunis and the nearby American School. Two

29. In 2006 a small group of armed Tunisians known as the Suleiman Group was allegedly trained by the Salafi Group for Preaching and Combat (GSPC), which became AQIM. The group infiltrated Tunisian territory with the alleged aim of conducting terrorist attacks.

30. Tarek Amara and Erika Solomon, "Gunmen Kill Eight Tunisian Troops as Political Tensions Rise," Reuters, July 29, 2013, http://www.reuters.com/article/2013/07/29/us-tunisia-protests-idUSBRE96S12A20130729.

31. Tarek Amara, "At Least 14 Tunisian Troops Killed in Mountain Attack," Reuters, July 17, 2014, http://uk.reuters.com/article/2014/07/17/uk-tunisia-violence-idUKKBN0FL2V420140717.

32. Nesma TV, for example, hosted telethons to raise money for families, and billboard adds were also used to create a sense of solidarity with the security forces.

rioters were killed in clashes with police.[33] The Tunisian government accused Ansar al Shari'a leaders of ordering the protests, though it is unclear to what extent the attack was directed by the group's leadership.[34] Then, in February 2013, opposition parliamentarian Chokri Belaid was gunned down outside his home. Tunisia's security environment was quickly deteriorating, and the assassination increased pressure on the Ennahda-led government to rein in extremism.

The political assassinations combined with rising attacks against security forces were a turning point. Ennahda's inclusive strategy had become a political liability, forcing it to shift its approach. The government replaced its polarizing Interior Minister Ali Laarayedh in February (though he later became prime minister) in an attempt to depoliticize the security response, and it moved more forcefully to evict jihadi-salafi preachers from mosques across the country. But it was only after a second political assassination—of opposition politician Mohammed Brahmi in July 2013—and the ensuing political crisis that the Ennahda-led government moved more forcefully to combat violent extremism. By then however, the political tide was already turning against Ennahda.[35]

In mid-2013 Tunisian security forces launched intensive operations against militants around the Chaambi Mountains. While these efforts focused primarily on the Okba ibn Nafaa Brigade, the assaults thrust other Islamist groups, including Ansar al Shari'a, into the media spotlight, and Ansar al Shari'a was now marked as a primary target. Government forces clashed with

---

33. See Tarek Amara, "Two Dead as Protesters Attack U.S. Embassy in Tunisia," *Reuters*, September 14, 2012, http://www.reuters.com/article/2012/09/14/us-protests-tunisia-school-idUSBRE88D1802012O914.

34. The Tunisian government accused Abu Iyadh al-Tunsi of orchestrating the attacks. "Twenty Sentenced over US Embassy Attack in Tunis," *France24*, May 29, 2013, http://www.france24.com/en/20130529-jail-sentenced-usa-embassy-attack-tunisia-islamists-film-salafists/.

35. It is possible that even once Ennahda decided to confront violent extremists, its efforts were not accurately or fully reported on by the media. According to some sources, once Mehdi Jomaa's government took office in January 2014, the media began reporting on raids on safe houses and weapons caches on a regular basis.

Ansar al Shari'a activists, arresting several hundred of them; the government suppressed Ansar al Shari'a preaching events in many cities and banned the movement's annual conference, which undermined its ability to openly organize and recruit.[36] In August 2013 the Ennahda-led government declared it a terrorist group and accused it of links to the Okba ibn Nafaa Brigade and involvement in the assassinations of Belaid and Brahmi.[37] Though the terrorist designation was vague and initially not fully enforced, it signaled a shift toward treating both models of jihadi-salafism—that of Ansar al Shari'a and that of the Okba ibn Nafaa Brigade—as one threat. Whether this was by design or not, the government needed a clear address to explain the rising violence.

Despite the chain of events and Ansar al Shari'a's involvement in sporadic violence, it is unlikely that the movement was prepared to move to a phase of open confrontation with the state in 2013. Its experiment with using social and political activism to promote its da'wa remained undeveloped and untested. Even after Tunsi went underground and reportedly fled to Libya following the U.S. embassy attack, he called for restraint and exhorted both the Tunisian government and his youthful followers to avoid violence toward each other. In a pronouncement on August 5, 2013, he urged Tunisian authorities to "protect" salafi youth from presumably violent outcomes following the July assassination of Brahmi.[38] After a series of confrontations in

36. Mohammad Yassin al-Jalassi, "Is the End Coming for Ennahda's Salafist Ties?" *Al Monitor*, May, 2013, http://www.al-monitor.com/pulse/politics/2013/05/tunisia-salafist-ennahda-relations.html#; "Tunisia Arrests 200 in Salafist Crackdown, Says PM," *Al Arabiya*, May 20, 2013, http://english.alarabiya.net/en/News/middle-east/2013/05/20/Tunisia-arrests-200-in-Salafist-crackdown-says-PM.html.

37. Tarek Amara, "Tunisia Blames 'Terrorist' Ansar al-Sharia for Killings," Reuters, August 27, 2013, http://www.reuters.com/article/2013/08/27/us-tunisia-crisis-ansar-idUSBRE97Q0EW20130827. See also "Tunisia: Branding Ansar Charia as Terrorist Organisation Based on Established Facts, Investigations—Interior Ministry," *Tunis Afrique Presse*, August 28, 2013, http://allafrica.com/stories/201308290732.html.

38. See, for example, "Abou Ayadh appelle les sheikhs à soutenir les jeunes salafistes," *MosaiqueFM*, August 8, 2013, http://www.mosaiquefm.net/fr/index/a/ActuDetail/Element/24610-abou-iyadh-appelle-les-cheikhs-a-soutenir-les-jeunes-salafistes.

May 2013, other jihadi-salafists such as the Jordanian-born Mohammed al-Maqdisi also urged Ansar al Shari'a and salafi youth to be cautious of clashing with security forces. But increased security operations against Ansar al Shari'a likely pushed the group toward a premature transition from prioritizing da'wa activities to violently confronting the state. With public activities and organizing closed off due to pressure from security services, the group's committed activists had few options.

Since the crackdown, most Ansar al Shari'a activists have gone underground, and the government has increasingly sought to demonstrate that Ansar al Shari'a and the Okba ibn Nafaa Brigade are effectively the same organization. In early October 2014, for example, after arresting a group it accused of plotting major terrorist attacks in Tunis in the lead-up to the parliamentary elections, the Tunisian Ministry of the Interior claimed to have found solid evidence of a close operational link between Okba ibn Nafaa and Ansar al Shari'a.[39] The actual extent of Ansar al Shari'a's relationship to Okba ibn Nafaa is difficult to ascertain. The murkiness of this relationship, coupled with the government's inability to crack down effectively on Okba ibn Nafaa, has encouraged the government to repress where it can, with Ansar al Shari'a feeling the brunt of this thrust.[40]

---

39. "Cell Providing Logistical and Financial Support to Ansar Al-Sharia and 'Okba Ibn Nafaa' Brigade Dismantled," *Tunis Afrique Press*, October 14, 2014, http://www.tap.info.tn/en/index.php/politics2/21755-cell-providing-logistical-and-financial-support-to-ansar-al-sharia-and-katiba-oqba-ibn-nafaa-dismantled. The same day, the Ministry of the Interior stated that it had arrested a 20-year-old woman who admitted to working on propaganda and managing social media accounts for both groups and to being in direct contact with Abu Iyadh al-Tunsi. "Young Girl Led Propaganda Cell of Ansar Al-Sharia and Okba Ibn Nafaa Brigade," *Tunis Afrique Press*, October 14, 2014, http://www.tap.info.tn/en/index.php/politics2/21756-young-girl-led-propaganda-cell-of-ansar-al-sharia-and-okba-ibn-nafaa-brigade.
40. Although Ansar al Shari'a's activities in Tunisia may be largely constrained by the government crackdown, some scholars suggest that it is finding a new home in Libya, where Tunsi, the group's leader, is believed to be. Aaron Zelin has suggested that Ansar al Shari'a is rebranding itself as Shabab al-Tawhid (the Youth of Pure Monotheism). On March 4, 2014, Shabab al-Tawhid Media, a new online media outlet calling itself the "pulpit of the Sunni people in Tunisia," was established. Shabab al-Tawhid members in Libya are thought to be involved in operational activities, such as the kidnapping of Mohamed Bechikh, a Tunisian embassy

Since Ennahda stepped down in December 2013, the government's strategy to contain jihadi-salafism in urban centers has intensified. Persistent individual raids have been carried out against suspected terrorists, such as a raid on February 4, 2014, that killed seven militants, including Kamel Gadhgadhi, a primary suspect in the 2013 assassinations. These raids have allegedly thwarted several major terrorist attacks aimed at tourists in Tunisia; a raid on December 9, 2013, for example, revealed an alleged plot to carry out an attack on the island of Djerba, a popular European tourist destination,[41] and several alleged plots in Tunis. More broadly, Interim Prime Minister Mehdi Jomaa's government prioritized security upon entering office. The government used the media more effectively to advertise its efforts, and the tension between the Ministry of the Interior and government that plagued Ennahda's tenure improved as Jomaa made personnel changes in the security arena. Moreover, greater cooperation with allied governments, including the United States and Algeria, has also given the government new tools in its fight against militants.[42]

---

employee, in Libya on March 21. Following the kidnapping, Shabab al-Tawhid Media posted a video addressed to the Tunisian government demanding as ransom the release of Libyan militants captured in Tunisia in 2011. According to Zelin, the group's Facebook content shows its members in Tunisia engaged in a concerted effort to maintain Ansar al Shari'a networks in Tunisia even though the movement is now illegal: "The main purpose of this shift is to help adherents maintain solidarity and preserve their ability to organize and continue *dawa* work on a smaller scale." Aaron Y. Zelin, "Shabab al-Tawhid: The Rebranding of Ansar al-Sharia in Tunisia?" Washington Institute for Near East Policy, May 9, 2014, http://www.washingtoninstitute.org/policy-analysis/view/shabab-al-tawhid-the-rebranding-of-ansar-al-sharia-in-tunisia.

41. See Daveed Gartenstein-Ross, Bridget Moreng, and Kathleen Soucy, "Raising the Stakes: Ansar al-Sharia in Tunisia's Shift to Jihad," ICCT Research Paper, International Centre for Counter-Terrorism–The Hague, February 2014, http://www.icct.nl/download/file/ICCT-Gartenstein-Ross-Moreng-Soucy-Raising-the-Stakes-ASTs-Shift-to-Jihad-Feb-2014.pdf.

42. The Tunisian government is allegedly creating the Technical Agency for Telecommunications, described by some as a unified professional spying service and centralized intelligence agency that will include mass monitoring of telecommunications and Internet traffic. See Tom Stevenson, "NSA-Style: Tunisia Setting Up Counterterrorism Unit That Will Also Spy on Citizens," *International Business Times,* February 26, 2014, http://www.ibtimes.com/nsa-style-tunisia-setting-counterterrorism-unit-will-also-spy-citizens-1558013.

Despite the crackdown and the government's more focused counterterrorism approach, violence in Tunisia has continued to surge. Between January and November of 2014, at least 35 Tunisian security personnel (soldiers or police) died in confrontations with militants, nearly double the number killed in 2013.[43] The first half of the year was marked by periodic confrontations between government forces and militants, mostly in the Chaambi region. Some attacks also occurred near Jendouba and Kasserine, including a May 27, 2014, attack on Interior Minister Lofti Ben Jeddou's home in Kasserine, which resulted in the deaths of four policemen.[44] Security personnel have been killed at roadblocks, as a result of landmine explosions, in operations to detain jihadi-salafists, and in ambushes by militants. The deadliest attack to date came on July 16, 2014, when 14 Tunisian soldiers were killed near Mount Chaambi in a militant attack for which the Okba ibn Nafaa Brigade claimed responsibility on social media platforms.[45]

In response, the government formed a crisis group made up of representatives from the army, police, Ministries of Foreign Affairs and Religious Affairs.[46] This group suspended at least 157 civil associations with "alleged links to terrorism" in July 2014, and also shut down a TV channel, a radio station, and several websites accused of promoting violence. Twenty mosques were also shuttered for preaching a call to jihad. Specifically, the prime minister's office released a statement saying the mosques in question were not under control of the authorities and had celebrated the deaths of the soldiers. More than 60 Islamists

---

43. Compiled from various media reports.
44. "Four Policemen Killed in Attack on Tunisian Minister's Home," BBC, May 27, 2014, http://www.bbc.com/news/world-africa-27599299.
45. Tarek Amara, "At Least 14 Tunisian Troops Killed in Mountain Attack," Reuters, July 17, 2014, http://uk.reuters.com/article/2014/07/17/uk-tunisia-violence-idUKK-BN0FL2V420140717.
46. Bouazza Ben Bouazza and Paul Schemm, "Tunisia Crackdown Raises Fear of Rights Rollback," Associated Press, August 22, 2014, http://bigstory.ap.org/article/tunisia-crackdown-raises-fears-rights-rollback.

linked to the militants have been arrested since the attacks.[47] Other reports list up to 1,000 arrests.[48]

Links among militant groups in Tunisia and across North Africa have only grown murkier. In January 2014 AQIM leader Abdelmalek Droukdal reportedly announced the creation of a new AQIM branch in Tunisia and Libya that would merge the Okba ibn Nafaa Brigade and Ansar al Shari'a. The new branch is reportedly headed by Khaled Chaieb (aka Lokman Abou Shakr).[49] After playing only a minor role in Tunisia throughout most of the last three years, AQIM is trying to assert itself and organize militant groups by reinforcing linkages among fighters in Algeria, Tunisia, Libya, and perhaps other neighboring countries. It is likely that some members of Ansar al Shari'a have joined the Okba ibn Nafaa Brigade or the new AQIM branch, but it is unclear whether the leadership of Ansar al Shari'a has made a formal decision to merge with these other groups. There are reports of an "Allegiance Act" between Tunsi and AQIM leader Abdelmalek Droukdal, but it is not clear whether this act constitutes an official *ba'ya*, or oath of allegiance (the Tunisian government claims that it does).

Further complicating the issue of links between different militant groups and the chain of command is the impact that the Islamic State's rebellion against al Qaeda has had on North African jihadi-salafists. According to some sources, the Okba ibn Nafaa Brigade has sworn allegiance to the Islamic State, though there is little evidence to substantiate this at the moment.[50] Given the Islamic State's growing appeal, such a move is possible. However, given the Islamic State's limited capabilities in

47. Tarek Amara, "Tunisia Orders Crackdown after Militants Kill 14 Soldiers," Reuters, July 19, 2014, http://www.reuters.com/article/2014/07/20/us-tunisia-violence-idUSKBN0FO10420140720.
48. Ben Bouazza and Schemm, "Tunisia Crackdown Raises Fears."
49. On January 9, 2014, the Tunisian government announced that Chaieb was wanted for attacks against security forces.
50. See Adam al-Sabiri, "Is an 'Islamic State in the Maghreb' Following in the Footsteps of ISIS?" *Al-Akhbar English*, October 23, 2014, http://english.al-akhbar.com/node/22161. The article refers to a claim by a Tunisian Ministry of the Interior spokesman that "pro-ISIS elements in the Ansar al-Sharia group—in reference to the Uqba bin Nafi Brigade—had declared an emirate in southern Tunisia."

Tunisia and Algeria at the moment, any move by the Okba ibn Nafaa Brigade that cuts its ties with AQIM would likely undermine Tunisian jihadi-salafi capabilities and access to important networks in the short term. The return of Tunisians who fought with the Islamic State in Syria and Iraq could create more local networks sympathetic to the Islamic State. Tunisian security officials claim that 400 Tunisians have returned to date and that thousands have been prevented from leaving the country, though there is no clear data.[51] The presence of so many Tunisian jihadi-salafists sympathetic to the Islamic State could eventually create a base for the movement's expansion in Tunisia.

THE IDEOLOGICAL BATTLE

While Tunisia's counterterrorism strategy evolved, there also emerged an ideological struggle to control the country's mosques and religious institutions and shape a new Islamic identity after half a century of state-imposed secularism. This ideological effort, which complemented the security response, sought to create an alternative to extremist discourse and ideology. For Ennahda, this meant attempting to redefine traditional Tunisian Islam and correcting the "historic mistake" (as political Islamists refer to it) of imposing secularization after independence.[52] Promoting traditional Islam became a tool for constraining both nonviolent salafists who posed a political challenge (by pushing for more-conservative clauses in the constitution) and the jihadi-salafists who had become a security threat and a political liability.[53]

---

51. Interview with Tunisian security official, November 24, 2014, Tunis.
52. Interestingly, Ennahda leader Rachid al-Ghannouchi rejects the notion of "traditional Tunisian Islam"; he has asserted that "Islam is one, the Qur'an and Sunna are one" and referred instead to "Tunisian Islamic culture." Interview with Rachid al-Ghannouchi, February 26, 2014, Washington, DC.
53. For a detailed analysis of Ennahda-salafi relations, see International Crisis Group, "Tunisia: Violence and the Salafi Challenge," Middle East/North Africa Report Number 137, Brussels, February 13, 2013, http://www.crisisgroup.org/~/media/Files/Middle%20East%20North%20Africa/North%20Africa/Tunisia/137-tunisia-violence-and-the-salafi-challenge.pdf.

Rulers and governments have historically attempted to control and define religion as a way to bolster their own legitimacy and their citizens' obedience. By controlling the ulema and religious discourse, rulers in the Muslim world have attempted both to create a religious establishment that legitimizes political authority and to shape religious subjects who obey that authority. Across the Maghreb, the Maliki school of jurisprudence, one of Sunni Islam's four schools of law, plays an important role in government efforts to centralize religious authority.[54] Malikism accepts the importance of local social and political context. In practice this has meant that Maliki jurisprudence coexists with local cultural practices and traditions, most importantly Sufism.[55]

The struggle to promote traditional Islam has a bureaucratic and institutional component as well as an ideological one. On the institutional level, when it led the government Ennahda moved to assert control over Tunisia's 5,000 mosques[56] and combat what the minister of religious affairs at the time described as "chaos in the mosques."[57] How many mosques were controlled by jihadi-salafists when the interim government took office in November 2011 is difficult to ascertain. Most government sources claim that at the time, nongovernment preachers controlled

---

54. Malikism is a school of law based on the teachings of Imam Malik bin Anas, who died at the end of the eighth century in Medina. Malikism prioritizes the Hadiths of the Medinan period and the "companions of the Prophet" over other parts of the Sunna. It also accepts that the context of time and place must be part of *ijtihad*, or the interpretation of issues not directly addressed in the Qur'an and Hadith; this position is not unique but is accepted in principle by other schools of law. See "Mālikiyya," *Encyclopaedia of Islam*, 2nd ed. , ed. P. Bearman, Th. Bianquis, C. E. Bosworth, E. van Donzel, and W. P. Heinrichs, Brill Online, 2014, http://referenceworks.brillonline.com/entries/encyclopaedia-of-islam-2/malikiyya-COM_0652.
55. Sufism, including the folk practices of venerating saints and visiting tombs, is found throughout North Africa, though it was largely eradicated on the Arabian Peninsula in the nineteenth and twentieth centuries by the followers of Muhammad ibn Abd al-Wahhab, who considered the practice akin to polytheism.
56. In most Arab countries mosque preachers are appointed by the government and receive government salaries. Unofficial imams and preachers also exist primarily in unlicensed prayer and study meetings.
57. Interview with senior adviser to the minister of religious affairs, November 20, 2013, Tunis; and AFP, "Extremists Control Hundreds of Tunisia's Mosques: Religious Affairs Minister," *Al Arabiya*, March 31, 2012, http://english.alarabiya.net/articles/2012/03/31/204431.html.

approximately one-fifth (nearly 1,000) of all mosques and that 1,000 new imams had appointed themselves.[58] A 2013 Reuters article cites a similar figure and claims that "radicals took over around 1,000 mosques," but it fails to define "radical." According to the Ennahda-affiliated minister of religious affairs at the time, salafists had taken over approximately 400 mosques, with 50 of those controlled by jihadi-salafists.[59] The actual numbers were likely higher, given that the government sought to downplay its lack of control.

Some of these new preachers had no formal religious training or credentials, and some espoused violence and jihadi-salafi ideology.[60] What is likely is that these mosques were taken over by a combination of salafists, jihadi-salafists, and nonaffiliated preachers or people who appointed themselves as preachers. As it sought to re-assert control, many of the preachers Ennahda installed in their stead were scripturalist salafi and conservative preachers loyal to Ennahda.[61] According to one preacher who was critical of Ennahda, the movement used its power not only to root out jihadi-salafism, but more broadly to suppress any religious ideas that did not conform to its positions, including Sufism.[62]

By early 2014 Ministry of the Interior officials claimed approximately 150 mosques remained under the control of ji-

58. According to a senior advisor to the minister of religious affairs, after the revolution many mosque preachers appointed by the old regime were either evicted from their communities or dismissed, though some were reappointed, and over 1,000 imams appointed themselves to positions within mosques. Interview with advisor to the minister of religious affairs, November 20, 2013, Tunis.

59. Tom Heneghan, "Ambiguous Religion Policy Backfires on Tunisia's Ruling Islamists," Reuters, September 3, 2013, http://www.reuters.com/article/2013/09/03/us-tunisia-crisis-religion-idUSBRE9820C920130903.

60. According to one report in the London-based pan-Arab daily *Al Hayat*, a taxi driver became the imam of a local mosque in the Monastir governorate and began recruiting youth to fight in Syria. See Hazim al-Amin, "Tunisia: The Road to Jihad in Syria Paved by the Muslim Brotherhood and Jihadist-Salafism," October 18, 2013, accessed from *BBC Worldwide Monitoring*.

61. International Crisis Group, "Tunisia: Violence and the Salafi Challenge."

62. Interview with Sufi imam, November 22, 2013, Tunis. The imam claimed that he had been removed from his mosque position after criticizing the Ennahda government, and was given 24-hour police protection after receiving multiple death threats.

hadi-salafists.[63] Despite government efforts, asserting control will remain an ongoing challenge. Mosque preachers or Friday prayer leaders are only the most visible manifestation of influence in mosques, and there are certainly more mosques where jihadi-salafists give classes or lead prayers informally than those where they preach or lead Friday prayers, though exactly how many is unknown. Tunisia, like every country, also has private, unlicensed mosques, where the Ministry of Religious Affairs has no oversight of preaching and education.

As a result, exerting central control over Tunisia's mosques—both as a way to influence religious values and explicitly to counter jihadi-salafi ideology—has taken on increased significance.[64] As it cracked down on jihadi-salafi activity, Ennahda realized it needed to reestablish centralized control over the appointment of preachers and over the messages they disseminated, primarily during classes and Friday communal prayers. The Ministry of Religious Affairs appointed a commission to address the issue and used a combination of police, legal, and bureaucratic actions to reassert authority. The day-to-day efforts to reshape the religious landscape unfolded primarily within the Ministry of Religious Affairs and Ministry of Higher Education.[65]

Tunisia's most prized religious institution, the Zaytouna Mosque, is at the center of this struggle. Though Zaytouna has been stripped of its religious authority, it remains a national symbol, and it has strong brand appeal, even among secular Tunisians. While there is a broad consensus across the religious spectrum that Zaytouna should be revived as part of the effort

63. Interview with senior Tunisian security official, April 2, 2014, Washington, DC; and Sana BenAbda, "Tunisia: 149 mosques under the control of radical salafists," *The Tunis Times*, March 14, 2014, http://www.thetunistimes.com/2014/03/tunisia-149-mosques-under-the-control-of-radical-salafists-51526/.

64. Interview with adviser to minister of religious affairs, November 20, 2013, Tunis.

65. The Ministry of Religious Affairs is responsible for appointing mosque imams or prayer leaders, monitoring the messages preached in mosques, and approving the criteria for qualifying religious scholars and imams, while the Ministry of Higher Education oversees the religious studies department at the University of Tunis.

to counter violent extremism, few agree on the roles Zaytouna should assume or the curriculum it should teach. A key question dividing Tunisians is whether Zaytouna should remain solely a mosque or should resume its function as a university. Many political Islamists affiliated with Ennahda and more conservative elements within Tunisian society wish to revive Zaytouna as a mosque-university that awards degrees. Some religious scholars who were appointed under the Ennahda government have proposed that the Zaytouna Mosque focus on religious and theological sciences as well as da'wa.[66] Because under Bourguiba and Ben Ali religion was an academic subject taught only in universities, restoring Zaytouna's status as a university—and thereby restoring Islamic study in Tunisia to a religious framework—would symbolize the rejection of the secularization carried out under Bourguiba.

Many secular-minded Tunisians as well as devout Tunisians who want to separate religion from politics fear that reviving Zaytouna as a university could create an education system parallel to the secular one, which would be shaped and politicized by more conservative religious scholars. The imam of the Zaytouna Mosque, Sheikh Hussein Obeidi, has in the past expressed intolerant views and incited violence, though he has kept his post.[67] Disputes over control of Zaytouna, its function, and its outlook will remain a source of tension among a range of religious and political actors for the foreseeable future. The stakes of this struggle are high. Given Zaytouna's historical importance in Tunisian national identity, whoever controls the religious out-

---

66. Interview with researcher at the Islamic Studies Center of Kairouan, November 20, 2013. The center is loosely affiliated with the religious studies department at the University of Tunis.

67. Sheikh Obeidi reportedly issued a fatwa arguing that a group of artists exhibiting what he deemed sacrilegious art were infidels and could be killed according to Islamic law. In June 2012 the exhibit, entitled "The Art Spring," sparked two days of riots in Tunis that led to at least one death and over 160 arrests. See Tarek Amara and Lin Noueihed, "Tunisian Salafi Islamists Riot Over 'Insulting' Art," Reuters, June 12, 2012, http://www.reuters.com/article/2012/06/12/us-tunisia-salafis-clash-idUSBRE85B0XW20120612.

look and doctrine of Zaytouna will have considerable influence in shaping religious values across the country.[68]

Though Ennahda led the struggle to define traditional Tunisian Islam while it headed the government, the issue transcends any single political or religious movement. A variety of political and religious actors increasingly see Tunisian Islamic traditions, which draw on the country's rich history and religious legacy, as integral to combatting extremist ideology. In interviews, a wide range of religious and political actors—including political Islamists and Ennahda leaders,[69] state-employed imams,[70] and Sufis—all affirmed the importance of reviving Tunisian Islam to combat extremism. Even some salafi leaders sympathetic to jihadi-salafists speak of reviving Tunisian Islam to counter extremism, yet their definition of extremism and traditional Islam is less clear.[71] This debate is being carried out among religious scholars and political leaders, but it will shape the religious values that are taught and promoted in Tunisia's schools and mosques for the next generation.

CHALLENGES OF CREATING NATIONAL ISLAMIC IDENTITY

The struggle to redefine traditional Tunisian Islam remains highly politicized and will likely be contested by a range of actors for the foreseeable future. Competition between Ennahda,

---

68. Reviving Zaytouna's educational role could give the ulema overseeing the Zaytouna Mosque considerable influence over the religious sphere, since it would involve them in controlling a nationwide network of charities, associations, mosques, and preachers. Before independence, Zaytouna had branches across Tunisia, and reopening those branches would give religious scholars more outlets for promoting religious education throughout the country.

69. Interview with Said Ferjani, member of Ennahda political bureau, November 18, 2013, Tunis.

70. Interview with Taieb Ghozi, Friday imam at Okba ibn Nafaa Mosque, November 20, 2013, Kairouan.

71. According to Adel al-Ilmi, the head of a conservative salafi group originally named the Group for the Promotion of Virtue and the Prevention of Vice, all four *madhhabs* are correct but only the Maliki *madhhab* should be taught. Interview with Adel al-Ilmi, November 19, 2013, Tunis. Critics of Tunisian salafists, however, argue that salafists merely talk about promoting the Maliki *madhhab* for fear of alienating more traditional Muslims.

the new government, secular political forces, and salafists means that no single actor can determine religious policy and the messages that are propagated. Despite its election defeat, Ennahda will remain an important political force in Tunisia, but its ability to independently guide religious policy will be constrained by the new government.

Several challenges loom ahead. For one, the specific ideological character of traditional Islam remains murky. However effective the government may be in controlling mosques and physical space, shaping ideology is more complicated. The credibility of state religious institutions has eroded over time, in part because their leaders are often reluctant to address challenges of daily life that are inherently political: poor governance, economic exclusion, and corruption. By steering to safe topics, state clerics undermine their credibility with young people, who are looking for more open discourse, particularly in the post–Arab uprising political environment.

Part of the problem is also a generation gap and communication gap between the older ulema and young people. These gaps are not a problem for jihadi-salafi preachers, on the other hand, who appeal to disenfranchised youth looking for order and meaning in their lives. They preach about injustice, humiliation, and inequality, and they provide means for young people to take action. They understand what motivates young people and focus on education and social work, which is empowering for many young people who feel marginalized.

A younger generation of scholars and thinkers in the region understands that combatting violent religious discourse requires addressing the needs of the young. Imams must be able to talk to younger generations, understand their needs, and have the tools and skills necessary to fulfill those needs. But training such imams will be a long-term process.

Marketing and messaging are also important components of spreading non-violent traditional Islamic values. Governments in the region, including Tunisia, have increased state-run religious television and radio programming to compete with preachers from the Gulf and Egypt found on satellite television. The challenge is that state-run television is generally dull compared to the more fiery programming available on the Internet or by satellite. State ulema seek to inculcate respect for authority, but that message is largely out of step with the mood of North Africa, where society and politics have been permeated with the rebelliousness of the Arab uprisings.

Most importantly, these issues raise the question of whether a secular government, and one headed by a political party (Nidaa Tounes) committed to state secularism and led by many individuals affiliated with the previous regime, can successfully control the state religious bureaucracy and create a legitimate and authoritative religious identity and discourse which satisfies the needs of the majority of Tunisians. Election results in October 2014, which gave Ennahda nearly 30 percent of the Parliament, illustrate that a sizeable minority of Tunisians seek a public role for religion. Tunisia's history demonstrates that repressing nonviolent religious discourse, or failing to create a discourse that resonates with young people in particular, ensures that extremist voices will fill the void. Can Ennahda serve as a bridge between the new government and the religious establishment, or will political competition complicate state-religious interaction? How the new government moves forward in shaping its religious policy including education and asserting control over the religious bureaucracy and whether it can work with a wide spectrum of nonviolent Islamist voices, including Ennahda, will determine whether defining a new religious identity becomes a source of strength for Tunisians or further divides them.

LOOKING FORWARD

Despite rising violence, Tunisia's two-pronged effort to combat extremist violence and ideology prevented further destabilization at a time of heightened political uncertainty and regional turmoil. Yet extremism will continue posing a challenge. Ongoing violence and state failure make neighboring Libya a sanctuary for Tunisian and other jihadi-salafists who seek to launch attacks inside the country.[72] Moreover, the ongoing war in Syria and Iraq creates a steady stream of jihadi-salafi propaganda. As of November 2014 an estimated 3,000 Tunisians have gone to fight with al Qaeda–linked groups as well as the Islamic State, making Tunisians one of the largest foreign national groups fighting in Syria. Hundreds are reportedly returning home. Many of the broader developments shaping the jihadi-salafi landscape across the region, including the Islamic State rebellion and jihad in Syria, cannot be addressed by Tunisia's government alone. But the government can influence several factors that will shape the country's future stability.

First, if security forces excessively harass or abuse Islamists or salafists, it could deepen sympathy for jihadi-salafists, especially in poorer urban areas where salafists and jihadi-salafists are part of the communal framework. Past repression has tended to strengthen Islamist groups' appeal, and renewed government harassment could encourage more young people to embrace violence. Since the beginning of 2014 Tunisia's security forces have intensified their operations and cast a wide net against potential extremists. More than 150 organizations and associations have been shut down for alleged links to terrorism, and over 1,500 people have been arrested.[73] Under the draft terrorism law that the new parliament will continue debating, civil society organizations may be subject to persecution for broadly defined terrorist acts. Abuses and mistakes by security forces have also prompted anger. In September, forces in Kasserine accidentally shot two young women driving by a checkpoint.[74] In

72. According to some reports, Tunisian security forces have begun arresting smugglers believed to be trafficking fighters from Tunisia to Libya. See "Tunisia Detains Six Traffickers," *Magharebia*, October 7, 2014, http://magharebia.com/en_GB/articles/awi/newsbriefs/general/2014/10/07/newsbrief-01.
73. Human Rights Watch, "Tunisia: Suspension of Associations Arbitrary," August 13, 2014, http://www.hrw.org/news/2014/08/13/tunisia-suspension-associations-arbitrary; Tarek Amara, "Tunisia cracks down on jihadists as elections loom: PM," Reuters, October 11, 2014, http://www.reuters.com/article/2014/10/11/us-tunisia-security-idUSKCN0I00F120141011.
74. Human Rights Watch, "Tunisia: Investigate Fatal Police Shooting," September 3, 2014, http://www.hrw.org/news/2014/09/03/tunisia-investigate-fatal-police-shooting.

October, local police allegedly tortured and murdered a young man from Tunis, reviving accusations that the government has not reformed the security sector or addressed the other grievances against state abuses of power that helped fuel the 2011 uprising.[75]

Second, how the government integrates returning fighters will have an impact on jihadi networks in the prison system and in the general population. If returning fighters or others who support jihad in Syria are treated simply as criminals to be prosecuted rather than rehabilitated, they are more likely to form a future threat. Those who return from Syria genuinely disillusioned by the jihadi project should be rehabilitated, but determining which returnees are redeemable and which mean to cause more harm will require careful government investigation. Lumping all returnees in one basket and punishing them will likely create more extremists. As of late 2014 the government had not articulated a plan for addressing the threat of returnees from jihad in Syria and Iraq.

Third, the ability of the existing political framework to incentivize political compromise and competition and make space for legitimate opposition including political Islamists is crucial. There should be some political space for nonviolent salafists as well as more conservative elements of Ennahda who may distance themselves from the movement, whether they choose to participate in formal politics or not. As the new government regulates religious space, it must strike a balance between promoting its own values and repressing other nonviolent interpretations. Salafism has existed in some form in the Maghreb for centuries, and it is likely to remain a social, religious, and (potentially) political force. The challenge is to provide enough space for nonviolent salafists to remain part of the system rather than adopting violence as a tool and strategy.

Fourth, it will matter whether Tunisia's state religious leadership can rebuild the credibility of the country's traditional reli-

---

75. Human Rights Watch, "Tunisia: Suspicious Death in Custody," October 13, 2014, http://www.hrw.org/news/2014/10/13/tunisia-suspicious-death-custody-0.

gious institutions and values in a way that resonates with young people and that depoliticizes religion. The new constitution addresses only broadly the role of religion in society. It cannot resolve complicated ideological and institutional divisions that will shape the future religious landscape. That task will be left to competing religious and political actors. How the new government approaches the religious establishment as well as Ennahda, which has religious objectives, and whether these groups can reach a consensus on a new Tunisian Islamic identity will have far-reaching implications for the country's future stability.

While Tunisia has a long history as a center of Islam, its modern history has been one of repression of Islam as a social and political force. Now Tunisia faces the difficult process of confronting violent extremism while moving away from the repression of the past—all in an environment where violence could easily destabilize the road ahead. As it navigates forward, it must balance between these competing historical tendencies. Tunisia has come a long way in a short period of time and despite its many challenges holds the promise of greater stability, representative government, and personal freedoms. As it moves forward in fighting extremism and finding an appropriate role for religion in public life, Tunisia can draw on its past religious traditions and a new appreciation for political compromise. The path forward will not be easy. But in order to succeed Tunisians must embrace both.

5. EGYPT: THE SEARCH FOR STABILITY

Jon B. Alterman and William McCants

When Cairo's Islamic Art Museum was devastated by a car bomb in January 2014, the attack represented a new face of an old problem in Egypt. The country's rulers—whether European colonial powers, Ottoman khedival administrations, or Egyptians themselves—have struggled against what they perceived to be religiously inspired radicalism for more than two centuries. The museum is located across the street from a security complex that was the real target of the attack. Amidst the rubble, shattered medieval mosque lamps and splintered millennium-old prayer niches were potent symbols of how little is protected in the confusing and often violent struggle. The government swiftly blamed its nemesis, the Muslim Brotherhood, for the attack, while a Sinai-based militant salafi group, Ansar Beit al-Maqdis, claimed responsibility. Each side took the attack and the reaction to it as proof of the underlying radicalism of its opponents. Each resolved to fight even harder for its survival.

The endurance of radicalism in Egypt is a puzzle, since the downfall of President Hosni Mubarak in February 2011 was broadly interpreted as a possible end to the region's violent struggles. The Egyptian government had fought a jihadi uprising for much of the 1990s, and Egyptians always constituted much of the muscle behind al Qaeda. Jihadists had justified their violence by calling it the only pathway to change, as Arab governments would brook no compromise with their opponents. The diverse coalition that helped displace Mubarak—secular liberals, Muslim Brothers, the youth, and parts of the business community—held out the prospect of a new model of governance. When ultraconservative salafi candidates took more than a quarter of the seats in Egypt's first postrevolutionary parliament, their success provided evidence to all sides: to liberals, it demonstrated that salafists were willing to share power, and to salafists it demonstrated that they could gain power by participating in elections. Most of the fundamental premises of the jihadi argument were eviscerated.

Yet prospects for a new model of governance have faded, and violence in Egypt appears to be on the upswing. The newly elected government of President Abdel Fattah al-Sisi seeks to reimpose order in Egypt. Former militants and other Islamist-leaning groups are deciding how to position themselves vis-à-vis the new government. While Egypt's government hopes to pacify the country as the Mubarak government did in the 1990s, many skeptics warn that traditional coercive methods are unlikely to prove as effective in the aftermath of the Arab uprisings as they did two decades ago, and in the current regional environment could even make matters worse.

ISLAMISM AND RADICALISM IN EGYPT

There is no consensus in Egypt on what constitutes a radical group in the current environment. Egypt's jails bulge with the secular and religious alike, and the relationship of religious groups to those who carry out acts of violence is contested. In many ways, Egypt is facing two different radicalism problems, though some see these as just two sides of the same coin. The threat that seems most imminent to the government is the one that it sees emanating from the Muslim Brotherhood, a nationwide movement with deep roots in Egypt's cities throughout the country. The second is the threat from violent groups such as Ansar Beit al-Maqdis. Though now mostly based in the Sinai Peninsula, these groups have not only attacked government targets in Sinai, they have also moved against targets in the Nile valley itself.

The Muslim Brotherhood was founded in Ismailiya in 1928 as a nationalist youth group and blended social services, religious self-improvement, and attacks on occupying British soldiers. Repression of the organization preceded—and followed—the Brotherhood's 1948 assassination of Prime Minister Mahmoud Nuqrashi Pasha, who feared the organization was seeking power in tumultuous postwar Egypt. Many of the military officers who seized power in 1952 (including future presidents Gamal Abdel Nasser and Anwar Sadat) had Brotherhood affiliations, and the Free Officers reportedly offered to include the group in the post-monarchical government. The Brotherhood's leader, Hassan al-Hudaybi, refused the offer, arguing that the Brothers should not be in power until society was completely Islamized.[1] Nasser and Hudaybi repeatedly clashed and reconciled until a member of the Brotherhood's armed wing tried to assassinate Nasser in October 1954. In the aftermath, the government arrested thousands of Brotherhood members and executed several of them.[2] In Nasser's jails, Brotherhood members such as Sayyid Qutb became further radicalized and developed the doctrinal underpinnings of jihadi-salafism.

The rise of salafism in Egypt dates back to the 1920s and occurred alongside the rise of the Muslim Brotherhood. Dedicated to stripping Islam of its cultural accretions and rediscovering the path of the Prophet Muhammad, salafists as a group were political quietists for much of their history. They believed party politics divided the Muslim community, and they viewed parliaments as illegitimate bodies that usurped God's role as legislator. Quietist salafi groups have been allowed to operate and organize over the decades—in part as an Islamist counter to the avowedly political Muslim Brotherhood.[3]

1. Richard P. Mitchell, *The Society of the Muslim Brothers* (New York: Oxford University Press, 1993), 96–104.
2. Ibid., 148–62.
3. Stéphane Lacroix, "Sheikhs and Politicians: Inside the New Egyptian Salafism," Brookings Doha Center Policy Briefing, June 2012, 2, http://www.brookings.edu/~/media/research/files/papers/2012/6/07%20egyptian%20salafism%20lacroix/stephane%20lacroix%20policy%20briefing%20english.pdf.

After Nasser's death in 1970, President Anwar Sadat sought to rehabilitate the Brotherhood and use it as a tool to counter other political opponents. Facing opposition to his efforts to dismantle Arab socialism and empower a new capitalist class, Sadat freed many Brotherhood members from jail and allowed the broader Islamist community to organize openly.[4] But the Islamists and Sadat soured on each other after Sadat began overt diplomatic overtures to Israel. Despite its disappointment in Sadat and harassment from his government, the Brotherhood kept its pledge of nonviolence. Some of Egypt's salafists, however, began organizing themselves to overthrow the regime in the mid- to late-1970s, and one of the resulting groups, Egyptian Islamic Jihad (or al-Jihad), was responsible for Sadat's assassination.[5]

This turn to violence by some salafi groups continued through the 1980s. The violence—much of which started among those imprisoned under Nasser and Sadat—both fed into and drew power from the involvement of Egyptians in the Afghan jihad and in the formation of what would become al Qaeda. Al Qaeda's global jihadi doctrine integrates elements of Egyptian and Saudi salafism, taking from the former Sayyid Qutb's emphasis on overthrowing renegade Muslim rulers and from the latter a more ultraconservative religious outlook. Ayman al-Zawahiri, who was Osama bin Laden's close associate and took over leadership of the global organization after bin Laden's death, was an admirer of Qutb's. Under Zawahiri's leadership in the late 1980s, the return of veterans from the Afghan jihad provided the justification as well as the muscle for a violent puritanical movement targeting the Egyptian government. Partly through coercion and partly through co-optation, the Egyptian government successfully contained the violent jihadi threat.

---

4. Gilles Kepel, *Jihad: The Trail of Political Islam* (Cambridge, MA: Harvard University Press, 2002), 83–87. For more detailed analyses of the period, see Omar Ashour, *The De-Radicalization of Jihadists: Transforming Armed Islamist Movements* (New York: Routledge, 2009) and Gilles Kepel, *The Prophet and the Pharaoh: Muslim Extremism in Egypt* (London: Saqi Books, 1985).
5. Ashour, *De-Radicalization*; Kepel, *Pharaoh*.

In the 1980s and 1990s, Sadat's successor, Hosni Mubarak, waged a brutal campaign against the Gama'a Islamiyya, a group that embraced the militancy advocated by Sayyid Qutb, built an armed wing, attacked Christians, and even seized a Cairo neighborhood.[6] The Egyptian security services rounded up tens of thousands of militants and suspected militants and deployed extensive firepower in Upper Egypt, where the group had its strongest base of support. Yet the government's response was not all at the end of a gun. In an effort to provide jobs and infrastructure to a population that felt starved of both, Mubarak directed that millions of pounds of resources be poured into Upper Egypt. The third leg of the government's strategy was ideological, as it sought to persuade militants of the theological errors in their thinking. In the 1990s, the government elicited from group members public recantations of their theology, in part through an extensive effort by orthodox theologians, and perhaps enabled by the personal animus felt by some Gama'a leaders toward al Qaeda deputy Ayman al-Zawahiri.[7] As the dust settled, most members of the Gama'a renounced violence and recognized the state's authority. The government's uncompromising attitude also led a major faction of al-Jihad, the group that assassinated Sadat, to renounce its campaign against the government.[8] Throughout this period, salafi groups that accepted the state's authority and renounced violence (such as the Salafi Call in Alexandria) were allowed to carry on with their missionary activism, though they suffered occasional low-level harassment by the authorities.

Mubarak alternately tolerated and repressed the Brotherhood. In return for releasing its members from jail, the organization endorsed Mubarak for president in 1988,[9] and he allowed the Brothers to establish hospitals and schools and to dominate many of the professional syndicates in the country. The Broth-

---

6. Ashour, *De-Radicalization*, 45–50.
7. Lawrence Wright, "The Rebellion Within," *New Yorker*, June 2, 2008, 36–53, http://www.newyorker.com/magazine/2008/06/02/the-rebellion-within.
8. Ashour, *De-Radicalization*, 90–109.
9. John Walsh, "Egypt's Muslim Brotherhood: Understanding Centrist Islam," *Harvard International Review* 24, no. 4 (Winter 2003): 32–33.

erhood also had a small but vocal minority in parliament; these men had run not as members of the Brotherhood (which was neither a recognized organization nor a legal political party), but in alliance with established parties or as independents.[10] The Brotherhood's persistent inability to gain legal status allowed the government to modulate its approach to the Brotherhood, and when desired, to arrest Brotherhood members and seize assets at will.[11] In practice, the government managed the organization through alternating co-optation and coercion. For many in Egypt, and for many at senior levels of the U.S. government and the intelligence community, it appeared not only that the strategy was working adequately, but also that it consolidated the Brotherhood's decisions to give up its violent past.[12]

AFTER THE UPRISING

After Mubarak's fall, his successors, the Supreme Council of the Armed Forces (SCAF), calculated that their survival depended on placating the most organized element of the opposition—the Islamists. Following Sadat's and Mubarak's playbook, the SCAF ordered the release of several prominent Islamist political prisoners (such as Muslim Brotherhood leaders Khairat al-Shater

---

10. Nancy J. Davis and Robert V. Robinson, *Claiming Society for God: Religious Movements and Social Welfare* (Bloomington: Indiana University Press, 2012), 32–61.
11. The Brotherhood was not officially recognized until it registered as a nongovernmental organization in 2013 in response to a lawsuit brought by its opponents in Parliament. By then, of course, the Brotherhood had already come to power through the Freedom and Justice political party it established in 2012. See "'No Decision' in Egypt on Dissolving Muslim Brotherhood," BBC, September 6, 2013, http://www.bbc.com/news/world-middle-east-23985622. The fact that Nasser had given verbal rather than written orders to dissolve the Brotherhood led to some controversy in 2012 when a non-Brotherhood member of parliament asserted that the group still operated illegally. See Noha El-Hennawy, "Muslim Brotherhood: Operating Outside the Law?" *Egypt Independent*, February 16, 2012, http://www.egyptindependent.com/news/muslim-brotherhood-operating-outside-law; "Brotherhood Mulls Legal Status, Name Change," *Egypt Independent*, February 26, 2013, http://www.egyptindependent.com/news/brotherhood-mulls-legal-status-name-change.
12. Bruce Reidel, "Don't Fear Egypt's Muslim Brotherhood," Brookings Institution, January 28, 2011, http://www.brookings.edu/research/opinions/2011/01/28-egypt-riedel.

and Hassan Malek) as well as some jihadi-salafists.[13] The SCAF also allowed many Islamists to return from exile[14] and permitted the Brotherhood and other Islamist groups to form political parties. Following the SCAF's lead, the Ministry of the Interior cooperated with the Brotherhood as well.[15]

While some salafists had begun to consider political activity in the 2000s, the real pivot in salafi thinking about politics did not come until after the fall of Mubarak.[16] Prior to 2011, the salafists often styled themselves as the "pure" Islamic alternative to the Muslim Brotherhood, which they characterized as hopelessly compromised by their participation in rigged elections and a powerless parliament.[17] But when they faced an opportunity to run in free elections and perceived that their competitors would reap the rewards of power while compromising on the establishment of an Islamic state, the salafists began founding political parties. The Salafi Call established the Nour Party; the reformed jihadi Gama'a Islamiyya established the Construction and Development Party; and two Cairo salafi personalities established their own small parties. The parties formed a coalition—dominated by Nour—to compete against

13. "Two Senior Brotherhood Members Released Today," *Ahram Online*, March 3, 2011, http://english.ahram.org.eg/NewsContent/1/64/6898/Egypt/Politics-/Two-senior-Brotherhood-members-released-today.aspx; "Egyptian Court Acquits Mohamed Zawahiri and Brother of Sadat's Assassin," *Al-Arabiya*, March 19, 2012, http://english.alarabiya.net/articles/2012/03/19/201778.html.
14. "Convicted Militant Islamists Return to Egypt Seeking Rehabilitation," *Ahram Online*, September 4, 2011, http://english.ahram.org.eg/News/20240.aspx.
15. Karim Medhat Ennarah, "The End of Reciprocity: The Muslim Brotherhood and the Security Sector," *South Atlantic Quarterly* 113, no. 2 (2014): 410–13.
16. William McCants, "Lesser of Two Evils: The Salafi Turn to Party Politics in Egypt," Brookings Middle East Memo, May 2012, 2–3, http://www.brookings.edu/~/media/Research/Files/Papers/2012/5/01%20salafi%20egypt%20mccants/0501_salafi_egypt_mccants.pdf; Hussam al-Wakil, "Anba' 'an khawd al-salafiyyin intikhabat majlis al-sha'b ba'd mubadarat rafd al-dimuqratiyya" [News about the salafists' particpation in elections after an initiative refusing to espouse democracy], *Al-Dustur*, February 16, 2010, http://www.dostor.org/politics/alexandria/10/february/15/6578.
17. Muhammad Isma'il al-Muqaddam, "Silsila hawl dukhul al-barlaman tariq al-barlaman al-ra'y wa-l-ra'y al-akhar" [A series about entering parliament by means of parliament, point and counterpoint]. Transcript of lecture, undated, available at http://audio.islamweb.net/audio/index.php?page=FullContent&audioid=163387. Based on excerpts posted on salafi forums, the lecture dates from no later than 2009. See http://alsalfy.com/vb/showthread.php?t=812.

the Brotherhood, and went on to capture nearly 24 percent of the seats in parliament.

When Muslim Brotherhood candidate Mohammed Morsi was elected president in May 2012, the military and security services appeared cooperative at first. But after Morsi's constitutional declaration on November 21, 2012, which was widely interpreted as a power grab, the situation changed. Morsi fired his minister of the interior for not cracking down hard enough on demonstrators protesting the declaration, and when the replacement minister brutally repressed demonstrations in the relatively quiet Port Said, the army had to intervene to calm the situation. Protests spiraled out of Morsi's control, and the rationale for further military intervention grew stronger. Morsi was already at odds with private media and the judiciary—powerful supporters of the old regime. And although Nour had cooperated with Morsi on drafting the constitution, its relationship with him and the Muslim Brotherhood was in general acrimonious. Many Nour members felt the Muslim Brotherhood shut them out, and the party forced out its principal founder in January 2013 for being too close to the Brotherhood.[18] The loss of the military's confidence in Morsi's ability to govern, combined with his failure to establish a broad-based ruling coalition, proved fatal.[19]

Following large public protests, the military stepped in on July 3, 2013, and put Morsi and many of his top advisers under house arrest. On July 24, then-General Sisi (still head of the Supreme Council of the Armed Forces) sharpened his rhetoric against the Brotherhood. In a speech delivered at a military parade, Sisi accused the Brotherhood of arming itself against

---

18. Zeinab El Gundy, "Salafist Splits Bring New Choices, Complications for Voters," *Ahram Online*, January 23, 2013, http://english.ahram.org.eg/NewsContent/1/64/62908/Egypt/Politics-/Salafist-splits-bring-new-choices,-complications-f.aspx; Michael Collins Dunn, "The Salafi Nour Party Split," Middle East Institute, January 3, 2013, http://mideasti.blogspot.com/2013/01/the-salafi-nour-party-split.html; Sarah El Deeb, "Egypt's Largest Ultraconservative Party Splits," Associated Press, January 1, 2013, http://bigstory.ap.org/article/egypts-largest-ultraconservative-party-splits.

19. Ennarah, "End of Reciprocity," 413–16.

the regime and asked the public for a "mandate" to allow him "to confront terrorism and violence."[20] After millions heeded his call to demonstrate on his behalf on July 26, in August Sisi ordered the military and the national police to demolish two of the most popular pro-Morsi camps in Cairo. The police and military killed somewhere between 600 and 2,600 civilians.[21] A September 2013 court ruling banned the Muslim Brotherhood, which had the effect of freezing the group's assets[22] and crushing its economic infrastructure.[23] A December 2013 proclamation branding the organization a terrorist group (in response to a bombing in the Nile delta for which Ansar Beit al-Maqdis claimed responsibility) tightened the noose further. Since then, Egyptian courts have sentenced over 1,000 Muslim Brotherhood supporters to death; over 200 of those sentences have been upheld, including that of Brotherhood leader Muhammad Badie, who also faces several sentences to life in prison.[24]

Following Morsi's fall, the salafi movement split even more deeply. While the clear end of Islamist rule in Egypt has alarmed many salafists, the Nour Party leadership has preached patience and circumspection. As one leader explained, "It is a matter of managing losses and choosing the least bad option. The reality is that people support this new government—or are at least giving

20. "Excerpts from General Abdel Fattah al-Sisi's Speech," *Egypt Independent*, July 24, 2013, http://www.egyptindependent.com/news/excerpts-general-abdel-fattah-al-sisi-s-speech.

21. Manar Mohsen, "Health Ministry Raises Death Toll of Wednesday's Clashes to 638," *Egypt Daily News*, August 16, 2013, http://www.dailynewsegypt.com/2013/08/16/health-ministry-raises-death-toll-of-wednesdays-clashes-to-638/; "Egypt's Brotherhood to Hold 'March of Anger,'" *Al Jazeera*, August 16, 2013, http://www.aljazeera.com/news/middleeast/2013/08/201381522364486906.html.

22. Patrick Kingsley, "Muslim Brotherhood Banned by Egyptian Court," *Guardian*, September 23, 2013, http://www.theguardian.com/world/2013/sep/23/muslim-brotherhood-egyptian-court.

23. Interview with Issandr El Amrani, May 4, 2014, Cairo.

24. "Badie and 14 MB Leaders Sentenced to Life for Giza Clashes," *MadaMasr*, September 15, 2014, http://www.madamasr.com/content/badie-and-14-mb-leaders-sentenced-life-giza-clashes; United Nations Office of the High Commissioner for Human Rights, "Egypt: UN Experts 'Outraged' at Confirmation of 183 Death Sentences," June 30, 2014, http://www.ohchr.org/EN/NewsEvents/Pages/DisplayNews.aspx?NewsID=14801&LangID=E.

Sisi enough legitimacy to maneuver. It is the will of the people and the will of the military." He added, "You only make gains if you stay in the struggle."[25] Nour's salafi opponents make precisely the opposite arguments. One prominent salafi leader has argued that by supporting the overthrow of a democratically elected Islamist president, Nour irrevocably damaged its long-term credibility as a serious opposition party.[26]

In 2014, Sisi made elimination of the Brotherhood a key plank in his successful bid for president. In an interview on Egyptian TV in May, Sisi vowed to finish off the Brotherhood.[27] Once elected—with 97 percent of the vote—Sisi continued his hard-line policy, refusing to reconcile with those who "committed crimes" or "adopted violence as a methodology." He emphasized that there would be "no cooperation or appeasement for those who resort to violence and those who want to disrupt our movement to the future."[28] Even if Sisi wanted to reconcile with the Brotherhood, his supporters would find such a move difficult to accept, given this rhetoric.[29] Some of those supporters include conservative governments in the Gulf, which are providing billions of dollars to keep Egypt's economy afloat. These governments see the Brotherhood as a mortal threat to their own rule, and they are increasingly active in regional efforts to undermine the organization.

In response to the crackdown against it, the Brotherhood has repeatedly rejected, officially, any endorsement of violence. Its members assert that the organization has no paramilitary wing and that its leaders do not sanction the violent overthrow of the Egyptian government. A prominent youth secretary in the Freedom and Justice Party stated in March 2014 that "the Brotherhood's youths are committed to creative peacefulness

25. Interview with Nour Party leader, May 5, 2014, Cairo.

26. Interview with prominent salafi political leader, May 6, 2014, Cairo.

27. "Egypt's Sisi Vows Muslim Brotherhood 'Will Not Exist,'" BBC, May 5, 2014, http://www.bbc.com/news/world-middle-east-27285846.

28. "At Swearing-In, Ex-General Vows 'Inclusive' Egypt," *New York Times*, June 8, 2014, http://www.nytimes.com/2014/06/09/world/middleeast/sisi-sworn-in-as-egypts-president.html?_r=0.

29. Interview with Ibrahim al-Houdaiby, May 4, 2014, Cairo.

in their anti-coup defiance. They will never attack any Egyptian in any way whatsoever."[30] Muhammad Ali Bisher, a member of the Brotherhood's Shura Council, released a statement in May in which he denounced violence against soldiers.[31] "The Muslim Brotherhood does not know violence," asserted the group's Supreme Guide Muhammad Badie in a June court appearance.[32] When the Cairo subway was bombed, the Brotherhood denied the government's charge that it was responsible and asserted that it would "not be dragged into violence and destruction, notwithstanding the systematic violence used by coup authorities since the beginning of the coup to the present day."[33] The true perpetrator, the Brotherhood argued, was likely the regime, which seeks to discredit the Brotherhood by falsely accusing it of violent acts.

Despite these assertions by Brotherhood representatives, it appears that individual members do not always follow suit. Fury at the regime for its massacre of Brotherhood members has increased the rank and file's appetite for violence.[34] The arrest of the regime's leadership has also left the Brothers—members of a very hierarchical organization who are used to guidance from the top—to their own devices.[35] The unprecedented regime violence and mass arrests have led members to engage in what analysts have called "micro"[36] or "lower-profile"[37] violence against

---

30. "Youth Leader: Muslim Brotherhood Committed to Non-Violence Notwithstanding Coup Atrocities," *Ikhwanweb*, March 17, 2014, http://www.ikhwanweb.com/article.php?id=31601.

31. "Muslim Brotherhood's Bishr Reiterates Commitment to Non-Violence," *Ikhwanweb*, May 2, 2014, http://www.ikhwanweb.com/article.php?id=31648.

32. "Egypt's Brotherhood Leader Says Committed to Nonviolence," *Middle East Eye*, June 5, 2014, http://www.middleeasteye.net/news/egypts-brotherhood-leader-says-committed-nonviolence.

33. "Muslim Brotherhood Denounces Dubious Subway Bombings in Cairo June 25," *Ikhwanweb*, June 26, 2014, http://www.ikhwanweb.com/article.php?id=31690.

34. Interview with Ibrahim al-Houdaiby, May 4, 2014, Cairo.

35. Ibrahim al-Houdaiby, "A Nonviolent Muslim Brotherhood?" Middle East Institute, October 4, 2013, http://www.mei.edu/content/nonviolent-muslim-brotherhood#_ftn1.

36. Ibid.

37. Eric Trager, "Egypt's Invisible Insurgency," *New Republic*, March 19, 2014, http://www.newrepublic.com/article/117072/egypts-young-islamists-use-facebook-organize-violence.

government installations and nonhuman civilian targets. The violence still falls within parameters prescribed by the Brotherhood's jailed leadership, its proponents claim, because it does not target humans. In a post circulated on a Brotherhood Facebook page popular among the protestors ahead of the July 3 anniversary of the coup, the author called on the "supporters of legitimacy to carry anything that will be useful for self-defense and not for killing," suggesting that fires be lit to disrupt metro travel in order to spark widespread clashes with the police.[38]

Worried it will lose control, the Brotherhood leadership tolerates this type of action to give breathing room to angry members and prevent splintering.[39] But not all Brotherhood members have limited themselves to this kind of "micro" violence. Some have threatened to assassinate government officials. Others—members of the so-called "Molotov Movement"—issued a statement on March 9 threatening to kill policemen in Luxor.[40] There are also rumors of Brotherhood members setting up military training camps in Sudan and Libya.[41] The government, for its own part, sees a Brotherhood hand in virtually all of the violence going on in the country, ascribing Brotherhood inspiration and support to actions claimed by jihadi-salafi groups in the Sinai and elsewhere.[42]

MILITANCY IN THE SINAI

In reality, the security problem in the Sinai is its own beast, and it is in the Sinai that the government's second radicalism problem is starkest. Underdeveloped, isolated, militarily occupied, and home to antigovernment militants, the Sinai resembles ungoverned spaces in other parts of the world more than it resembles

38. Hani al-Arjundi, "Al-Tariq ila 3 Yulyu" [The path to July 3], Facebook, July 1, 2014.
39. Interview with Ibrahim al-Houdaiby, May 4, 2014, Cairo.
40. See Trager, "Egypt's Invisible Insurgency"; "Harakat 'Mulutuf' tuhaddid bi-ightiyal 40 shakhsiyya" [The Molotov Movement threatens to assassinate 40 individuals], *al-Mesryoon*, March 9, 2014.
41. Interview with Issandr El Amrani, May 4, 2014, Cairo.
42. Louisa Loveluck, "Sisi Says Muslim Brotherhood Will Not Exist under His Reign," *Guardian*, May 5, 2014, http://www.theguardian.com/world/2014/may/06/abdel-fatah-al-sisi-muslim-brotherhood-egypt.

other parts of Egypt. Political and economic grievances against the government in Cairo—including the overthrow of Morsi—have driven some militancy in the Sinai, but other factors are at play as well. Northern Sinai has long been home to a range of militant groups, and these movements have proliferated and grown bolder in the past few years. The political uncertainty, constrained and distracted government in Cairo, and steady supply of weapons from Libya that are a legacy of the uprisings created ideal conditions for jihadi-salafi expansion in the Sinai.

For the marginalized Bedouin in the Sinai, long-standing grievances against the Egyptian government, military, and security services contribute to militancy. Sinai's Bedouin populations felt general contempt toward the Mubarak government for its neglect of development in the Sinai apart from a few tourism-oriented areas. Persistently, local inhabitants also perceived that emigrants from the Nile valley were advantaged over them in an array of economic and legal matters. Making matters worse, the Ministry of the Interior consistently exercised a heavy hand in Sinai, while Egypt's General Intelligence Service was focused on gathering informants at any cost.[43] The result was endemic violence, corruption, and a perception that many of the area's most malign actors operated with impunity. The Mubarak government also conducted harsh and sometimes indiscriminate crackdowns on Bedouin populations following the terrorist attacks in Dahab, Taba, and Sharm al-Sheikh in the mid-2000s. These experiences left a legacy of hostility toward Egypt's central government that post-Mubarak governments have not overcome.

Grievances against Cairo alone do not explain the proliferation of militants in Sinai since 2011, however. The most lethal jihadi-salafi group operating in Sinai is Ansar Beit al-Maqdis, made up largely of Egyptians and Palestinians.[44] Created in

43. Steven A. Cook, "Al Qaeda's Expansion in Egypt," statement before the Committee on Homeland Security, Subcommittee on Counterterrorism and Intelligence, U.S. House of Representatives, February 14, 2014, 3.

44. "Profile: Egypt's Militant Ansar Beit al-Maqdis Group," BBC, January 24, 2013, http://www.bbc.co.uk/news/world-middle-east-25882504.

the wake of the 2011 uprisings,[45] it has since claimed responsibility for a wave of high-profile violent attacks, most of them in the wake of the overthrow of Morsi.[46] In addition to Ansar Beit al-Maqdis, known or suspected groups in the Sinai include the Muhammad Jamal Network, al Qaeda in the Sinai Peninsula, the Mujahideen Shura Council in the Environs of Jerusalem, and al Tawhid wal Jihad, the group blamed for the 2004–2006 bombings in Taba, Sharm al-Sheikh, and Dahab. Analysts have variously argued that the latter attacks were linked to the Israeli-Palestinian conflict[47] or that they were the work of al Qaeda–linked jihadists who had originally come from Upper Egypt,[48] where the Mubarak government had fought jihadi-salafi violence throughout the 1990s.

It remains difficult to determine the exact nature of these groups' affiliation (or lack thereof) with al Qaeda. Some groups, such as al Qaeda in the Sinai Peninsula, have openly aligned themselves with al Qaeda leader Ayman al-Zawahiri, and he in turn has praised the activities of Ansar Beit al-Maqdis.[49] Zawahiri opposed the Muslim Brotherhood, and the endorsement suggests that attacks by Ansar Beit al-Maqdis—while they have increased since July 2013—have not been driven solely by Muslim Brotherhood–military dynamics. A powerful Sinai tribal leader claimed in September 2013 that around 1,000 al Qaeda fighters, composed of Libyans, Palestinians, and Ye-

---

45. "Terrorist Designation of Ansar Bayt al-Maqdis," U.S. Department of State, April 9, 2014, http://www.state.gov/r/pa/prs/ps/2014/04/224566.htm.

46. In January 2014 alone, it was responsible for the Cairo bombings (January 24), the downing of a military helicopter in Sinai with a man-portable air defense system (MANPAD) (January 27), and the assassination of an aide to the Egyptian interior minister (January 28).

47. International Crisis Group, *Egypt's Sinai Question*, January 30, 2007, 3, http://www.crisisgroup.org/~/media/Files/Middle%20East%20North%20Africa/North%20Africa/Egypt/61_egypts_sinai_question.pdf.

48. Lucas Winter, "The Abdullah Azzam Brigades," *Studies in Conflict and Terrorism* 34, no. 11 (November 1, 2011), 883–95.

49. Zawahiri also called on Egyptians to oppose Sisi. See "Update: Zawahiri Praises Chechen Fighters as Models for Jihad, Reflects on Egyptian Revolution," SITE Intelligence, January 26, 2014, https://news.siteintelgroup.com/Jihadist-News/zawahiri-praises-chechen-fighters-as-models-for-jihad.html.

menis, were operating in the Sinai.[50] In late 2014, Ansar Beit al-Maqdis reportedly pledged allegiance to the Islamic State and changed its name to Wilayat Sinai, although actual linkages between the two groups remain unclear.[51]

The situation in the Sinai is further complicated by the amorphous and poorly understood links between local jihadi-salafi groups and the Islamists and jihadists in neighboring Gaza. Gaza's population shares many ties with the Bedouin of northern Sinai.[52] The bombings at Sinai resorts in the mid-2000s were blamed on militants with ties to Palestinian organizations. Sinai has at times served as a safe haven for Gazan militants, and the smuggling tunnels between Egypt and Gaza have been an economic boon to residents on both sides of the border. The Mubarak regime's cooperation with the Israeli government in maintaining the blockade of Gaza contributed to anti-Mubarak sentiment in the Sinai,[53] and the Sisi government's aggressive effort to close down the tunnels has had a similar effect. At least one Gaza-based group, the Mujahideen Shura Council in the Environs of Jerusalem, which primarily attacks Israeli targets, has also attacked Egyptian security forces in relation to their cooperation with Israel.[54]

The current Egyptian government has generally attributed violent acts in Egypt to the Brotherhood, rather than to jihadi-salafi groups operating in the country. While some caution is warranted in evaluating the charge, there seems to be little doubt that the jihadi-salafi forces fighting from Sinai have been strengthened both by an unknown number of prisoners

---

50. Mohannad Sabry, "Al Qaeda Emerges amid Egypt's Turmoil," *Al Monitor*, December 4, 2013, http://www.al-monitor.com/pulse/originals/2013/12/al-qaeda-egypt-sinai-insurgency-growing-influence.html.

51. An *Al Monitor* Correspondent in Sinai, "After joining IS, Ansar Bayt al-Maqdis expands in Egypt," *Al Monitor*, December 1, 2014, http://www.al-monitor.com/pulse/originals/2014/12/egypt-ansar-maqdis-sinai-spread.html.

52. Nicolas Pelham, "Sinai: The Buffer Erodes," Chatham House, London, September 2012, 1.

53. Ibid., 10.

54. Seth G. Jones, *A Persistent Threat: The Evolution of Al-Qaida and Other Salafi Jihadists* (Santa Monica, CA: RAND Corporation, 2014), 28, http://www.rand.org/pubs/research_reports/RR637.html.

escaping from jail in Mubarak's final days and by subsequent governments' decisions to release hundreds of prisoners who had spent decades in Egyptian jails for violent crimes under Mubarak. In June 2011, one report suggested that the SCAF had released more than 400 political detainees in the four months it had been in office.[55] Upon taking office, President Morsi continued to free dozens of prisoners, including several who had been condemned to death for violent acts in the past.[56]

Perhaps surprisingly, jihadi-salafists also launched devastating attacks against Egyptian security forces even during Morsi's tenure. Morsi had a complicated relationship with the jihadi-salafists revolting in the Sinai. The revolt began under the SCAF when some militants there took advantage of the chaos surrounding Mubarak's fall to try to push the Egyptian military out of the peninsula and to assist militants in Gaza. Morsi first attempted to dissuade the jihadists from their campaign, appealing to their shared Islamist ideals and working through salafi intermediaries to establish a rapport.[57] When those talks failed, he ordered the military to crack down.[58] In August 2012, Morsi launched Operation Eagle II to secure the Sinai,[59] and he increased the government's efforts to destroy the tunnels to

55. Heba Afify, "Victims of Mubarak's War on Islamists Still Serving Jail Time," *Egypt Independent*, June 1, 2011, http://www.egyptindependent.com/news/victims-mubaraks-war-islamists-still-serving-jail-time.

56. See Tom Perry, "Egypt's Mursi Frees Islamists Jailed by Mubarak," Reuters, July 31, 2012, http://www.reuters.com/article/2012/07/31/us-egypt-mursi-pardon-idUSBRE86U13K20120731 and "Morsy's Pardon Decree 'Includes 25 Jamaa al-Islamiya, Islamic Jihad leaders,'" *Egypt Independent*, July 21, 2012, http://www.egyptindependent.com/news/morsy-s-pardon-decree-includes-25-jamaa-al-islamiya-islamic-jihad-leaders.

57. Avi Issacharoff, "Egypt's Morsi Using Former Islamists as Intermediaries in Negotiations with Sinai Militants," *Haaretz*, August 29, 2012, http://www.haaretz.com/news/middle-east/egypt-s-morsi-using-former-islamists-as-intermediaries-in-negotiations-with-sinai-militants-1.461453.

58. Nancy Youssef, "Egypt's Morsi Dispatches Army to Sinai after Suspected Islamists Snatch Soldiers," *McClatchy*, May 20, 2013, http://www.mcclatchydc.com/2013/05/20/191735/egypts-morsi-dispatches-army-to.html.

59. Ahmad Eleibah, "Egypt's 'Operation Eagle': Army Boasts 'Successes' as Criticisms Mount," *Ahram Online*, September 2, 2012, http://english.ahram.org.eg/NewsContent/1/64/51761/Egypt/Politics-/Egypts-Operation-Eagle-Army-boasts-successes-as-cr.aspx.

Gaza in February 2013.[60] Morsi's willingness to use force against the jihadists contradicts Sisi's claim that Morsi kept the military sidelined in Sinai during his entire presidency; indeed, Sisi privately counseled Morsi in 2012 to avoid a crackdown in the Sinai on the grounds that it would stir further violence against the government.[61]

Since Morsi was ousted, jihadi-salafi attacks against Egyptian security forces have increased in scale and frequency and spread beyond the Sinai. The seeming return of the status quo ante in July 2013 has not only reinvigorated long-standing complaints against Cairo; it has also led to grassroots criticism that the peninsula's tribal leaders were both unprincipled (in shifting allegiances toward whoever was in power in Cairo) and ineffective (in failing to derive tangible benefits for their communities in exchange for their support).[62] Periodic security operations—targeted at extremists, but reportedly also hitting civilians—have added to anger. Anti-state sentiment has grown so strong that there has been a sharp rise in the northern Sinai in the use of locally run shari'a courts, which circumvent state laws as well as formal legal authority. In addition, government buildings in the area have come under repeated attack.[63] For local Bedouin, many of whom are inclined not to be religious, jihadi-salafi groups not only help frame a broader indictment of Egypt's central government, but also provide a means to strike that government in anger.

---

60. Fares Akram and David Kirkpatrick, "To Block Gaza Tunnels, Egypt Lets Sewage Flow," *New York Times*, February 20, 2013, http://www.nytimes.com/2013/02/21/world/middleeast/egypts-floods-smuggling-tunnels-to-gaza-with-sewage.html?_r=0.

61. David Kirkpatrick, "Egypt's New Strongman, Sisi Knows Best," *New York Times*, May 24, 2014, http://www.nytimes.com/2014/05/25/world/middleeast/egypts-new-autocrat-sisi-knows-best.html.

62. Rani Geha, "Sinai Tribal Elders Lose Local Support," *Al Monitor*, April 2014, http://www.al-monitor.com/pulse/originals/2014/04/egypt-sinai-tribal-leaders-lose-local-support.html.

63. See for example "Egypt pleas for help after deadly Sinai attacks," *Al Arabiya*, October 26, 2014, http://english.alarabiya.net/en/News/middle-east/2014/10/26/Palestinians-say-Gaza-truce-talks-in-Cairo-postponed.html.

CONCLUSION

The Arab uprisings temporarily reduced the power of the old elite in Egypt and prompted the Brotherhood and its Islamist supporters to create a new one. Traditional elites took umbrage at the Brotherhood's power grab and want to ensure it does not happen again. The Brotherhood miscalculated its level of popular support and its ability to withstand the old elite stepping back in. Other salafi and jihadi actors in Egypt have reacted to the Brotherhood's fall by variously abjuring politics, lining up with the Sisi government, joining the Brotherhood's rejection of the Sisi government, or launching violent attacks against the state.

Now that Sisi is in control, he has to weigh the risks of keeping Morsi's supporters outside of the political tent. So far, the Sisi regime has calculated that it can deal with its nonviolent Islamist opponents in the way Mubarak dealt with his violent Islamist opponents in the 1990s—through mass arrests and violence. This marks a shift in the state's definition of Islamist radicalism. Sisi's predecessors had made violence the touchstone for determining who was an extremist and which of them merited absolute repression. Now, Sisi has changed the definition to hinge on political ambitions rather than ideological or violent commitments. Taking such a position against a group like the Brotherhood, which professes nonviolence and which many observers feel is not committed to violence, risks pushing it or factions of it into a long and bloody revolt against the state. Such a scenario played out in Algeria, after the government nullified the Islamists' gains in parliamentary voting in the early 1990s.[64] Sisi faces the additional challenge of a failed state—Libya—in his backyard, which can provide a safe haven to his enemies.

When talking to visitors, Sisi's administration frequently characterizes his counterterrorism policy as a continuation of his predecessors' policies toward violent Islamist groups. That would be right if the Brotherhood were a violent Islamist group.

---

64. See Mohammed Hafez, *Why Muslims Rebel: Repression and Resistance in the Islamic World* (Boulder, CO: Lynne Rienner, 2003) for an explanation of what triggers revolution in Muslim-majority countries.

But compared to the groups that launched terrorist attacks in Egypt in the 1990s or 2000s, it is not. Prior to the Arab uprisings, the military leaders who ran Egypt tolerated Islamist organizations as long as they did not use violence against the state. Today, in order to perpetuate the justification for a crackdown on the Brotherhood, the government suggests whenever possible that the Brotherhood bears responsibility for violence in Egypt. In July, for example, Ansar Beit al-Maqdis killed 22 soldiers and border guards near Libya.[65] True to form, the Egyptian military insinuated that Qatar was behind the attack, presumably because Qatar supports the Brotherhood and the Brotherhood allegedly controls the salafi militants in Egypt.[66]

For the moment, nonviolent salafi political activists are allowed a seat at the table as long as they do not threaten the power of the old guard. Sisi has allowed the Nour Party to continue engaging in politics, which blunts charges that the regime is anti-Islamic and weakens the Brotherhood's hold over the Islamist vote. The Nour Party has endorsed the new political reality because it anticipates outsized influence over Islamist politics if it is the only official and well-organized Islamist party. But if Nour cannot run in future elections, which is a real possibility,[67] the party's strategy of accommodation will have completely backfired. Further, it is difficult to imagine the current government passing laws of which Nour's base would approve, so the party will likely have to justify its continued participation in a government unresponsive to a salafi political agenda.

---

65. "Ansar Bayt al-Maqdis Claims Responsibility for New Valley Attack," *Egypt Independent*, July 22, 2014, http://www.egyptindependent.com//news/ansar-bayt-al-maqdis-claims-responsibility-new-valley-attack.
66. The military spokesman said an "international intelligence service" used mercenaries to carry out the attack. See "Al-Dakhiliyya al-Misriyya tattahim mukhabarat duwaliyya bi-l-wuquf wara' majzarat al-Farafra" [The Egyptian Interior Ministry accuses an international intelligence service of standing behind the al-Farafra massacre], *al-Arab Online*, July 25, 2014, http://www.alarabonline.org/?id=28836.
67. "News Analysis: Islamic Parties at Stake as Egypt Dismantles Brotherhood's Political Wing," Xinhua, August 10, 2014, http://www.philstar.com/world/2014/08/10/1356011/news-analysis-islamic-parties-stake-egypt-dismantles-brotherhoods-political.

The more distant future is even more unfathomable. Islamist opponents might be permitted to reenter Egyptian politics in a weakened state. Returning to procedures from the Mubarak era, the government might allow the Muslim Brothers to field candidates as independents in rigged elections, a move that might mollify some of the opposition. The government could also prohibit the Brothers' political participation altogether but tolerate their continued existence as long as they remained nonviolent and stayed out of politics, a policy that served Sisi's predecessors well. Given the heterogeneous nature of the Islamist coalition against Sisi and the generational divides within it, the responses will vary. Some leaders of the Brotherhood may want to reconcile, but many younger members are in no mood to bargain.

The Brotherhood's nonviolent salafi allies are also conflicted, as demonstrated by a rift in the Gama'a leadership over the question of negotiations with the regime. Although the Gama'a leaders sided with Morsi and against the coup, they have remained committed to nonviolence[68] and have denounced attacks on Christians and churches.[69] In June, one of the group's most important figures, Aboud al-Zomor, urged the Gama'a and the Brotherhood to accept Sisi's presidency, arguing that the jailed Morsi could not provide leadership to the nation. He also called on them to sponsor candidates in upcoming parliamentary elections. The Gama'a and its political party rejected al-Zomor's initiative, although they admitted that the Brotherhood has been deaf to criticism of its maneuverings since the crackdown.[70]

---

68. "Egypt Al-Gamaa Al-Islamiya Says Group Won't Return to Violence," *Ahram Online*, October 23, 2013, http://english.ahram.org.eg/NewsContent/1/64/84599/Egypt/Politics-/Egypt-AlGamaa-AlIslamiya-says-group-wont-return-to.aspx.

69. "Al-Gamaa Al-Islamiya Denies Role in Church Attacks," *Ahram Online*, August 15, 2013, http://english.ahram.org.eg/NewsContent/1/0/79134/Egypt/AlGamaa-AlIslamiya-denies-role-in-church-attacks.aspx; "Egyptian Political and Religious Figures Condemn Warraq Church Attack," *Ahram Online*, October 21, 2013, http://english.ahram.org.eg/NewsContent/1/64/84375/Egypt/Politics-/Egyptian-political-and-religious-figures-condemn-W.aspx.

70. "Inqisam 'ala 'walayat Mursi' yufarriq Al al-Zumur' wa yashuqq 'al-Jama'a al-Islamiyya' bi-Misr" [Division over the "governance of Morsi" splits the Zumur family and divides the Jama'a Islamiyya in Egypt], CNN Arabic, June 24, 2014, http://arabic.cnn.com/middleeast/2014/06/24/egypt-brotherhood-zomor;

Meanwhile, Egypt's violent jihadi-salafists are unlikely to abate their activities. They will continue to network with other jihadi-salafists across the region, destabilize the Sinai Peninsula, threaten the Sisi government with large-scale attacks, and regularly target policemen and soldiers in the Sinai, the Delta, and Cairo. The genuine security challenge posed by these groups—and by the ideological alternative they present to young Egyptians frustrated with Morsi's overthrow, governance under Sisi, or various economic and social ills—will remain a threat to Egyptian peace and stability.

Sisi's current policy of denying many of his Islamist opponents any access to the political system after they have been mobilized politically is likely, intentionally or not, to push some into violent opposition. Sisi is unlikely to change his calculation about the Brotherhood in the short term. His policy is supported by two of his most generous patrons, Saudi Arabia and the United Arab Emirates, both of which urge the destruction of the Brotherhood. The two states have risked billions of dollars and the ire of their own Islamists to ensure Sisi succeeds in his campaign. Sisi also has the support of a large part of the Egyptian public and the old guard, which does not want the Brotherhood to return to power. Sisi could change his strategy in the long term if his opponents continue to destabilize the country and scare away Western investment. But Gulf money and the state of emergency have tempered public anger toward the president, which means he does not have much incentive to change course.

The problem of religiously inspired radicals who urge violence against the Egyptian state and its supporters is unlikely to disappear soon. Sorting out the religious and political roots of violence, and understanding which of those roots to address through persuasion and inclusion in lieu of brute coercion, will take time. If this effort is successful, it might allow the Egyptian state to avoid creating new grievances and inspiring new

"Islamist Hardliner El-Zomor Backs Transition of Power Following Morsi's Ouster," *Ahram Online*, June 24, 2014, http://english.ahram.org.eg/NewsContent/1/64/104667/Egypt/Politics-/Islamist-hardliner-ElZomor-backs-transition-of-pow.aspx.

ideologues. If unsuccessful, it could sow the seeds of the current government's downfall. Whatever the political future of Egypt looks like, its leaders will need to have a strategy to confront this problem.

6. SAUDI ARABIA: ISLAMISTS RISING AND FALLING

Jon B. Alterman and William McCants

Since its inception, the Saudi state has not defined radicalism in terms of the violent, autocratic, or regressive content of an ideology. Instead, the state evaluates ideologies in terms of the challenge or support they offer to Saudi rule. In doing so, the state variously accommodates, co-opts, delegitimizes, and represses different political and religious actors at different times. These actors include a range of violent and nonviolent salafists, Islamists, and jihadists, as well as reformers who seek to moderate the role of religion in the Saudi political system.

Over the decades, religious movements within Saudi Arabia have fractured and reorganized, alternately adopting quietism (or withdrawal from politics), nonviolent political opposition, or violent action against the state. Various actors have competed for the attention of the state and control of official religious institutions. Even those who have opposed the Al Saud's political monopoly and who share basic creedal principles with one another disagree over how to engage the state politically.[1] Historically, the state has tolerated radical or militant groups that do not attack it directly or challenge its legitimacy, while cracking down harshly on those who do either. The archetypal crackdown occurred when King Abdul Aziz ibn Saud crushed Wahhabi

---

1. For an account of those creedal principles, see Bernard Haykel, "On the Nature of Salafi Thought and Action," in *Global Salafism: Islam's New Religious Movement*, ed. Roel Meijer (New York: Columbia University Press, 2009), 33–57.

Ikhwan militants—originally his own strike force—in 1929.[2] Within this context, the Arab uprisings in 2011 presented two new challenges to Saudi Arabia. One stemmed from the Muslim Brotherhood's electoral successes across the region, raising the specter that political Islamists inside the Kingdom would demand reforms or even revolution. The second challenge emerged from the proliferation of militant groups operating in Syria against the Assad regime and later in Iraq. The former situation posed principally a political threat, while the latter posed principally a security threat. The Saudi state has treated them both as security threats.

So far, Saudi Arabia's counterterrorism policies—together with the distraction of Shi'a clashes in the Eastern Province— have muted domestic opposition to Saudi rule. But anger at the regime is high among those opposed to the government's stance against the Muslim Brotherhood, its suppression of private support for jihadists in Syria and Iraq, and its recent alliance with the United States to attack the Islamic State. Over 2,500 Saudi youth have gone to fight with jihadi groups in Syria, and many of them have joined the Islamic State.[3]

THE SAUDI STATE

The legitimacy of the Saudi state is built on the Al Saud family's alliance with the descendants of Muhammad Ibn Abd al-Wahhab and adherents to the Wahhabi religious path, an ideology that other governments in the region and around the world consider radical. Ibn Abd al-Wahhab was an eighteenth-century religious reformer who sought to purify Islam of the innovations in be-

---

2. While the Ikhwan had helped King Abdul Aziz expand and cement his territorial control, by 1929 they were continuing to fight on into Kuwait and Iraq, which angered the British and annoyed the king. He enlisted British assistance in bringing an end to their independent activities.

3. The 2,500 figure is from Richard Barrett, *Foreign Fighters in Syria*, Soufan Group, June 2014, 13, http://soufangroup.com/wp-content/uploads/2014/06/TSG-Foreign-Fighters-in-Syria.pdf. A spokesman for the Ministry of the Interior recently stated that between 2,000 and 2,100 Saudis have gone to Syria and Iraq since 2011. Angus McDowall, "Riyadh fears Islamic State wants sectarian war in Saudi Arabia," Reuters, November 18, 2014, http://www.reuters.com/article/2014/11/18/us-mideast-crisis-saudi-idUSKCN0J21CX20141118.

lief and practice that he deemed alien to the earliest community of Muslims. He endorsed the political leadership and military campaigns of Muhammad ibn Saud in an alliance that built a large state in the Arabian Peninsula by the early nineteenth century. Ottoman military campaigns emanating from Egypt ultimately destroyed this state in 1818, but Ibn Abd al-Wahhab's influence on religious practice in the region remained. A second Saudi state rose and fell in the mid-nineteenth century. In the early twentieth century, Abdul Aziz ibn Saud—an adherent of the creed Ibn Abd al-Wahhab had spread and a descendant of Muhammad ibn Saud—reestablished the Saudi state and, with the help of the Ikhwan militants, gradually gained power over most of the Arabian Peninsula. Since then, Saudi political legitimacy has rested on two foundations: political commitment to upholding Wahhabism as religious creed, and the religious establishment's endorsement of the Al Saud's rightful role as temporal leaders. Saudi foreign policy has also encouraged proselytization around the world and, at times, tolerance of militant actions by Saudis directed abroad.

There are, of course, other important dimensions to the Saudi state and its political power. These include traditions of loyalty and patronage that predate the discovery of oil, historical relationships among Arab tribes, and the massive expansion of a central administrative state—upon which the people of Saudi Arabia depend for their livelihoods and which the Al Saud family controls—that the discovery of oil enabled. The Saudi state today draws on a combination of religious, administrative, economic, and military power to maintain its stability and advance its aims.

SAUDI SALAFISM

The alliance between Ibn Saud and Ibn Abd al-Wahhab in the eighteenth century, revived by their descendants in the twentieth century, bound the legitimacy of the Saudi state to the version of salafism Ibn Abd al-Wahhab propagated. He vehemently opposed the expression of cultural practices not sanctioned by

Islam and anything he perceived to contradict the unity of God (*tawhid*—Wahhabis would refer to themselves not as Wahhabis but as Muwahhidun, or those who adhere to *tawhid*). While in theory Ibn Abd al-Wahhab criticized strict adherence to any of the four schools of traditional Sunni Islamic law, in practice one of the schools, the Hanbali, informs many Wahhabi interpretations and judgments.[4]

The descendants of Ibn Abd al-Wahhab, known as the Al al-Shaykh (or the family of the sheikh, Ibn Abd al-Wahhab himself) control the religious establishment in Saudi Arabia, which ensures that religious policy and practice adhere to Wahhabi orthodoxy. Religious scholars run Saudi Arabia's legal system based on their Wahhabi interpretations of the Qur'an, Hadith, and other legal traditions. They control religious education and practice throughout the Kingdom and play a significant role in the education system more broadly. They issue a formal religious judgment (fatwa) to stamp various behaviors as permissible, impermissible, or necessary. Through the institution of committees to "command virtue and forbid vice," the Mutawwa' (religious police) monitor public behavior and enforce strict Wahhabi norms.

Yet officially sanctioned Islam in Saudi Arabia is no monolith. The political and social space in Saudi Arabia has produced loyal salafists and Wahhabis who support the Saudi state and argue for political obedience to the Al Saud; "Islamo-liberals" critical of state Wahhabism but supportive of a continued role for religion in Saudi public life;[5] the Muslim Brothers who participated in the organized Sahwa (or "Awakening") movement to curtail the state's powers; hard-line Wahhabis critical of social, economic, and political reform that in their view undermines Saudi Arabia's authentically Islamic character; and jihadi-salafists who join or support transnational jihadi organizations, in-

---

4. David E. Long and Sebastian Maisel, *The Kingdom of Saudi Arabia*, 2nd ed. (Gainesville: University Press of Florida, 2010), 26.

5. The term "Islamo-liberal" was coined by Stéphane Lacroix, "Between Islamists and Liberals: Saudi Arabia's New 'Islamo-Liberal' Reformists," *Middle East Journal* 58, no. 3 (Summer 2004): 345–65.

cluding al Qaeda (which rejects the legitimacy of the Saudi state) or, more recently, rebel jihadi groups fighting in Syria and Iraq, including the self-declared Islamic State. The state's relationship with each of these currents has ebbed and flowed over time in line with perceived challenges to the state's power and legitimacy.

DIRECTIONS WITHIN SAUDI ARABIA

The Quietists and Islamo-Liberals
Most religious scholars in Saudi Arabia preach obedience to the state run by the Al Saud. The most supportive religious figures confirm the Saudi claim to be ruling justly over the home of the two holy cities in Islam, Mecca and Medina, by ensuring Islamic governance of the Arabian Peninsula. Others, even if they privately harbor disloyal thoughts, still do not preach disobedience. Like other salafists across the region who preach an apolitical approach to religion, they cite religious texts and traditions that forbid rebellion against a ruler who is even nominally Muslim, because to rebel is to cause *fitna*, or chaos and disunity, within the Muslim community. Many also view politics as a distraction from religious practice in both thought and behavior.

Quietists do not always refrain from criticizing Saudi policy. In the 1980s and 1990s, for example, the Ahl al-Hadith (scholars who base religious practice on the Sunna, or traditions of the Prophet and his companions)[6] rejected official calls for Saudis to

---

6. Ahl al-Hadith ("the people of Hadith") is a medieval school of thought that emphasized the role of Sunna in determining religious rulings for which the Qur'an provided no explicit direction. The movement was revived in the nineteenth century by the Syrian-born Mohammed Nasir al-Din al-Albani. Al-Albani rejected the practice of imitation (*taqlid*) that was characteristic of the four canonical schools of Islamic law. Instead, al-Albani advocated the use of independent reasoning (*ijtihad*) based on the Qur'an and Sunna. Although the Saudi jurisprudential tradition claims no explicit link to any of the four schools, in practice it follows the Hanbali line. While al-Albani's outspoken criticism of *taqlid* earned him many foes within the Saudi religious establishment, he was also able to amass a number of "self-proclaimed disciples" who in turn adopted the name Ahl al-Hadith. "By relying on al-Albani's positions for legitimacy, they broke both with the traditional Wahhabi religious establishment and with the Sahwa." Stéphane Lacroix, *Awakening Islam: The Politics of Religious Dissent in Contemporary Saudi Arabia*, trans. George Holoch (Cambridge, MA: Harvard University Press, 2011), 85. For more on the Ahl al-Hadith see ibid., 81–89.

join the jihad in Afghanistan, insisting that the Afghans, who belonged to the Maturidi school of Islamic thought, needed proper creedal guidance more than military support.[7] In terms of their creedal approach, the Ahl al-Hadith do not differ significantly from other groups that have embraced a turn toward militancy—in fact, the leader of the 1979 Grand Mosque attack drew heavily on their teachings.[8] Yet in the early 1990s, the Saudi state carefully co-opted offshoots of this movement to protect itself from political threats: followers of two loyalist sheikhs, Muhammad Aman al-Jami and Rabi' al-Madkhali, gained notoriety for their critical stance toward the Muslim Brotherhood and the Sahwa, and the state was quick to enlist their support. The government facilitated the rise of prominent individuals from the Jami and Madkhali movements in Islamic universities, from which they could launch a counteroffensive against the Sahwa.[9]

The Saudi state has also shown it can accommodate those whose ideologies may deviate from the Saudi Wahhabi orthodoxy. In the 1990s, a group of activists became intellectually and politically critical of the dominant Wahhabi orthodoxy. While these "Islamo-liberals" advocated religious reform, they did not reject salafism as such.[10] They have advanced two interrelated positions. Intellectually, Islamo-liberals take a steadfastly anti-Wahhabi position. Politically, they argue for the adoption of democratic practices, viewing democracy almost exclusively as a procedural scheme rather than a value-laden ideology.[11]

---

7. Ibid., 116. Lacroix notes, however, that the Saudi state also appreciated the Ahl al-Hadith's stance against the jihad in Afghanistan as they grew more concerned about potential blowback against Middle Eastern regimes from jihadists fighting there.

8. Stéphane Lacroix, "Between Revolution and Apoliticism: Nasir al-Din al-Albani and His Impact on the Shaping of Contemporary Salafism," in *Global Salafism: Islam's New Religious Movement*, ed. Roel Meijer (New York: Columbia University Press, 2009), 74.

9. Ibid., 77.

10. Rather, they maintain that in order to arrive at a state of "real" salafism, the latter must be divorced from its Wahhabi and Ibn Taymiyyan intermediaries. In other words, Islamo-liberals argue for an innovative and dynamic form of salafism—one that agitates for a "return to the methodology of the pious ancestors and not simply to their productions, with a clear vision of what the *maqasid* (objectives) of the *shari'a* ought to be." Interview with Abdullah al-Hamid; quoted in Lacroix, "Between Islamists and Liberals," 349–50.

11. Ibid., 347.

The Islamo-liberal reformist movement began to consolidate and formalize its demands in the aftermath of the September 11, 2001, attacks. In their 2003 charter, "Vision for the Present and the Future of the Homeland," a group of Islamo-liberal intellectuals, including both Sunnis and Shiʻa, demanded "the separation of powers; the implementation of the rule of law; equal rights for all citizens regardless of regional, tribal, and confessional background; the creation of elected national and regional parliaments (*majlis al-shura*); and complete freedom of speech, assembly and organization to allow the emergence of a true civil society."[12] Then-Crown Prince Abdullah was at first receptive to these demands: he invited 40 of the signatories to his palace and offered his support for their cause, created a national dialogue conference to facilitate debate about and refinement of the charter, and in October 2003 announced the introduction of partial municipal elections to be held in 2004.[13]

The Muslim Brotherhood and the Sahwa

The Saudi government has had an ambiguous yet interdependent relationship with the Muslim Brotherhood since the movement unofficially established a branch in the Kingdom in 1937.[14] The annual pilgrimage traffic to Mecca and Medina made Saudi Arabia an inviting target for the Brotherhood's expansion because it offered easy access to potential recruits from around the world.[15]

12. Ibid., 360–61.

13. Ibid., 363. The municipal elections were delayed and eventually took place in 2005.

14. The relationship between Saudi Arabia and the Muslim Brotherhood began in 1936 when Hassan al-Banna, the founder of the Muslim Brotherhood, went to the Kingdom to solicit the new ruler's permission to establish a local chapter of the Islamic fraternal order. Banna had called Abdul Aziz "one of the hopes of the Islamic world for restoration of its grandeur and a recreation of its unity." *Five Tracts of Hasan Al-Banna (1906–1949)*, trans. Charles Wendell (Berkeley: University of California Press, 1978).

15. King Abdul Aziz did not permit the Muslim Brotherhood to recruit openly, but did not prohibit recruitment altogether. The king also bought numerous volumes of the Brotherhood's edition of a classical Islamic text, which helped finance the publishing endeavor. Banna, in turn, wrote editorials urging the Saudi king to lead Muslim public opinion. But as the Brotherhood's fortunes rose in the late 1930s, the Brotherhood's newspaper became more critical of the king for his allegedly un-Islamic behavior while abroad. See William McCants, "Derivatives of the Mus-

For the next several decades, relations between Saudi Arabia and the Egyptian Muslim Brotherhood waxed and waned depending on whether the Brotherhood was being persecuted by Arab nationalists at home. In 1954, after Gamal Abdel Nasser's crackdown on the Muslim Brotherhood in Egypt, the Saudis welcomed the Brothers and offered citizenship to many of their prominent members. The Saudis badly needed the many professionals among the Brotherhood members to build and maintain the Kingdom's educational and financial infrastructure, which oil revenues were rapidly expanding.[16] The Saudis also viewed Nasser's socialism and Arab nationalism as a threat to the legitimacy of the Kingdom's identity and system of governance, and so considered his enemies as their allies.[17]

The Muslim Brotherhood's hold on the Saudi education system afforded the movement its greatest and most lasting im-

lim Brotherhood: Saudi Arabia," Center for International Issues Research, January 2, 2007; Brynjar Lia, *The Society of the Muslim Brothers in Egypt: The Rise of an Islamic Mass Movement 1928–1994* (Reading, UK: Ithaca Press, 1998), 140–43, 219; Umar al-'Izzi, "Al-Ikhwan al-Sa'udiyyun... Al-Tayyar al-ladhi lam yaqul kalimatahu ba'd!" ['The Saudi Brotherhood': The trend which has not said its piece yet], *Al-Asr*, July 25, 2004, http://alasr.ws/articles/view/5547; Husam Tammam, "Al-Ikhwan fi al-Sa'udiyya: Hal daqqat al-sa'a" [The Brotherhood in Saudi Arabia: Has the time of separation arrived?], *Islamismscope*, December 3, 2002, http://www.islamismscope.net/index.php?option=com_content&view=article&id=119:2010-02-09-13-12-44&catid=37:articles&Itemid=67.

16. One of the first Muslim Brothers to arrive in Saudi Arabia was Manna al-Qattan, an Egyptian scholar who came to the Kingdom in 1953 and served on various committees directing religious schools and educational policy. Qattan was the head of the Saudi Brotherhood until his death in 1999 and the intermediary between the Saudi government and the Brotherhood in Egypt. In that capacity, he frequently met with the interior minister, Prince Naif, and his deputy Prince Ahmad bin Abdul Aziz, in addition to Crown Prince Salman bin Abdul Aziz, then the governor of Riyadh. See McCants, "Derivatives of the Muslim Brotherhood: Saudi Arabia"; Muhammad al-Majdhub, "Sheikh Manna' al-Qattan," *Odabasham*, undated, December 18, 2007 http://www.odabasham.net/show.php?sid=8353; Yusuf al-Qaradawi, "al-Halaka al-Thalitha: al-Ikhwan fi Kharij Masr," [Section Three: The Brotherhood outside Egypt], *Islamonline*, October 2003; Ali Ashmawi, *Al-Tarikh al-sirri li-jama'at al-Ikhwan al-Muslimin* [The secret history of the society of Muslim Brothers] (Cairo: Dar Al-Hilal, 1993), 62.

17. McCants, "Derivatives of the Muslim Brotherhood; Tammam, "Al-Ikhwan fi al-Sa'udiyya"; Thomas Hegghammer and Stéphane Lacroix, "Rejectionist Islamism in Saudi Arabia: The Story of Juhayman al-'Utaybi Revisited," *International Journal of Middle East Studies*, 39, no. 1 (2007): 103–22.

pact on political Islam in Saudi Arabia.[18] This is nowhere more evident than in the rise of the so-called Sahwa or Awakening movement in the 1980s and 1990s. In essence this movement represented a marriage between the doctrinal conservatism of Wahhabism and the "political consciousness" of the Muslim Brotherhood.[19] Influenced by the political vocabulary of the Muslim Brotherhood, this movement over time assumed its own unique identity.[20] The ideology of the Sahwa as such did not perturb Saudi authorities, but when the Sahwa movement openly critiqued Saudi policy in the early 1990s, the Saudi government's attitude toward it shifted accordingly.

In 1991, when the Muslim Brotherhood in Saudi Arabia opposed the stationing of U.S. troops on Saudi soil in the wake of Iraq's invasion of Kuwait, the Sahwa launched a national campaign demanding political reforms through a series of open letters to the king.[21] In response, the Saudi government cracked

---

18. Muslim Brothers also established charitable and missionary institutions that extended Saudi influence around the world, such as the Islamic Bank for Development, the Muslim World League (a Wahhabi missionary organization), and the World Assembly of Muslim Youth (a youth mission organization headquartered in Saudi Arabia). On the Islamic Bank for Development see Qaradawi, "Brotherhood outside Egypt"; 'Ala' Matar, "Asrar 'audat madaris al-Ikhwan," [Secrets of the return of Brotherhood schools], *Katibatibia*, December 18, 2007; Sulayman bin Salih al-Kharashi, "Arba't 'ibar… min mudhakarat ahad rumuz jama'at al-Ikhwan al-Muslimin," [Four lessons from the memoirs of one of the prominent members of the Muslim Brotherhood], *Sayd al-Fuad*, undated, http://saaid.net/Warathah/Alkharashy/27.htm. For details on the Muslim World League, see J. Millard Burr and Robert O. Collins, *Alms for Jihad: Charity and Terrorism in the Islamic World* (New York: Cambridge University Press, 2006), 19, 33, 34–35. See also Thomas Hegghammer, *Jihad in Saudi Arabia: Violence and Pan-Islamism since 1979* (Cambridge: Cambridge University Press, 2010): 38–58.

19. See Haykel, "On the Nature of Salafi Thought and Action," 50.

20. Stéphane Lacroix, "Saudi Arabia's Muslim Brotherhood predicament," *Washington Post*, March 20, 2014, http://www.washingtonpost.com/blogs/monkey-cage/wp/2014/03/20/saudi-arabias-muslim-brotherhood-predicament/. For example, even though one of the Sahwa groups referred to itself as "the Saudi Muslim Brotherhood," organizational links between this group and the mother organization were weak and informal. More importantly "its members did not pledge allegiance to the general guide in Cairo"—because they had already pledged allegiance (*bay'a*) to the Saudi King.

21. For example, in the famous *Letter of Demands* presented by the Sahwa leaders in 1991, out of the 12 points outlined, only one makes implicit reference to the stationing of U.S. troops in Saudi: "Build a foreign policy that preserves the interests

down, and it largely succeeded in silencing the movement. In an attempt to frame the episode as an intrusion of foreign origin, the Saudi government exaggerated the link between the Muslim Brotherhood and the Sahwa, and in the process exiled Egyptian members of the former while imprisoning those of the latter.[22]

In the late 1990s the Sahwa movement reemerged weakened and fractured. A significant number of its former leaders and scholars had broken off and espoused alternate political and ideological positions, ranging from the extreme to the "liberal" and from the active to the quietist. Salman al-'Awda, one of the movement's most prominent and prolific scholars, toned down his opposition to Saudi rule and policy in exchange for official tolerance for his views. Mitigating circumstances—the deaths of two of the most respected figures in the state religious establishment—facilitated the rapprochement.[23] In this "theological power vacuum" the government co-opted members of the Sahwa movement to serve as an alternative source of legitimacy.[24]

The Grand Mosque Attack, Anti-Saudi Wahhabism, and Jihadism
The co-optation of different components of the Muslim Brotherhood and Sahwa movements at various points in Saudi Ara-

---

of the *umma*, far removed from the alliances contrary to God's law, and that joins in Muslim causes." The rest of the document demands the creation of an independent advisory council, rulers' accountability, the fair distribution of wealth, etc. Quoted in Lacroix, *Awakening Islam*, 180.

22. This theme would reemerge in 2002 when Prince Naif bin Abdul Aziz lamented: "The Brotherhood has done great damage to Saudi Arabia . . . All of our problems come from the Muslim Brotherhood . . . The Muslim Brotherhood has destroyed the Arab World." Quoted in "Naif says Muslim Brotherhood Cause of Most Arab Problems," *Arab News*, November 28, 2002, http://www.arabnews.com/node/226291. It would emerge yet again in 2014 when, for example, Khalid al-Faisal, the Saudi Minister of Education, said of the Brotherhood: "We offered them our children, and they took them hostage . . . The society left the stage open for them, including schools." See "Saudis Arrest Professors Linked to Brotherhood: 'We Offered Them Our Children . . . '" *World Tribune*, May 27, 2014, http://www.worldtribune.com/2014/05/27/saudi-arrests-university-professors-linked-muslim-brotherhood/.

23. The two were Abd al-Aziz bin Baz (died May 13, 1999) and Muhammad bin 'Uthaymin (died January 10, 2001).

24. Hegghammer, *Jihad in Saudi Arabia*, 83; Lacroix, "Saudi Arabia's Muslim Brotherhood Predicament."

bia's recent history served the overarching goal of countering accusations from within Saudi Arabia that the Al Saud's political rule failed to uphold a sufficiently Islamic form of governance or failed to protect the holiest sites in Islam.

The Saudi government faced such accusations on the morning of November 20, 1979, when a group of several hundred apocalyptic militants led by Juhayman al-Utaybi laid siege to Mecca's Grand Mosque and Islam's holiest site, the Ka'ba. The attack initially provoked confusion and questioning among many Saudis, both as to whether the Mahdi (or savior) had actually arrived, and as to whether fighting in Mecca, expressly forbidden in a reliable prophetic tradition, was permissible to dislodge the rebels (some Saudi soldiers refused to attack).[25] In response, the regime was quick to enlist the support of the Council of Ulema, which, on November 24, 1979, issued a fatwa permitting the use of force within the mosque.[26] The Saudi authorities launched a two-week offensive against the insurgents, and by December 4, they had reclaimed control of the mosque and its surroundings. Al-Utaybi was captured and the alleged Mahdi, his brother-in-law Muhammad Abdullah al-Qahtani, was killed. Although the exact number of casualties is not known, estimates place the death toll in the hundreds, if not as high as a thousand. On January 9, 1980, the Saudi state executed 63 people across eight different cities in connection with the siege.[27] Following that incident, the government began to exercise tighter control over religious institutions within Saudi Arabia and pursued a policy of "re-Islamizing" society by clamping down on unreligious behaviors and expressions such as music and song on television

---

25. Yaroslav Trofimov, *The Siege of Mecca* (New York: Doubleday, 2007), 85–86.

26. See Joseph A. Kechichian, "The Role of the Ulama in the Politics of an Islamic State: The Case of Saudi Arabia," *International Journal of Middle East Studies* 18, no. 1 (February 1986): 53–71.

27. In the wake of the incident, government officials were quick to blame foreign ideological influences for Utaybi's actions. Specifically, the government singled out Egyptian groups such as Jama'at al-Muslimin (the Society of Muslims), also known as al-Takfir wa-l-Hijra (Excommunication and Emigration). See Hegghammer and Lacroix, "Rejectionist Islamism in Saudi Arabia," 113.

and immodest dress by women. In addition, beginning in 1982, the state required every mosque orator to receive official authorization from the Ministry of Hajj and Waqf,[28] and a number of informal religious groups were banned. One immediate consequence was to strengthen the position of the Sahwa movement, which at that time was more "institutionally integrated" than other Islamist movements.[29]

Al-Utaybi's movement, a singular blend of radical Wahhabism and messianism, had few adherents, and therefore represented a short-term security threat more than an existential challenge to the Saudi state. Nevertheless the government did see a need in the aftermath of the attack to bolster its Islamic credentials. The shock of the attack, combined with concerns about an oversupply of trained clerics in the country, the recent Islamic Revolution in Iran, and growing criticism from the religious establishment—including leading cleric Abd al-Aziz bin Baz—of the Kingdom's rapid modernization,[30] contributed to the Saudi government's decision to support Arab jihadists in the fight against the Soviet occupation of Afghanistan in the 1980s. Working with Pakistani and U.S. intelligence agencies, Saudi Arabia provided institutional support (including recruitment and funding) as well as religious sanction for what became the jihad in Afghanistan.[31] In addition to the Afghan jihad, the Saudis also supported jihadi activity in Chechnya. Saudi sheikhs legitimized the Chechen resistance, and private donors and Islamic charities in Saudi Arabia offered financial support to the cause.[32] The state neither intervened in nor curtailed these ef-

---

28. Lacroix, *Awakening Islam*, 103.
29. Hegghammer and Lacroix, "Rejectionist Islamism in Saudi Arabia," 113.
30. Trofimov, *Siege of Mecca*, 27.
31. For example, the grand mufti, Sheikh Bin Baz, issued a fatwa sanctioning the jihad against communism and referring to it, in religious terms, as a *fard kifaya* (incumbent on the Muslim community as a whole). The state, for its part, provided logistical and financial support to the effort. The Saudis also afforded a space for private, unofficial contributions in the form of Islamic charities, mosque collections, and private donations. Madawi Al-Rasheed, *Contesting the Saudi State: Islamic Voices from a new Generation* (Cambridge: Cambridge University Press, 2007), 107.
32. Hegghammer, *Jihad in Saudi Arabia*, 56.

forts. Many of the fighters wounded in Chechnya received medical treatment in Saudi Arabia.[33]

Osama bin Laden emerged from the fight in Afghanistan at the head of a network of jihadists looking for a new fight. While bin Laden's ambitions were global, he held a particular antipathy toward the Al Saud, especially after their collaboration with the United States during the first Gulf War. Bin Laden's diatribes against the Al Saud found a receptive audience within Saudi Arabia. Many fighters returned from Afghanistan feeling empowered and enthusiastic to fight on behalf of Islam. From the early 1990s through the 2000s, Saudi Arabia confronted rising numbers of domestic *takfiris*, Muslims who rejected the Saudi leadership as un-Islamic. Rejection of the state was based both on opposition to domestic policy reforms seen as Westernizing or un-Islamic, and on foreign policy decisions—including alliance with the United States and the decision to allow U.S. troops to be stationed within Saudi Arabia—seen as antithetical to the state's claim to be protecting Islamic holy sites and Muslims. A new movement known as the Shu'aybi school, whose leadership was made up almost entirely of former Sahwa leaders, provided significant intellectual support for the domestic jihadi movement that began to gather momentum in the 2000s in the wake of the U.S.-led military campaign in Afghanistan.[34] According to Thomas Hegghammer, the movement was fueled by the so-called Jenin Battle in the spring of 2002, the build-up to the Iraq War in late 2002, the Saudi regime's crackdown on possible militant action during the Iraq War, and the circulation of images from Guantánamo Bay.[35]

Sometime in 2002, bin Laden ordered al Qaeda networks in Saudi Arabia to prepare for attacks within the country.[36] At the time, the Saudi security apparatus was underprepared and

---

33. Ibid.
34. Among the leaders of the movement were Hamud al-Shu'aybi and Ali al-Khudayr. According to Hegghammer, *Jihad in Saudi Arabia*, 148, there is little evidence indicating that the Shu'aybis were aware of the jihadists' operational schemes.
35. Ibid., 143–47.
36. Thomas Hegghammer, "Islamist Violence and Regime Stability in Saudi Arabia," *International Affairs* 84, no.4 (2008): 709.

weak relative to the operational capability of the local al Qaeda network.[37] Bin Laden also had Yusuf al-Uyayri in his arsenal of Saudi-based personnel. Unlike other jihadi leaders before him, Uyayri was from the conservative stronghold of Burayda in Najd, and he was able to significantly broaden the scope of al Qaeda recruitment and fundraising within Saudi Arabia. His family ties to Najd linked him—and by extension al Qaeda—to the most conservative and well-respected religious scholars in the country, among whom were the members of the Shu'aybi movement.[38] Around this time, Nasir al-Fahd, a leading scholar of the Shu'aybi school, issued a fatwa declaring that visas could no longer guarantee the safety of Western visitors, and he published documents that sanctioned the targeting of Westerners as well as Saudi security forces in violent attacks.[39]

Saudi officials' overt concern about terrorist activity grew not after the September 11, 2001, attacks in the United States, but after May 12, 2003, when multiple suicide car bombs were detonated in Riyadh at several residential compounds housing non-Saudi contractors and their families. In total, 34 people were killed and another 200 were injured. The declared and immediate aim of the attacks was to rid the Arabian Peninsula of the U.S. presence there.[40] Over the next several years, an unprecedented and sustained wave of attacks was carried out across the country; by mid-2005, over 91 civilians and 118 militants had been killed and nearly 800 others injured.[41] In response, the regime first launched a nationwide crackdown on suspected militants, questioning thousands and arresting at least 800 on suspicion of terrorist activity,[42] and then instituted a rehabili-

---

37. Ibid., 703.

38. Hegghammer, *Jihad in Saudi Arabia*, 121, 148–55.

39. Ibid., 153.

40. Ibid., 105. There are also statements from bin Laden and Uyayri (al Qaeda's leader in Saudi Arabia) to this effect.

41. John Bradley, "Kingdom of Peace Transformed into al-Qa'eda's Latest War Zone," *Telegraph*, August 1, 2005, http://www.telegraph.co.uk/news/worldnews/middleeast/saudiarabia/1495290/Kingdom-of-peace-transformed-into-al-Qaedas-latest-war-zone.html.

42. "Initiatives and Actions Taken by the Kingdom of Saudi Arabia to Combat Terrorism," Royal Embassy of Saudi Arabia in Washington, DC, December 2006, http://www.saudiembassy.net/files/PDF/KSA_WOT_Report_Dec06.pdf.

tation and reeducation program. The program sought not only to address the behavior of suspected terrorists directly but also to portray the latter as "errant" and religiously misguided, suffering from a sort of "illness." By defining the attackers as misguided and terrorism as a "fatal disease," the authorities attempted to deny the attacks' political relevance and frame them as a social challenge.

AFTER THE UPRISINGS

The Arab uprisings confronted Saudi Arabia with two principal challenges related to religious ideology and militancy: First, the success of the Muslim Brotherhood in Egypt and Ennahda in Tunisia emboldened political Islamists across the region—including a variety of salafi and Islamist Saudis critical of the state and the Al Saud. Second, the civil war in Syria fostered the emergence of a radical Islamic group, the Islamic State, which is not just a military concern but an ideological one—specifically, the Islamic State's claims to authentic religious authority over all Muslims threaten the Saudi state's legitimacy. Saudi Arabia has responded to the first challenge by framing the political opposition of the Muslim Brotherhood (and others) as a terrorism threat that must be addressed through police and counterterrorism efforts. As for the second threat, the Saudis have countered the dual challenge posed by the Islamic State with combat operations and with religious scholarship that seeks to delegitimize the Islamic State's religious and ideological claims. While in the past, the Saudi government dealt with various oppositional movements as they emerged periodically, the Arab uprisings presented the Saudis with the threat of a resurgence of oppositional sentiments en masse. This was a novel situation, but the techniques used by the Saudis to to address it were old ones: the conflation of political threats with security threats, and the framing of all political opposition as foreign intrusion in domestic affairs.

The most credible threat came from the Saudi Muslim Brotherhood and Sahwa, which continue to be the only organized and popular activist groups. Notable Sahwa figures, such as Salman al-'Awda and Nasir al-Umar, expressed their support for the revolutions taking place across the region, despite the Kingdom's official position.[43] Activists and intellectuals closely associated with the Sahwa movement established Saudi Arabia's first political party, the Islamic Umma Party *(Hizb al-Umma al-Islami)*.[44] Intellectuals of various religious and political stripes put forward reform proposals; one petition that garnered widespread support demanded "an elected parliament... and the appointment of a prime minister distinct from the king and accountable to a parliament."[45] One of the only oppositional groups that refused to sign the petition was the salafi Sururis,[46] who objected that the petition was not "Islamic" enough. However, this did not stop a number of figures associated with the Sururi movement from signing the petition individually. Overall, the petition garnered nearly 9,000 signatures within a few weeks of being posted online.[47]

---

43. The Kingdom's grand mufti described the demonstrations in Egypt and Tunisia as "planned and organized by the enemies of the Umma" in order to "strike the Umma and destroy its religious, values and morals." Quoted in Stéphane Lacroix, "Saudi Islamists and the Arab Spring," Kuwait Programme on Development, Governance and Globalisation in the Gulf States, London School of Economics and Political Science, London, 2014, http://eprints.lse.ac.uk/56725/1/Lacroix_Saudi-Islamists-and-theArab-Spring_2014.pdf, 3.

44. Lacroix, "Saudi Islamists and the Arab Spring," 8–9. The SCPRA was established in 2009 as Saudi's first fully independent human rights nongovernmental organization. Lacroix notes that the founders of the party were influenced by the writings of the Kuwaiti religious scholar Hakim al-Mutayri, who "attempted to justify democratic practices using Salafi references."

45. Ibid.

46. Sururis (so-called by their opponents) adhere to the teachings of Muhammad Surur Zayn al-Abidin, a former Syrian Muslim Brother who blended the thought of Sayyid Qutb and Ibn Abd al-Wahhab. Because the Sururis share an intellectual pedigree with the Brotherhood, they compete with them for recruits, royal patronage, and control of Saudi Arabia's religious and educational institutions. See 'Izzi, "Al-Ikhwan al-Su'udiyyun'"; Faris bin Hazzam, "Sibaq bayna Islamiyyin wa Islamiyyin: Intikhabat al-Dammam tush'il fatil 'al-Sururiyya' wa 'al-Ikhwan'," [The race between the Islamists and the Islamists: The elections of Al-Dammam ignite the fuse between the Sururis and the Ikhwanis], Al Arabiyya, February 28, 2005, http://www.alarabiya.net/articles/2005/02/28/10767.html.

47. Lacroix notes that most signers were young Saudis in their 20s and 30s. See Lacroix, "Saudi Islamists and the Arab Spring," 11–12.

The government's initial response included both forceful intervention and compromise. On February 23 and again on March 18, 2011, the king decreed two aid packages that targeted the most disaffected members of society, namely the poor and the young. Together the packages amounted to a total of around US$130 billion.[48] The government gave civil servants—around two-thirds of the Saudi workforce—a 15 percent raise and an extra two months' pay.[49] The government also sought to intimidate the opposition. According to a person with contacts in the Saudi Brotherhood, Crown Prince Naif and future Crown Prince Salman gathered the more vocal Islamists and threatened them into silence.[50] Around this time, 'Awda lost his weekly television show.[51] Seven out of the 10 founding members of the Islamic Umma Party were arrested,[52] and security forces were deployed around the country. Echoing its past practices, the government also argued that opposition movements were the product of an Iranian conspiracy aimed at "destabilizing the Kingdom."[53] By designating activists as foreign agents, the government has been able to subsume all forms of opposition under the umbrella of terrorism. The promulgation of a broadly termed antiterrorism law in 2014 confirmed the government's investment in this strategy. Under the guise of enforcing this law, Saudi authorities have arrested and tried activists of all stripes.[54]

---

48. "Saudi stocks soar after king's spending spree," Agence France-Presse, March 20, 2011, http://english.ahram.org.eg/NewsContent/3/12/8119/Business/Economy/Saudi-stocks-soar-after-kings-spending-spree.aspx.

49. Ayesha Daya and Vivian Salama, "OPEC's $1T Cash Quiets Poor as $100 Oil Fills Coffers," Bloomberg, September 20, 2011, http://www.bloomberg.com/news/2011-09-19/opec-s-1t-cash-quiets-poor-on-longest-ever-100-oil.html.

50. Interview with a former member of the Muslim Brotherhood, March 2, 2014, Jeddah.

51. Stéphane Lacroix, "Is Saudi Arabia Immune?" *Journal of Democracy* 22, no. 4 (October 2011): 48–59.

52. Lacroix, "Saudi Islamists and the Arab Spring," 13.

53. Ibid.

54. Most recently, the human rights activist Waleed Abul al-Khair was sentenced to 15 years in prison and a 15-year travel ban, in addition to a fine in the amount of 200,000 riyals. The charge included, inter alia, "assembling international organisations against the Kingdom"; "creating and supervising an unlicensed organisation, and contributing to the establishment of another"; and "preparing and

Back in 2011, when the Saudi government viewed these domestic developments in the context of events taking place
around the region, it became increasingly focused on the Muslim
Brotherhood as a political threat. The Saudis determined early
on that the Islamists would be the revolutions' primary ben-
eficiaries, and the regime worried that they would try to export
their revolution to the Arab monarchies. The *Wall Street Journal*
reported as far back as February 4, 2011, that "President Barack
Obama's attempt to abruptly push aside Egyptian President
Hosni Mubarak in favor of a transition government has sparked
a rift with key Arab allies Saudi Arabia and United Arab Emirates, which fear the U.S. is opening the door for Islamist groups
to gain influence and destabilize the region."[55]

The regimes' fears were partially confirmed when Ennahda
in Tunisia and the Muslim Brotherhood's Freedom and Justice
Party in Egypt dominated the voting. Saudi supporters of the
Muslim Brothers lauded the open elections, a thinly veiled criticism of the Saudi regime. Next door in the United Arab Emirates
(UAE), some Muslim Brothers also put their names to a petition
demanding that the UAE's advisory council be empowered and
that real elections be held.[56] There is no evidence that the Brotherhood in Egypt was pushing its fellow travelers in the Gulf to
challenge the monarchies, but officials in the most politically
closed of the Gulf states—Saudi Arabia and the UAE—interpreted the agitation as a conspiracy or at least part of a regional
zeitgeist they disliked.

While Saudi Arabia and the UAE kept one eye on domestic
Brotherhood unrest at home, they also watched the Muslim
Brotherhood in Egypt. There the group was attempting to wrest
control of the Mubarak state apparatus from the old guard and

---

storing information that will affect public security." "Update—Saudi Arabia: Mr.
Waleed Abu Al-Khair Receives Lengthy Prison Sentence and Travel Ban," Frontline
Defenders, July 7, 2014, http://www.frontlinedefenders.org/node/26509.

55. Adam Entous, Julian Barnes, and Jay Solomon, "U.S. Pressure on Mubarak
Opens a Rift with Arab Allies," *Wall Street Journal*, February 4, 2011, http://online.
wsj.com/articles/SB10001424052748704376104576122610828648254.

56. Lori Plotkin Boghardt, "The Muslim Brotherhood on Trial in the UAE," Washington Institute for Near East Policy, April 12, 2013, http://www.washingtoninsti-
tute.org/policy-analysis/view/the-muslim-brotherhood-on-trial-in-the-uae.

shift away from the Saudi camp to a more neutral position vis-à-vis Saudi Arabia's enemy Iran. According to one intermediary between the Saudi government and the Egyptian Brotherhood, the Saudis were furious that the Brotherhood refused to share power with other members of the opposition.[57] This refusal reinforced their view that the Brotherhood is an intrinsically expansionist organization that seeks total power when the opportunity presents itself.[58] After Morsi followed his fund-raising visit to the Kingdom with an attempted rapprochement with Iran, the Saudi government began to suffocate the new Egyptian government by withholding its promised financing. Just two months before the overthrow of Morsi, Saudi Arabia had sent only US$1 billion of the US$3.5 billion in aid it had promised after Mubarak's overthrow.[59]

Tensions between the regime and the Saudi Muslim Brothers flared again in the summer of 2013 after the Saudi government supported the coup against Morsi. The Saudis immediately promised US$5 billion in aid, together with US$3 billion from the UAE and US$4 billion from Kuwait. The Saudi king, Abdullah, also publicly supported the military's bloody crackdown on Brotherhood members protesting Morsi's ouster, characterizing it as a justified action against terrorists.[60] Brotherhood members and sympathizers in the Kingdom responded by criticizing their government's backing of the coup and decorating their Twitter avatars with symbols supporting the Egyptian Brotherhood pro-

---

57. Interview with Anwar Eshqi, March 3, 2014, Jeddah.

58. Interview with Angus McDowall, March 5, 2014, Riyadh.

59. One French journalist was told by a Saudi official that the Kingdom would spend billions to keep the Muslim Brotherhood from coming to power. He was told by numerous Egyptian journalists and officials that Saudi Arabia and the UAE view the Brotherhood as a strategic threat and will therefore continue sending money to Sisi for his social programs so that the Brotherhood cannot claim to provide services not provided by the government. Interview, May 5, 2014, Cairo. See also "Finance Minister Requests Aid from Saudi Arabia," *Daily News Egypt*, May 19, 2013, http://www.dailynewsegypt.com/2013/05/19/finance-minister-requests-aid-from-saudi-arabia/.

60. Tariq Al-Homayed, "Opinion: King Abdullah's Egypt Speech Was Like a Surgeon's Scalpel," *Asharq Al-Awsat*, August 19, 2013, http://www.aawsat.net/2013/08/article55314019.

testors.[61] Muhammad bin Nasir al-Suhaybani spoke out against those who supported the coup during a sermon at the Prophet's Mosque in Medina.[62] Brotherhood sympathizer Salman al-'Awda barely concealed his criticism of the Saudi government, tweeting "It is clear who is driving Egypt to its destruction out of fear for their own selves."[63] The Brotherhood's spiritual leader, Yusuf al-Qaradawi, accused Saudi Arabia's close ally, the UAE, of standing against Islamist regimes.[64]

By March 2014, the Saudis and the Emiratis had had enough. They refused to send ambassadors to Qatar, a state they held responsible for funding, harboring, and giving media exposure to the Brotherhood. They also joined Egypt in declaring the Muslim Brotherhood a terrorist organization. The liberal Saudi prince, Alwaleed bin Talal, removed popular Brotherhood member Tareq al-Suwaidan from al-Risala TV for criticizing the killing of Brotherhood protestors, accusing him of being part of the "terrorist Brotherhood movement."[65] The government also banned books by Suwaidan and 'Awda.[66] According to a State Department source, there was also a brief campaign by the Ministry of the Interior to detain Islamists at the local ministry branches and force them to sign a pledge agreeing to cease criticism of

---

61. Interview with Angus McDowall, March 5, 2014, Riyadh.

62. "Kalima 'an ahwal Misr," [A word on the situation in Egypt], YouTube video, posted by "Bandar Bouresly" August 16, 2013, https://www.youtube.com/watch?v=desfNSSjd4k; Marc Lynch, "Gulf Islamist Dissent over Egypt," *Foreign Policy*, August 18, 2013, http://www.foreignpolicy.com/posts/2013/08/18/gulf_islamist_dissent_over_egypt.

63. Salman al-'Awda, Twitter post, August 15, 2013, https://twitter.com/Salman_Al_Odah/status/368022839666167808.

64. "UAE Summons Qatar Envoy over Qaradawi Remarks," *Al Jazeera*, February 2, 2014, http://www.aljazeera.com/news/middleeast/2014/02/uae-summons-qatar-envoy-over-qaradawi-remarks-20142215393855165.html.

65. Habib Toumi, "TV Manager Fired over Muslim Brotherhood Links," *Gulf News*, August 18, 2013, http://gulfnews.com/news/gulf/saudi-arabia/tv-manager-fired-over-muslim-brotherhood-links-1.1221473; Marc Lynch, "Gulf Islamist Dissent over Egypt."

66. "Muslim Brotherhood-Affiliated Authors' Books Pulled in Saudi Arabia," *Gulf News*, June 2, 2014, http://gulfnews.com/news/gulf/saudi-arabia/muslim-brotherhood-affiliated-authors-books-pulled-in-saudi-arabia-1.1342080.

the Saudi state. Since then, most Islamists have become more circumspect on Twitter. The popular cleric Muhammad al-Arifi, for example, has focused on personal piety or Muslim suffering abroad, for example in Burma.[67] He was reportedly recently arrested[68] and forbidden to teach at King Saud University.[69]

Even before the Saudis' official announcement designating the Brotherhood a terrorist organization, news of the decision had already spread in the Kingdom. A former member of the Brotherhood related that the 25,000 or so Brothers in the Kingdom were reacting by keeping a low profile and canceling some of their gatherings so as not to anger the government. At the time, they anticipated that the decree was just a warning and that the government would not arrest local Brothers en masse.[70] So far, they have been right.[71]

Despite the calm surface, the Brotherhood's anger at the Saudi regime recalls that of the early 1990s, when unrest associated with the Sahwa movement shook the Kingdom.[72] Based on their earlier experience in the Sahwa, the elder Brothers and Brotherhood sympathizers like 'Awda know they do not have the broad-based political support to defy the state security apparatus. Rather, they are biding their time until factions in the royal family work out their differences.[73] But the younger Brotherhood members may be unwilling to play the long game, especially now that Saudi Arabia is ringed by revolutions.

67. Interview with U.S. State Department analyst, March 4, 2014, Riyadh.

68. "Usrat al-Da'iyya al-'Arifi tu'akkad khabr 'Itiqalihi munthu Usboa'" [The family of Al-Arifi confirms the news of his arrest a week ago], *Al-Watan*, October 15, 2014.

69. "Suhuf: Qarar bi-waqf al-'Arifi 'an al-tadris wa jasr li-l-'ashaq fi al-Basra" [Papers: Decision to remove al-Arifi from his teaching, and a bridge for lovers in Basra], CNN Arabic, October 21, 2014, http://arabic.cnn.com/middleeast/2014/10/21/arabic-papers.

70. Interview with former member of the Muslim Brotherhood, March 2, 2014, Jeddah.

71. To date, the government has only arrested nine Brothers, all of whom were university professors charged with being involved in "foreign organizations." See "Saudis Arrest Professors Linked to Brotherhood."

72. Interview with a former member of the Muslim Brotherhood, March 2, 2014, Jeddah; interview with Yousef al-Dayni, March 2, 2014, Jeddah.

73. Interview with former member of the Muslim Brotherhood, March 2, 2014, Jeddah.

The other group that has faced a crackdown rather than accommodation since 2011 is Saudi Arabia's Shi'a.[74] Events in Bahrain and Syria have dramatically increased the tension between the Sunni majority and the Shi'ite minority in Saudi Arabia. Prior to the Arab uprisings, Sunni critics of the government regularly met with Shi'ite leaders and argued that the regime was just trying to divide the Islamist opposition and prevent it from pushing for political reforms. Shi'ite and Sunni activists even planned a day of countrywide protests on March 11, 2011, though this collapsed when the Shi'a began promulgating narrow sectarian demands.[75] The resulting mutual distrust was compounded days later when the Saudis deployed troops to put down the uprising in Bahrain, and then when Hezbollah deployed its forces to Syria and rumors began circulating of Shi'ite youth from the Eastern Province going there to fight.[76] Regular Shi'ite protests in the villages of the Eastern Province harken back to the protests of the 1980s in the wake of the Iranian Revolution, leading one analyst to proclaim that the current unrest has pushed sectarian tensions to "arguably . . . the highest level" since the fall of the shah.[77]

A journalist in Riyadh related that his government contacts were not particularly worried about the Shi'a in the Kingdom, believing "they have the situation well in hand."[78] According to one Shi'ite activist, the government tries to redirect Sunni anger at the royal family toward the Shi'a. He cited as evidence the destruction of a Shi'ite village in Eastern Province early in 2014.[79]

---

74. The unwillingness of the Saudi regime to make mild concessions to the moderate Shi'a leadership has discredited the government in the eyes of many of the activist youth. As a consequence, many activists are embracing a radical program of political change, and their discredited leaders are adopting a more strident tone to maintain their leadership. Fred Wehrey, "Shia Days of Rage: The Roots of Radicalism in Saudi Arabia," *Foreign Affairs*, December 11, 2012, http://www.foreignaffairs.com/articles/138498/frederic-wehrey/shia-days-of-rage.
75. Ibid.
76. Interview with a U.S. State Department analyst, March 4, 2014, Riyadh.
77. Wehrey, "Shia Days of Rage."
78. Interview with Angus McDowall, March 5, 2014, Riyadh.
79. Interview with Shi'ite activist, March 5, 2014, Riyadh. Madawi al-Rasheed also concluded that the Shi'ite protests were "God-sent" for the regime. See "Egypt's

Although no such destruction has been reported in the media, it is certainly the case that the Saudis have killed Shi'ite protestors and gunmen during clashes in the province.[80] The incidence of armed clashes in the Eastern Province is increasing, "indicating that militants have improved access to firearms" and "signaling a growing risk of radical Shia opposition factions resorting to terrorism against the Saudi state."[81]

Even amidst the recent crackdowns on Sunni and Shi'ite opposition figures alike, there remain individuals and currents within Saudi Arabia that walk the line of criticism and ingratiation. One example is Nasir al-Umar, the leader of the salafi Sururi movement in Saudi Arabia and an anti-Shi'ite firebrand who called on Sunni Muslims to fight Americans in Iraq.[82] Umar has obliquely criticized Saudi Arabia's handling of the Arab uprisings by praising the ascent of Islamists to power in Egypt and Tunisia in 2012. Not an advocate of democratic reform before 2011,[83] Umar has come to view such reform as a positive if limited step toward realization of an Islamic state.[84] As for the

Coup and the Saudi Opposition," *Foreign Policy*, August 19, 2013, http://mideastafrica.foreignpolicy.com/posts/2013/08/19/egypts_coup_and_the_saudi_opposition.

80. "Saudi Forces Shoot Dead Shia Protester," Agence France-Presse, January 13, 2012, https://now.mmedia.me/lb/en/nownews/saudi_forces_shoot_dead_shia_protester; "Four Killed in Crossfire between Saudi Police, Gunmen," *Finland Times*, February 21, 2014, http://www.finlandtimes.fi/worldwide/2014/02/21/4985/Four-killed-in-crossfire-between-Saudi-police,-gunmen.

81. "Small-Arms Attacks Likely to Increase in Saudi Arabia's Oil-Rich Eastern Province," *IHS Jane's Intelligence Weekly*, February 26, 2014, http://www.janes.com/article/34681/small-arms-attacks-likely-to-increase-in-saudi-arabia-s-oil-rich-eastern-province.

82. "Interview: Sheikh Nasser al-Omar," *Frontline*, February 8, 2005, http://www.pbs.org/wgbh/pages/frontline/shows/saud/interviews/alomar.html.

83. Saud al-Sarhan, "The Neo Reformists: A New Democratic Islamic Discourse," Middle East Institute, Washington, DC, October 1, 2009, http://www.mei.edu/content/neo-reformists-new-democratic-islamic-discourse.

84. Yusuf al-Hazza, "Al-Sahawiyyun al-Sa'udiyyun yatalammasun atharan bi-l-thawrat wa-l-Hawali ila al-wajiha," *Elaph.com*, December 18, 2011, http://www.elaph.com/Web/news/2011/12/703390.html; interview with State Department analyst, March 4, 2014, Riyadh; "Jadal al-Dimuqratiyya . . . kitab jadid lil-shaykh al-'Umar" [The Controversy of Democracy . . . A new book by Shaykh al-'Umar"), *Almoslim.net*, February 10, 2013, http://www.islamicfinder.org/dateConversion.php?mode=hij-ger&day=29&month=3&year=1434&date_result=1.

ratification of the Egyptian constitution approved when the Brotherhood was in power, he seemed to consider it the lesser of two evils: "Infidelity is not permitted unless under duress. The jurist, however, is one who distinguishes between two corrupt positions by treading on the lesser one in light of that fact that (not voting) would do more to assist falsehood."[85]

Umar's support for elections abroad contrasts with his silence about the lack of political reforms at home. When the Saudi government supported the coup against Morsi, Umar thinly veiled his anger: "Don't those who support the Felul's revolution and the Tamarrud movement in #Egypt against their legitimate leaders know that by doing so they validate the legitimacy of revolution in their countries and revolt against their rulers!"[86] Although three days later he was careful to reaffirm his official stance of not supporting revolutions against the state,[87] after several weeks Umar again voiced his anger at the coup's supporters: "All those who carried out or aided the #slaughter_ Rabi'a_al-'Adawiyya, even if it was just a word, is falling under the promise [from the Qur'an]: 'his recompense is Gehennam, therein dwelling forever, and God will be wroth with him and will curse him, and prepare for him a mighty chastisement.'"[88]

ACCEPTABLE AND UNACCEPTABLE RADICALISM IN SYRIA AND IRAQ

Saudi ambivalence toward radicalism in general and hostility toward challenges to its power—from the Brotherhood and now via the claims of the Islamic State—have shaped its sup-

---

85. Abd Allah al-Rashid, "Al-Salafi al-Dimuqrati," *Asharq Al-Awsat*, March 25, 2013, http://classic.aawsat.com/details.asp?section=39&article=722183&issueno=12536#. U6nE6PldX7M.

86. Nasir al-Umar, Twitter post, July 5, 2013, https://twitter.com/naseralomar/status/353149894732685312. "Felul" refers to the "remnants" of the Mubarak regime seeking a return to power. Tamarrud was the name of the youth-led movement that called for mass protests to force Morsi from power.

87. Nasir al-Umar, "Bayan hawl ahdath Misr" [Statement on the events in Egypt], *Almoslim.net*, July 8, 2013, http://www.almoslim.net/node/186224?page=2. See also Stéphane Lacroix, "Saudi Arabia's Muslim Brotherhood Predicament."

88. Nasir al-Umar, Twitter post, July, 27, 2013, https://twitter.com/naseralomar/status/361220827397632000.

port for the Syrian rebels and the opposition in exile.[89] As one leader of the Syrian Muslim Brotherhood, Riad al-Shaqfa, has pointed out, "The Saudis say 'No to the Brotherhood,'" whereas the Qataris are "playing a positive role."[90] The tussle between Saudi Arabia and Qatar for control of the regional and ideological orientation of the opposition has had a profound effect on the coherence of the armed opposition fighting Assad inside Syria. Despite being united in supporting the armed overthrow of Assad in early 2012,[91] they have disagreed sharply on whom to fund. As they did with their support to the external opposition, the Qataris have favored funding Islamists with transnational agendas—typically the Brotherhood or salafi groups. Saudi Arabia, in contrast, has favored non-Islamists or so-called soft Islamists with a nationalist bent and often aligned with the Free Syrian Army.[92] With Qatar's help and Saudi Arabia's early

---

89. Saudi Arabia, for example, funneled a lot of its early money to Jamal Maarouf's Martyrs of Syria Battalion in Idlib because Maarouf disliked the Brotherhood. Maarouf's group would later form the backbone of the Syrian Revolutionaries Front (SRF), which began the winter 2013 push against the Islamic State in Iraq and al Sham (ISIS). Qatar's favorite rebel conglomeration, the Salafi Islamic Front, was much slower to act against ISIS, with which it often cooperated. It has also clashed at times with the Saudi-backed SRF. Marlin Dick, "FSA Alliance Pushes Back against Islamic Front," *Daily Star*, December 17, 2013, http://www.dailystar.com.lb/News/Middle-East/2013/Dec-17/241361-fsa-alliance-pushes-back-against-islamic-front.ashx#axzz2zXuLKY2R.

90. "How Qatar Seized Control of the Syrian Revolution," *FT Magazine*, May 17, 2013, http://www.ft.com/intl/cms/s/2/f2d9bbc8-bdbc-11e2-890a-00144feab7de.html#axzz2ub3wwt00. According to Anwar Eshqi (interview, March 3, 2014, Jeddah), the Saudis have extended only limited support to the Syrian Brotherhood as part of their aid to the exiled opposition because it has not met certain conditions.

91. "Syrian Opposition Praises Saudi FM Position," *Asharq al-Awsat*, February 25, 2012, http://www.aawsat.net/2012/02/article55243080; James Hider, "Gulf Countries 'Have Secret Arms Deal with Resistance,'" *Times* (London), January 26, 2012; Justin Vela, "Arab States Arm Rebels as UN Talks of Syrian Civil War," *Independent*, June 13, 2012, http://www.independent.co.uk/news/world/middle-east/exclusive-arab-states-arm-rebels-as-un-talks-of-syrian-civil-war-7845026.html.

92. Rania Abouzeid, "Syria's Secular and Islamist Rebels: Who Are the Saudis and the Qataris Arming?" *Time*, September 18, 2012, http://world.time.com/2012/09/18/syrias-secular-and-islamist-rebels-who-are-the-saudis-and-the-qataris-arming/; Phil Sands and Suha Maayeh, "Syrian Rebels Get Arms and Advice through Secret Command Centre in Amman," *National*, December 28, 2013, http://www.thenational.ae/world/middle-east/syrian-rebels-get-arms-and-advice-through-secret-command-centre-in-amman.

neglect,[93] the Syrian Brotherhood came to dominate the main exile organization, the Syrian National Council.

The Saudi regime has been very careful not to back rebel factions that may one day turn their sights on the Kingdom. But some factions within the regime have not been so cautious about citizens' support for those extremist groups. To be sure, the government has officially banned its citizens from fighting in Syria or sending money to rebel groups through private channels. The Senior Ulema Council ruled in June 2012 that Saudi citizens could not fight against the Assad regime. The Saudi Ministry of the Interior's security spokesman repeated the same prohibition in September 2012. Senior Saudi clerics forbade youth from going to fight abroad, and the government has warned religious scholars not to encourage defiance of the ban. Saudi's grand mufti repeated the prohibition in October 2013 and criticized religious scholars who did not heed the government's warning.[94]

The Saudi government has also tried to curb private funding for extremist rebel groups in Syria. In 2012, King Abdullah banned religious scholars from raising money for Syria without state sanction.[95] Salman al-ʿAwda called on his followers to circumvent the ban, and the popular cleric Muhammad al-Arifi publicly groused when the government forced him to sign a pledge to stop soliciting money for Syria[96] (a fund-raising effort that included support for Jabhat al-Nusra, according to a

93. Reportedly, the Saudis initially allowed the Qataris to take the lead role in shaping the exiled opposition. See Roula Khalaf and Abigail Fielding-Smith, "Qatar Bankrolls Syrian Revolt with Cash and Arms," *Financial Times*, May 16, 2013, http://www.ft.com/intl/cms/s/0/86e3f28e-be3a-11e2-bb35-00144feab7de.html#axzz2ub3wwt00.

94. Fred Wehrey, "Saudi Arabia Reins in Its Clerics on Syria," Carnegie Endowment for International Peace, Washington, DC, June 14, 2012, http://carnegieendowment.org/2012/06/14/saudi-arabia-reins-in-its-clerics-on-syria/bu10; Kevin Sullivan, "Saudis Line Up against Syria's Assad," *Washington Post*, October 7, 2012, http://www.washingtonpost.com/world/middle_east/saudis-line-up-against-syrias-assad/2012/10/07/7b06de8e-0e51-11e2-bd1a-b868e65d57eb_story.html; Ben Gilbert, "Saudi Arabia Walks a Fine Line in Backing Syrian Rebellion," *Al Jazeera America*, January 20, 2014, http://america.aljazeera.com/articles/2014/1/20/saudi-arabia-walksafinelinkinbackingsyriarebellion.html.

95. Interview with Anwar Eshqi, March 3, 2014, Jeddah.

96. Wehrey, "Saudi Arabia Reins in Its Clerics."

U.S. State Department source).[97] In the summer of 2012, King Abdullah sponsored a public fund-raiser for Syria,[98] donations to which were dispersed by the Ministry of the Interior. By the winter of 2013, the Ministry of the Interior threatened to arrest anyone who gave donations to unapproved fund-raisers.[99] This spring, the king vowed that anyone fighting abroad would be punished with up to 20 years in prison.[100]

The threats meant to discourage foreign travel or illicit fundraising have not worked, which suggests the government cannot or will not enforce its edicts. As of May 2014, some 2,500 Saudis had traveled to fight in Syria.[101] Saudi youth are motivated to fight for a variety of reasons. Some are enticed by the chance to be part of what they consider the final battles leading to the Day of Judgment.[102] Others have grown weary of patiently working their way up the ranks of Islamist study circles and are seeking to burnish their Islamist credentials by fighting in Syria.[103] Many of the young men going to fight are from Burayda, which has been a breeding ground of conservative Islamist activism for decades. A number of the men do not identify as radicals, but they strongly dislike the Saudi government.[104] They have been encouraged by clerics who coyly acknowledge the ban against

---

97. Interview with State Department analyst, March 4, 2014, Riyadh.

98. Sullivan, "Saudis Line Up"; Elizabeth Dickinson, "Saudi Arabia Almost Doubles Aid to War-Torn Syria with US $72M Donation," *National*, July 31 2012, http://www.thenational.ae/news/world/saudi-arabia-almost-doubles-aid-to-war-torn-syria-with-us-72m-donation.

99. "Saudi Warns against Illegal Fund Raising for Syria Refugees," Agence France-Presse, December 30, 2013, http://www.dailystar.com.lb/Article.aspx?id=242674.

100. "Saudi Arabia Jails 13 for Security Offences," *Al Jazeera*, April 24, 2014, http://www.aljazeera.com/news/middleeast/2014/04/saudi-jails-13-security-offences-20144145389450328.html; Theodore Karasik, "Saudi Arabia and the U.S. to Cooperate on Syria," *Al Arabiya*, February 23, 2014, http://english.alarabiya.net/en/views/news/world/2014/02/23/Saudi-Arabia-offers-U-S-solutions-over-Syria.html; interview with Anwar Eshqi, March 3, 2014, Jeddah.

101. Barrett, *Foreign Fighters in Syria*, 13.

102. Interview with State Department analyst, March 4, 2014, Riyadh; Mariam Karouny, "Apocalyptic Prophecies Drive Both Sides to Syrian Battle for End of Time," Reuters, April 1, 2014, http://www.reuters.com/article/2014/04/01/us-syria-crisis-prophecy-insight-idUSBREA3013420140401.

103. Interview with Yousef al-Dayni, March 2, 2014, Jeddah.

104. Interview with a former member of the Muslim Brotherhood, March 2, 2014, Jeddah.

encouraging youth to fight in Syria while also saying youth who do fight would be martyrs.[105]

The government has also been unable to completely stem the flow of illicit money to Syrian rebels. Saudis who want to circumvent the ban send money to other Gulf countries with lax counter-threat financing laws, especially Kuwait.[106] Bundlers in those countries routinely brag about receiving money from Saudi citizens.[107] Saudis also send money through *hawalas* (informal systems used to transfer assets).[108] Soon after the Saudi foreign minister called for aid to Syrian fighters, Nasir al-Umar tried to organize an online fund-raising campaign. The Saudis shut it down.[109] In December 2013, Umar and 71 other imams called on the government to throw its weight behind the Islamic Front,[110] implicitly criticizing the government's support for non-salafi groups. Saudi officials and non-Saudi diplomats have also admitted that the state has been unable to stem the flow of money.[111]

105. Ibid.

106. Gilbert, "Saudi Arabia Walks a Fine Line"; interview with U.S. State Department analyst, March 4, 2014, Riyadh; interview with Yousef al-Dayni, March 2, 2014, Jeddah.

107. Hay'at al-Zakat al-Sha'biyya, Twitter post, August 17, 2013, https://twitter.com/alhayahalshabyh/status/368827241293037569.

108. Interview with U.S. State Department analyst, March 4, 2014, Riyadh. Even the wife of the Ministry of the Interior spokesman Gen. Mansour al-Turki has received pleas for private donations. "She gets a text message or email, and I have to tell her, 'No, that's not legal, and you can do it through the approved channels.' We can't guarantee that the money will end up in the hands of the right people." Gilbert, "Saudi Arabia Walks a Fine Line."

109. "Lajnat al-'ulama' li-nusrat Suriyya ta'lin iqaf hamlat al-tabarru'at" [The committee of Ulema for helping Syria announces the end of the campaign for donations], *Almoslim.net*, May 28, 2012, http://www.almoslim.net/node/165719; Wehrey, "Saudi Arabia Reins in Its Clerics on Syria."

110. Gilbert, "Saudi Arabia Walks a Fine Line"; David Weinberg, "Saudi Clerics Endorse Jihadists in Syria," Foundation for Defense of Democracies, Washington, DC, December 5, 2013, http://defenddemocracy.org/media-hit/saudi-clerics-endorse-jihadists-in-syria. For text of the statement, see "Al-'Ulama' wa du'aat fi-l-mamlaka yasdurun bayanan li-ta'yiid 'al-Jabha al-Islamiyya' fi Al-Sham wa yad'un ila da'miha" [Religious scholars and missionaries in the Kingdom publish a statement in support of the "Islamic Front" in al-Sham and call for supporting it], *Almoslim.net*, December 5, 2013, http://almoslim.net/node/195146.

111. Interview with Angus McDowall, March 5, 2014, Riyadh.

Some observers have attributed the Saudis' schizophrenic counterterrorism policy to a rift in the royal family between the hawkish Prince Bandar, who had controlled the Syria file until recently, and the more reticent Prince Muhammad bin Naif, who took it up after Bandar fell ill.[112] In this interpretation, Bandar encouraged the Saudi government to turn a blind eye to private efforts to support the Syrian fighters, whereas bin Naif has tried to clamp down on private support because of the potential blowback in the Kingdom.[113] Other observers disagree with this interpretation and suggest that Bandar could take up the Syria portfolio again once his health improves.[114] The fact that Bandar was recently removed as head of Saudi intelligence gives more credence to the factional explanation for the Saudis' counterterrorism policy.[115]

In response to the emergence of the Islamic State as the focal point of regional concern over militancy, the official Saudi position toward the group has hardened, and the Saudi state has once again enlisted the support of the official ulema—this time to delegitimize the Islamic State while leaving open the possibility of Saudi aggression toward it. Abdulaziz Al al-Sheikh, the Saudi grand mufti, declared in August 2014 that the Islamic State and al Qaeda are "enemy number one of Islam" and that "extremist and militant ideas and terrorism which spread decay on Earth, destroying human civilization, are not in any way part of Islam . . . and Muslims are their first victims."[116] The grand mufti also referred to the Islamic State as a modern incarnation

112. Bruce Riedel, "Saudi Arabia Plans to Pitch Obama for Regime Change in Syria," *Al Monitor*, February 15, 2014, http://www.al-monitor.com/pulse/originals/2014/02/saudi-arabia-barack-obama-syria-fighters.html.

113. This reading is supported by sources in Riyadh. Interview with U.S. State Department analyst, March 4, 2014, Riyadh; interview with former member of the Muslim Brotherhoood, March 2, 2014, Riyadh.

114. Interview with Anwar Eshqi, March 3, 2014, Jeddah; interview with Angus McDowall, March 5, 2014, Riyadh.

115. Khalil al-Harb, "Al-Mufaja'at al-Sa'udiyya tatawali fusulan" [The Saudi surprises come one after another], *As-Safir*, May 15, 2014, http://www.assafir.com/Article/1/350659.

116. "Saudi Grand Mufti Denounces Iraq's Islamic State Group," Reuters, August 19, 2014, http://www.reuters.com/article/2014/08/19/us-iraq-security-saudi-mufti-idUSKBN0GJ11S20140819.

of the Kharijite movement in early Islam, a designation that rejects the group's claim to authority over the Muslim community and emphasizes its heresy instead.

CONCLUSION

Although the Saudi state sometimes characterizes its detractors as religious extremists, religious extremism is not really what worries the Saudi family; by Islamic standards, the Wahhabi religious establishment that supports the state prides itself on not being moderate on a range of issues. What really concerns the Saudis is perceived threats to their continued rule of the Kingdom, including challenges to the state's claim to represent Islamic legitimacy. The state's current zero tolerance for domestic dissent—whether Sunni or Shi'ite—and its effort to delegitimize the Islamic State's claims to authority indicate the depth of its concern.

The Saudi state employs the language and legal apparatus of counterterrorism to justify its repression of dissent, singling out the Muslim Brotherhood because of its early successes against Saudi Arabia's allies after the Arab uprisings. As in Egypt, nonviolent salafi activists who are critical of the Saudi government do not receive the same treatment as Brotherhood members unless they closely align with the group. Despite its nonviolent stance and longtime cooperation with Saudi authorities, the Brotherhood's organization and anti-autocratic message seem to pose a unique threat in the eyes of the Saudis after the Arab uprisings. But this threat is not principally related to the ideology or religious views of the Brotherhood; rather, it stems from the group's perceived political power and ambitions in the wake of the Arab uprisings.

Earlier Saudi leaders faced similar Islamist dissent and managed it with more velvet glove and less iron fist than today's leaders, who are worried with good reason. The last of the first generation of princes who have led the country since its founding could soon die, and a chaotic transition of leadership is possible, though by no means certain. The country's population continues to swell, placing greater strain on the state's coffers. Its neighbors to the north and west are battling insurgencies of low or high grade, the government in Yemen has been seized by Houthi rebels, and a major Shi'ite uprising took place in Bahrain, which has sporadically turned violent. The Saudi state could move to liberalize its political system, but its leaders doubtless judge that a move of this kind is too risky while a storm is raging in the region. Better to batten down the hatches and ride out the storm.

The royal family may not be able to wait long enough. The Islamic State now controls significant territory in neighboring Iraq, and a substantial number of its fighters are Saudi citizens. Until recently, the Saudis treated the Islamic State as a terrorism problem,[117] but it threatens to become an insurgency problem if the well-funded and well-armed extremist group decides to send a convoy into Saudi Arabia. "Tens of thousands" of Islamic State supporters and Saudi detractors retweeted the Arabic hashtag #IslamicStateOnSaudiBorder after the group captured the town of Rutba, 70 miles from the Jordanian and Saudi border. Islamic State supporters also posted maps indicating their desire for the group to push into the Kingdom.[118]

There is no question that the Saudis would eventually be able to beat back the challenge, especially with the aid of their allies;

---

117. Huda al-Saleh, "Saudi Arabia Arrests First ISIS-Related Terror Cell," *Asharq Al-Awsat*, May 7, 2014, http://www.aawsat.net/2014/05/article55332025. A good example of the current state of Saudi thinking about the threat posed by the Islamic State is offered by a recent article by Nawaf Obaid, a confidant of the hawkish Prince Turki. Although Obaid acknowledges the threat posed by the Islamic State and its seizure of territory, he recommends a counterterrorism approach at odds with the Islamic State's behavior as a sophisticated insurgency: "The advances by ISIS—an al Qaeda splinter group—are another reminder that a key element of any nation's defense must be a counter-terrorism capability. After all, the militant "legions" that have seized Iraq's second city among others are basically non-state actors. It is therefore essential that Saudi Arabia continue to invest in what is already one of the largest and most efficient counter-terrorism programs in the world to ensure that the threat is managed both within and outside the Kingdom's borders." Nawaf Obaid, "Why Saudi Arabia Needs a New Defense Doctrine," CNN, June 23, 2014, http://globalpublicsquare.blogs.cnn.com/2014/06/23/why-saudi-arabia-needs-a-new-defense-doctrine/.

118. Rachel Levy, "Could Saudi Arabia Be the Next ISIS Conquest?" *Vocativ*, June 23, 2014, http://www.vocativ.com/world/iraq-world/saudi-arabia-next-isis-conquest/.

the Saudis have already partnered with the United States for airstrikes against the Islamic State to curtail its ability to wage an insurgency inside the Kingdom. But should the Islamic State invade, it would not have to get far to cause a political upheaval in the Kingdom. Two other comparable events of this kind—the seizure of the Grand Mosque by salafi apocalyptists and Saddam's invasion of Kuwait—led to severe legitimacy crises for the regime because they challenged its competency to protect the holy places in the Hijaz. With the Saudi government keeping such a tight lid on domestic Islamist political pressure, an outside attack by an extremist Sunni group would cause a dramatic explosion with far-reaching consequences. Such an attack could be exacerbated by jihadi-salafists inside the Kingdom who are waiting for a propitious time to strike.[119]

As for the nonviolent Sunni opposition, its members are also biding their time, waiting for an opportunity to again press for political reform. The Saudi Muslim Brotherhood and its supporters know they now have to tread lightly given the threat of arrest for membership in the group and the lack of support from the masses. Nonviolent activist salafists like the Sururis also know they are on a short leash and have become more muted in their criticism of the Saudi government. Of course, a sudden political opening by the Saudi government would change their calculations. But that is unlikely because Saudi Arabia's leaders are convinced now is not the time to create space for domestic dissent. They are determined that the public pressure for political reforms that toppled their allies will not topple them, even if they end up creating more pressure for such reforms by smothering dissent.

---

119. In May, Saudi authorities arrested 62 members of an ISIS cell, 35 of whom were "Saudi nationals previously detained on terrorist-related charges." See Huda al-Saleh, "Saudi Arabia Arrests First ISIS-related Terror Cell."

7. CONCLUSION

Jon B. Alterman

While many observers of the Arab world had believed for years that change was inevitable, the Arab uprisings themselves came as a complete surprise. The idea that a self-immolating fruit seller in Tunisia could shake the political foundations of the Arab world to their core would have been thought ludicrous just the week before events unfolded. By March 2011, as uprisings churned in Libya, Syria, Morocco, Bahrain, and beyond, it seemed clear that these changes would prove transformational. The question was not whether change would come, but how complete it would be. After decades in which authoritarian governments secured themselves by protecting secular liberals and religious conservatives from each other, secular and religious groups were uniting with one another and with an unprecedentedly entrepreneurial generation of young people to rise up against authoritarianism.

And yet, as the months passed, the old authoritarian systems proved surprisingly durable. Some sitting governments were able to co-opt their populations through material reward or the promise of political reform; others were able to rally their populations against the prospect of insurgency. Still others revived repression. Most importantly, governments were able to learn from each other's mistakes. After an initial flurry of change, the process slowed. In some places, such as Bahrain, it seemed to be arrested. In Egypt, the process actually reversed.

While it was surprising to most observers that that Arab uprisings did not result in more-liberal political systems, what was more surprising was the way in which it revived radical movements. Indeed, almost four years after the fact, radical movements in the Arab world seem to have been even more invigorated by the Arab uprisings than liberal ones. This is in part because many of the radical movements embraced the idea of fighting, and the breakdown in order allowed more fighting to occur across the region. Ungoverned space in the Sahara and the Levant has created opportunities for radical groups to train and equip, and contested space has given them a forum for battle.

But there was a more worrying aspect to the resurgence of radical movements. Many of the radical groups learned potent lessons from the revolutionary political movements of the Arab uprisings. Experiments with social media that began in the laboratory of revolutionary Egypt and Syria found their way into extremists' tool kits. In the 2000s, websites and chat rooms were the somewhat static, one-to-many platforms for recruitment and communication. In the 2010s, private messages, Tweets, and videos dubbed into dozens of languages made jihad not only truly global but also infinitely customizable. Recruiters did not need to wonder how their messages were being received, because they were in constant and intimate contact with the recipients.

In a way, the religious radicals always had an advantage over the political revolutionaries. The latter sought mass support, hoping to rally majorities to their cause. They needed millions in the streets, and they needed diverse audiences to join in common cause. The rainbow that poured into Egypt's public squares in 2011—young and old, rich and poor, religious and secular—represented their dream. It soon proved difficult to sustain.

The religious radicals have always had a different model, one that is content to assemble a violent vanguard from disaffected communities around the world. They need not fill any squares, and they need not draw a diverse set of adherents. Judged as a mass movement, the radicals have failed; they have attracted only a tiny percentage of their audience. But becoming a mass movement was never central to their ambition. As a vanguard and fighting force they have found at least limited success, winning battles and rallying tens of thousands to their cause. What all of this means for the Middle East is a continuation of conflicts that many thought were coming to an end. The raging wars in Libya, Syria, and Iraq—all of which owe at least part of their origin to the Arab uprisings—have gathered existing religious, ethnic, and sectarian tensions into large and messy existential struggles. These conflicts not only radicalize young men in the affected countries, but they attract foreign fighters in search of a cause, or adventure, or spiritual reward. None of these conflicts appears close to ending.

Beyond the Middle East, the consequences are less clear. A few foreign fighters have emerged from war zones to commit hate crimes, such as the former Islamic State of Iraq and Syria fighter who opened fire in a Jewish museum in Brussels, Belgium, killing four.[1] Syria has already attracted more than twice as many foreign fighters as the decade-long anti-Soviet war in Afghanistan, and it seems possible that the raging conflicts in the Sahel and the Levant will spread new extremist techniques, reach new adherents, and connect new networks.

Yet many close observers of terrorism doubt that the West will be much affected by these foreign fighters. Some argue that the number of returnees is likely to be small, although they warn that those returnees will be more lethal after their foreign experience.[2] Others suggest most foreign fighters will die on the battlefield, and those who survive can be managed through robust intelligence activities.[3]

---

1. Anne Penketh, "Brussels Jewish Museum Shooting: Suspect with Islamist Links Arrested," *Guardian*, June 1, 2014, http://www.theguardian.com/world/2014/jun/01/suspect-arrest-brussels-jewish-museum-shooting.
2. Thomas Hegghammer, "Should I Stay or Should I Go? Explaining Variation in Western Jihadists' Choice between Domestic and Foreign Fighting," *American Political Science Review*, 107, no. 1 (February 2013): 1–15, doi:10.1017/S0003055412000615.
3. Daniel Byman and Jeremy Shapiro, "Homeward Bound?" *Foreign Affairs* 93, no. 6 (November/December 2014): 37–46.

Whatever the numbers of jihadists, the Arab uprisings seem to have increased the innovation and entrepreneurship of radical groups in the Middle East, at the same time that they increased the opportunities for radicals to gain battlefield experience. For those seeking to combat radicalism, the challenges will only grow more complex.

Most troubling for policymakers is the uncertainty about when the pitched battle against extremism will end. For the political revolutionaries of the Arab uprisings, it was relatively clear what "victory" would look like: the demise of the old order and a more pluralistic future for their countries. They sought to energize the streets. There would be little mystery about the outcomes. The battles would have to be fought, and victory would need to be found, in the relatively clear light of politics.

For radicals, victory is much more obscure. Some proclaim victory in their martyrdom-seeking operations, embracing their own deaths as an ennobling triumph. Some seek reward in a constant battle against mortal enemies. More recently, some have claimed victory in the establishment of their caliphate, a collection of impoverished, dusty cities ruled under the stern glare of religious police. What unifies their vision is an acceptance of the idea of deadly conflict stretching far into the future, fought by irregular forces arrayed against better-armed foes. It is a logic that rewards asymmetrical warfare and accepts heavy casualties. For the rest of the world, it is a daunting prospect.

INDEX

ABOUT THE AUTHORS

Jon B. Alterman is a senior vice president, holds the Zbigniew Brzezinski Chair in Global Security and Geostrategy, and is director of the Middle East Program at CSIS. Prior to joining CSIS in 2002, he served as a member of the Policy Planning Staff at the U.S. Department of State and as a special assistant to the assistant secretary of state for Near Eastern affairs. He is a member of the Chief of Naval Operations Executive Panel and served as an expert adviser to the Iraq Study Group (also known as the Baker-Hamilton Commission). In addition to his policy work, he teaches Middle Eastern studies at the Johns Hopkins School of Advanced International Studies. Before entering government, he was a scholar at the U.S. Institute of Peace and at the Washington Institute for Near East Policy. He received his Ph.D. in history from Harvard University.

Haim Malka is a senior fellow and deputy director of the Middle East Program at CSIS, where he oversees the program's work on the Maghreb. His principal areas of research include religious radicalization, government strategies to combat extremism, violent nonstate actors, and North African politics and security. Before joining CSIS in 2005, he was a research analyst at the Brookings Institution, where he concentrated on U.S. Middle East foreign policy. Malka spent six years living in Jerusalem, where he worked as a television news producer. He holds a B.A. from the University of Washington in Seattle and an M.A. from Columbia University's School of International and Public Affairs.

William McCants is a fellow in the Center for Middle East Policy and director of the Project on U.S. Relations with the Islamic World at the Brookings Institution. He is also adjunct faculty at Johns Hopkins University and the founder of Jihadica. com, an academic group blog focused on the global jihadi movement. From 2009-2011, McCants served as a U.S. State Department senior adviser for countering violent extremism. He has also held positions as program manager of the Minerva Initiative for the Department of Defense; as an analyst at the Institute for Defense Analyses, the Center for Naval Analyses, and SAIC; and as a fellow at West Point's Combating Terrorism Center. He earned his Ph.D. in Near Eastern studies from Princeton University.

Thomas Sanderson is codirector and senior fellow in the CSIS Transnational Threats Project, where he works on terrorism, transnational crime, global trends, Central Asia, and intelligence issues. He also serves as a course instructor and consultant for the U.S. government and the private sector on terrorism, China, and global threats. He has conducted fieldwork across 60 countries, engaging all manner of sources, including extremists, insurgents, foreign intelligence officials, nongovernmental organizations, and academics. His commentaries have appeared in the *New York Times*, the *Economist, Washington Post, West Point CTC Sentinel*, and *Harvard Asia Pacific Review.* He received a B.A. from Wheaton College and an M.A. from the Fletcher School at Tufts University.

ABOUT CSIS

For over 50 years, the Center for Strategic and International Studies (CSIS) has worked to develop solutions to the world's greatest policy challenges. Today, CSIS scholars are providing strategic insights and bipartisan policy solutions to help decisionmakers chart a course toward a better world.

CSIS is a nonprofit organization headquartered in Washington, D.C. The Center's 220 full-time staff and large network of affiliated scholars conduct research and analysis and develop policy initiatives that look into the future and anticipate change.

Founded at the height of the Cold War by David M. Abshire and Admiral Arleigh Burke, CSIS was dedicated to finding ways to sustain American prominence and prosperity as a force for good in the world. Since 1962, CSIS has become one of the world's preeminent international institutions focused on defense and security; regional stability; and transnational challenges ranging from energy and climate to global health and economic integration.

Former U.S. senator Sam Nunn has chaired the CSIS Board of Trustees since 1999. Former deputy secretary of defense John J. Hamre became the Center's president and chief executive officer in 2000.